Future

Anterior

Future Anterior
Volume XIX, Number 2
Winter 2022

Tao DuFour

Space and Heritage

On the Generativity of Environing Worlds

In his manuscript fragments on perception, the philosopher Edmund Husserl would speak of a certain thickening of temporal experience as an acquisition, that is, as a kind of *heritage* that takes the form of embodied habitus that is inherent to the lived experience of space. Husserl is here not using the German noun *Erbe* merely figuratively[1]; rather, what this sense of heritage points toward is a certain affective relation to the past that is conjured by spatio-environmental qualities. Heritage here takes the form of feelings, the auras of memories and moods. The articles, transcripts and photographic works featured in this special issue of *Future Anterior* speak with different timbres and through distinct contexts to the experience of heritage as spatially lived and felt. One of the key theoretical difficulties that, through their narrative and descriptive qualities, the pieces in this issue each in their own way address concerns the problem of showing how the affective quality of embodied sentiments and feelings are experienced intersubjectively and across generations as shared. This consideration of heritage as experienced *spatially*—in terms of the affectivity of embodiment—and in this way intersubjectively across generations was the focus of an interdisciplinary roundtable session that I organized as guest editor of this issue, which was hosted by the Department of Architecture and Clare Hall College at Cambridge University in the autumn of 2022. It initiated a discussion around one of the key thematic concerns of this issue, which is the significance of intergenerational relations in the constitution of heritage, and the basis of such relations on spatial experience. What is examined here is the phenomenon of heritage as subjectively constituted. It means that the status of the objects of reference—their "tangibility" or "intangibility"—emerge as consequential only in reference to the generativity of encounter. The concept of generativity (*Generativität*) is a phenomenological notion that thematizes problems concerning intersubjective and historical becoming, in the formation and transformation of intergenerational community.[2] Objects and their spatial situation take on significance in terms of contingent events tied to wider conditions that ultimately take the form of historical transformations. The concept of generativity, however, foregrounds situations at various thresholds of lived experiential relations and living memory, through which events, although experienced as past, retain emotive affective

Future Anterior
Volume XIX, Number 2
Winter 2022

force in the present and in this way only tentatively approach the category of the "historical."[3] Heritage cannot here be drawn out and set apart from subjective experience, inherent to which are common spatial horizons the significance of which is necessarily intersubjective and shared in immediate and mediated ways across generations.

The five articles published in this issue speak to its theme in ways that move beneath its philosophical framing, illuminating the lives of persons for whom heritage is tied to the spatiality of displacement, violence and trauma, but also of solidarity, care, and love. The abstracts that accompany each article will give the reader a sense of their content so that, rather than duplicating this, I would like to use this introduction to think through in a preliminary way the problem of generativity from the space of violence—specifically colonial and state sanctioned, which each article addresses in some way—handed over as living heritage. Each article takes us through in intimate detail particular concrete conditions, so that—inspired by their content—I will speak generally and conceptually in what follows. The philosophical framing of this issue—if one were to trace the genealogy of terms used in its title and the call for papers—derives its conceptual texture from Husserlian thought. At its conceptual depth, the problem concerns the ethical horizons that a phenomenological analysis of concrete spatial experiences opens up. When this concreteness implicates shared histories of violence, the lived experience of this as a peculiar tapestry of inheritances takes on a vague and nebulous quality. Here, the temporality of heritage as a lived spatial experience, drawing on the words of Romanian author Mihail Sebastian, "reaches far back and hangs like a haze over the horizon of our future."[4] Although clouded and indistinct as memory, this lived experiential relation to the historical past is not wholly abstract; rather, it has intimate dimensions. The past here can exist, to quote Stuart Hall, "like a pall of mist, enveloping us all, which no one could admit was there."[5] The task that each article takes on is to a significant extent a descriptive one that allows the relations between persons—living, ageing, deceased, and disappeared—to emerge in their qualitative and emotive dimensions on the ground of spatio-environmental affections. In this way, to linger with Hall's observations, the lives of those who had "slipped out of memory" in the wake of violent and even genocidal pasts come to visibility, emerging out of an opaque brume of forgetfulness through the latency-cum-affectivity of spatial horizons that persist.[6] These are the environing worlds that the articles in this issue illuminate. They are characterized by conditions of precarity that are a function of real, embodied spatial relations with others:

> the bounded and living appearance of the body is the condition of being exposed to the other, exposed to solicitation, seduction, passion, injury, exposed in ways that sustain us but also in ways that can destroy us. In this sense the exposure of the body points to its precariousness. At the same time [. . .] this precarious and corporeal being is responsible for the life of the other, which means that no matter how much one fears for one's own life, preserving the life of the other is paramount. [. . .] this is a form of responsibility that is not easy while undergoing a felt sense of precarity. Precarity names both the necessity and the difficulty of ethics.[7]

Here, Judith Butler directs us to the spatio-environmental bases of our ethical lives:

> If we try to understand in concrete terms what it means to commit ourselves to preserving the life of the other, we are invariably confronted with the bodily conditions of life and so, a commitment not only to the other's corporeal persistence but to all those environmental conditions that make life livable.[8]

If we consider the generative—in a phenomenological sense—implications of Butler's careful meditations, then the environmental conditions to which she refers are not merely sense perceptually affective. Inherent to the embodied perceptual experiences, which are necessarily spatial, lie temporal affections. These take the form of memories, emotions, and what Edith Stein terms "sensations of feelings" (*Gefühlsempfindungen*), "general feelings" (*Gemeingefühle*), and "moods" (*Stimmungen*).[9] What the articles in this issue show us are ways of approaching these spatial horizons whose affectivities are tied, for generations of persons, to forms of experiential conditions characterized by profound feelings of loss; they can be described, in the words of the Barbadian writer George Lamming, as "a certain state of feeling which is the heritage of the exiled and colonial" subject.[10] They are emotions that defy linguistic articulation and erupt thorough the sheer expressive force of one's spatio-corporeal being, as in moments of wailing. Yet, the essays in this issue also reveal the shared conditions of life that make the articulation of traumatic pasts possible and necessary. These conditions are difficult to state distinctly and completely, but they are not abstractions; rather, they have to do with feelings for and obligations toward those who have suffered, died, or disappeared—they can be feelings of love and longing, of shame and guilt, or even of forgiveness. They are tied inextricably to the affectivity of spatio-environmental horizons, and in this way the environing world takes on the lived-experiential quality of an inheritance. Conceptually and *concretely*, spatial experience is here an ethical problem that pertains to questions of intergenerational responsibility and justice.[11] In this special issue of *Future Anterior* the contributors ask us—directly or implicitly, each in their own way—to contemplate the sense and significance of heritage in this light.

Biography
Tao DuFour is Assistant Professor in History and Theory of Architecture at the University of Cambridge. His work investigates questions of embodied spatial experience, intersubjective and intergenerational understandings of architecture, landscape and territory, and the ways in which these both constitute and are embedded in the historicity of environments. DuFour's current research focuses on the regional context of the Caribbean and Guianas. He is the author of *Husserl and Spatiality: A Phenomenological Ethnography of Space* (Routledge 2022), which was awarded the Edward Goodwin Ballard Book Prize in Phenomenology. DuFour obtained his PhD from Cambridge University and is a Fellow of Trinity College.

Notes

[1] Tao DuFour, *Husserl and Spatiality: A Phenomenological Ethnography of Space* (London: Routledge, 2023), 116.

[2] See Anthony J. Steinbock, *Home and Beyond: Generative Phenomenology after Husserl* (Evanston, IL: Northwestern University Press, 1995) and Dan Zahavi, *Husserl and Transcendental Intersubjectivity: A Response to the Linguistic-Pragmatic Critique,* trans. Elizabeth A. Behnke (Athens: Ohio University Press, 2001).

[3] Tao DuFour, "Environmentality: A Phenomenology of Generative Space in Husserl," *Research in Phenomenology* 53, no. 3 (2023): 331–58.

[4] Mihail Sebastian, *For Two Thousand Years,* trans. Philip Ó Ceallaigh (London: Penguin Books, 2016), 215.

[5] Stuart Hall, *Familiar Stranger: A Life Between Two Islands* (Durham: Duke University Press, 2017), 73.

[6] Hall, *Familiar Stranger,* 73. I am indebted here to Dalibor Vesely's discussion of space in terms of what he termed the "latent world"; see Dalibor Vesely, *Architecture in the Age of Divided Representation: The Question of Creativity in the Shadow of Production* (Cambridge, MA: MIT Press, 2004), 378–89.

[7] Judith Butler, "Precarious Life, Vulnerability, and the Ethics of Cohabitation," *The Journal of Speculative Philosophy* 26, no. 2 (2012): 141.

[8] Butler, "Precarious Life," 147.

[9] See DuFour, *Husserl and Spatiality,* 79.

[10] George Lamming, *The Pleasures of Exile* (London: Pluto Press, 2005), 9.

[11] Matthias Fritsch, *Taking Turns with the Earth: Phenomenology, Deconstruction, and Intergenerational Justice* (Stanford, CA: Stanford University Press, 2018).

In This Issue

Trauma Heritage as Memory Justice: Sites and Dilemmas in Rwanda
Delia Duong Ba Wendel

After the 1994 genocide in Rwanda, killing sites were preserved as memorials to maintain evidence of crimes for public viewing. Rather than be seen as exceptional, those engagements in memory justice activism comprise part of a larger "era of trauma heritage" emerging largely from the Global South in the late twentieth century and continuing today. Trauma heritage refers to spatialized memories of violence that have been systematically marginalized or hidden. These are sites of truth-telling that aim to enact change in the contexts of impunity and gross negligence that they resist. But they are inordinately hard to see, both for those who are close and at a distance. Reflecting from Rwanda, this article engages the tensions inherent to trauma heritage and their potential as sites of repair.

Indigenous Heritage and Ontological Conflicts in the Southcentral Andes
Francesco Orlandi

Taking inspiration from the epistemological potential of the Aymara concept of taypi this contribution aims to show the persistence of Indigenous peoples' self-determination and community governance in contemporary heritage politics. A multisited archaeological ethnography across Tiwanaku (Bolivia) and the Calchaquí valleys (Tucumán, Argentina) brings to light the long memories of anti-colonial resistance in the south-central Andes and visualizes heritage-making practices in their ecological dimension, bridging multiple temporalities and territorial relatedness. The resulting picture figures a deep-seated tension between regulatory policies that adjust indigenous heritage to universal classifications and values embedded in the modern nation-state imaginaries, and emancipatory politics in which heritage claims are entangled with the social reproduction of community life and with the reparation of historical injustices. This twofold political dimension materializes in the legal artefact of the free, prior, informed consultation (FPIC), whose long memory of ambiguity is traced down to the early day of colonization. The article argues that consent-seeking mechanisms create an intermediate space where universal and place-based worldmaking designs converge. Locating these

Future Anterior
Volume XIX, Number 2
Winter 2022

grey areas in time and space is crucial for addressing intercultural histories and future-oriented practices of heritage rights.

"Our Auschwitz is the ESMA": Preservation and the Holocaust at the former Higher School of Mechanics of the Navy in Argentina
Valentina Rozas-Krause
The article examines the transformation of the Higher School of Mechanics of the Navy in Buenos Aires, ESMA for its Spanish initials, from one of the largest clandestine detention centers of the Argentine military dictatorship (1976–83), into a historical monument, museum, and a campus for human rights organizations. Starting in 2004, ESMA was symbolically and materially recovered. Following the debates that framed this transformation, it explores how the efforts to preserve the memories of the victims of the civic-military dictatorship were transmuted into the preservation of buildings, and how the local argentine heritage discourse became entangled with global Holocaust tropes. The preservation efforts of ESMA reveal the contradiction between building boundaries to protect the site's past, while at the same time responding to the functional demands of a campus dedicated to present-day human rights and memory activists. Finally, by analyzing the successful application of the ESMA site to the UNESCO World Heritage List, the article explores the tensions between global heritage and local demands for memory, justice, and reparation.

The Bunker, the Barracks, the Base, and the Border: Preservation as Resistance in South Lebanon
Batoul Faour and Meriam Soltan
About six kilometers from the Blue Line and twelve from the Syrian border, the southern town of Khiam sits at a frontline traversing constant regional turmoil. Its existence in Lebanon entirely was determined by the colonial nation-state division of the area following the end of World War II, a critical period in the establishment of Lebanon's independence and a time during which British control oversaw the construction of a series of defensive architectural fortifications within the town's landscape. These structures include a bunker, a barracks, and an airbase—all three of which were built in Khiam during World War II, given its strategic border location and the overlooking conditions of its mountain ranges. Their functions have since been transformed by events within Lebanon's regional and local history, including two Israeli invasions, and a neighboring civil war in Syria. This article, through a telling of encounters based on fieldwork within and around the sites, reanimates the collective history of intergenerational cycles of occupation, displacement, violence, and return in South Lebanon. It

situates the ephemeral lifespans of each of these structures and their embodied narratives as distinct reconstructions of time and place. Over the years, these reconstructions have been imposed by a diversity of actors and transgressors ranging from the imagination of a child to the strategic vision of a colonizer. Through a biographical quality inspired by personal experiences of the sites, it also takes a contextual approach situated in the geopolitics of the South as a contested borderland constantly being transgressed, and the intimacies of living under such precarious conditions.

The Intimacies of Restitution: Acts of Reinscribing the Dadaab Refugee Camps
Anooradha Iyer Siddiqi

In a consideration of restitution through the work of Edward Said, this article examines a critical archive of artworks that carry out acts of countermapping, of "drawing" the Dadaab refugee camps, free from any agenda to restrict or control the free migration of people. The Dadaab refugee camps, in northern Kenya near the border of Somalia, have been for much of their existence the largest-ever refugee-hosting site administered by the UNHCR. The settlements have been drawn and redrawn, by architects, by humanitarians, by aerial photographers, and by satellites. The works of art in this article—by Deqa Abshir, AbdulFatah Adam, Elsa MH Mäki, and Cave Bureau—reinscribe the Dadaab refugee camps by "drawing," renarrating them with altogether different aims. This article discusses the work of these concerned artists in light of Said's reflections on academic freedom, made in Cape Town in the wake of the struggle against apartheid, in the article "Identity, Authority, Freedom: The Potentate and the Traveler." This critical archive of works enables conceptualizations of restitution. This article examines the intimacies of restitution through these distinct critical acts of reinscribing the Dadaab refugee camps.

Figures 1 and 2. Residents living near Murambi, employed by the Genocide Memorial Commission, care for their children and clean the bones of genocide victims found in mass graves near Murambi, 1996. Image courtesy of Mario Ibarra, Chile.

Delia Duong Ba Wendel

Trauma Heritage as Memory Justice

Sites and Dilemmas in Rwanda

After the 1994 genocide against Tutsi in Rwanda, massacre sites were conserved as memorials to maintain evidence of crimes for public viewing. Churches, schools, and government offices—transformed by the killings they held—were suspended from use in quotidian life to serve as places of witness. Those efforts in conservation emerged as urgent priorities amid ongoing violence, displacement, and uneasy return.[1] Yet, the ethics that sought memory justice for victims and their relatives have increasingly sat at odds with state interests. The idea to conserve scenes of violence for future encounter was also driven by a post-genocide government seeking sovereignty and social control.[2] The phenomenon—the spatialization of hidden or normalized violence—is not unique to Rwanda. Neither are the ethical dilemmas that have emerged as a result. As an extreme example of a global phenomenon, then, Rwanda's genocide memorials reveal the tensions inherent in confronting violence and representing violent acts for political leverage, along with the sites' potential to enact forms of repair.

The individuals first involved in genocide memory work in Rwanda rarely spoke about memorialization.[3] Instead, they conceived of their work as means to care for the dead and "make history known."[4] They conserved the remains of victims in sites of killing to represent a minoritized history: the erasure of a people by mass violence and from global attention. For the individuals committed to it, the work was agonizingly, emotionally and physically, difficult. It was also rife with irresolvable paradoxes to do with the enduring presence of the dead in living communities, the coexistence of trauma and justice-seeking, and conflicting priorities of individual and collective memory. Their reflections prompt understanding the sites more as "trauma heritage" than memorial monuments.[5]

My concept of trauma heritage is related to a wider category of what sociologist Maurice Halbwachs called collective memory, or shared remembrance. Halbwachs claimed that all memory is socially constructed around some concept of place: he argued that only spatial imagery had the necessary historical stability that would allow groups to discover their past in the present.[6] These *lieux de memoire* (sites of memory), to expand on historian Pierre Nora's term, are not mere repositories of past experiences.[7] They are sites of discourse in which historical narratives become tangible—knowable—and passed on to others.

Future Anterior
Volume XIX, Number 2
Winter 2022

But trauma inflects memory in powerful ways, affecting the ways that it is spatialized. Theorist Cathy Caruth defines trauma as "doubled" injuries felt by both bodies and minds, which tell "the story of a wound."[8] Trauma heritage locates a third site where wounds are felt: the places associated with traumatic experiences and their afterlives. Trauma is a particular type of past representation: it haunts, recurs, persists unceasingly, and is fleeting, in turn and at once. The representation of violence is not always fully available to understanding. Enigmatic memories of violence become collective—located and remembered by groups that share traumatic experiences—in part through their presence in the landscape.

When made defiantly visible, as in the case of the first attempts to conserve genocide sites and victims' remains, trauma heritage tells subaltern truths about acts of violence. It is animated by what I call an "ethics of non-erasure": a set of values partly informed by human rights that seeks justice by emplacing violent histories. Survivors and victims' advocates that render trauma as heritage make disappearances, oppression, and destruction *visible*. Spatializing memory aims to challenge erasure and inattention, replacing narratives with landscapes, amplifying words with images. Those efforts come with significant personal costs. They are also put forward with expectations of actions beyond mere remembrance. Burdened and oriented thus, trauma heritage makes public space for silenced pain.

The origins and legacies of Rwanda's genocide memorials contain important lessons for understanding relationships between memories of injustice and forms of empowerment and repair. Reading genocide memorials solely as commemorative monuments misses the dilemmas and emotional and physical labor inherent in that memory work. Considering the sites, instead, as trauma heritage, forestalls hasty assumptions regarding the sites' political sensationalism. It also troubles the connections of that emotionally and physically challenging work to memory justice. In place of both conclusions, the following three vignettes, based on oral history interviews with genocide memory workers, residents living near the memorials, and photographs and videos of conservation work from 1994–98, seek to open up and ground the ethics and politics of trauma heritage.

Backstage

At Rwanda's most iconic genocide memorial today, the conserved and mummified bodies of victims on display make it difficult to see beyond the image of suffering. The Murambi Genocide Memorial in southwest Rwanda was formerly a technical school under construction where more than 35,000 people were killed. The perpetrators of those killings destroyed evidence of their crimes by moving victims into mass graves. The clay content in the soil effectively mummified hundreds of bodies. One year later, genocide survivors and Tutsi returning to the area from exile began to exhume and move the remains of victims back into the school buildings. These first experiments to conserve victims' remains shaped Rwanda's genocide heritage aesthetic.

In what follows, I describe two photographs and a video taken near the Murambi genocide site that provide a sense of what it was like to conserve genocide evidence in the years immediately following 1994. Images of violence are never easy to receive; they are overlaid with issues of vantage and power that can reproduce pain and harm. For many of us, these sites open landscapes of association and memory that we cannot help but see and feel. At the same time, scenes of massacre are the very substance of trauma heritage; they register the acts through which repair and justice are addressed.The reader of this essay may not be willing to regard images of violence in this way. That is certainly understandable. But I am primarily asking those of us unaccustomed to experiences of violence to look. Trauma heritage demands methods based on deep listening and seeing.[9] Learning to "read" trauma heritage fosters an ethics of seeing violence—of countering abstraction and inhumanity—and thereby of recognizing personhood and listening to struggle.

In two photographs taken in 1996, hands hold both the dead and the young (Figures 1 and 2). In one image, a woman's arms gently encircle a child who watches an infant playing with the grass at their feet. Blankets to keep the pair warm are close in case comfort is needed. She is resting and looking off to the distance, where another woman sits partially out of frame, holding a baby, nestled in a blanket, to her chest. In the second image, the camera centers in on many hands suspended over a sheet of plastic that holds soapy water. They rub human skulls to wash the dirt and remaining bits of hair, blood, and flesh from genocide victims found in a mass grave. The group is sitting in the same field as the children and their caregivers. Several groups are at work conserving hundreds of bones and skulls, some for display at the Murambi Memorial and others for burial in consecrated graves.

Photographs of this backstage work of conservation and mothering challenge a reading of genocide memorials solely as commemorative monuments, inviting questions as to the politics and emotional labor involved. Early conservation work at sites of killing was gruesome, difficult, and emotional. Most conservation workers were women, often young widows and genocide survivors whose young children accompanied them as they did their work. Conservation interweaved processes of grief and caregiving—for the young and the dead, at once.

Vestine is one of the women who was first involved in that conservation effort. She and I talked about what it was like to do that work some twenty years later. Vestine survived the genocide with two of her children. She and many other conservation workers were still grieving at the time. Conservation was done amid really difficult life situations and emotional states. The bodies and bones that they cleaned were heavy and smelled of decay. Yet, Vestine did the work because the job provided her and her children with some income. She was equally motivated because, as she put it, "they were our people."[10] Vestine cleaned the bodies of the dead to bring her kin, her relatives and fellow Tutsi, some measure of dignity. She continues to care for them today. Vestine has returned to the school buildings daily for the last three decades to clean the grounds and the bodies in the classrooms at the Murambi Genocide Memorial. This despite being laid off for a time by the government, and the recurring migraines and high blood pressure that doctors diagnosed as trauma related.

A video filmed in 1997 further illustrates what it was like to conserve genocide evidence, providing a window onto not only the personal, but also the necessarily social, nature of that memory work (Figure 3). Like the photographs above, it was recorded by Mario Ibarra, a Chilean human rights worker who first worked for the United Nations Human Rights Field Office in Rwanda (UN-HRFOR) and then directly for the Rwandan government's Genocide Memorial Commission until 1998. Mario brought his extensive expertise investigating human rights violations to the conservation effort. His keen sensitivity to cultural trauma, dispossession, and the non-acknowledgment of crimes derives from his own lived and collective memory, as a member of the Mapuche Indigenous people. Mario developed the conservation strategy at Murambi along with Dr. Célestin Kanimba Misago (or Dr. Kanimba as he was called), an archaeologist and director of the National Museum in Rwanda.

The video shows 6 individuals—4 women and 2 men—working with domestic tools—kitchen gloves, toothbrushes, bars of soap, buckets—to prepare skulls and other bones for conservation at Murambi. The rasps, scrapes, and water plunges produce a rhythm of work against the background of their crying children. They tease each other in Kinyarwanda, aware of the camera watching. Mario comes into view to inspect the bones and see if their experiments with household products are cleaning, and not damaging the remains. This prompts one woman to tease another in Kinyarwanda, "You are working with the white man!" The other woman cocks her head, looking slyly back and replies, "*Sha,* stop laughing at me!" Dr. Kanimba is behind the camera, out of frame. His voice interrupts the banter to translate the group's conversation to French for Mario. Dr. Kanimba

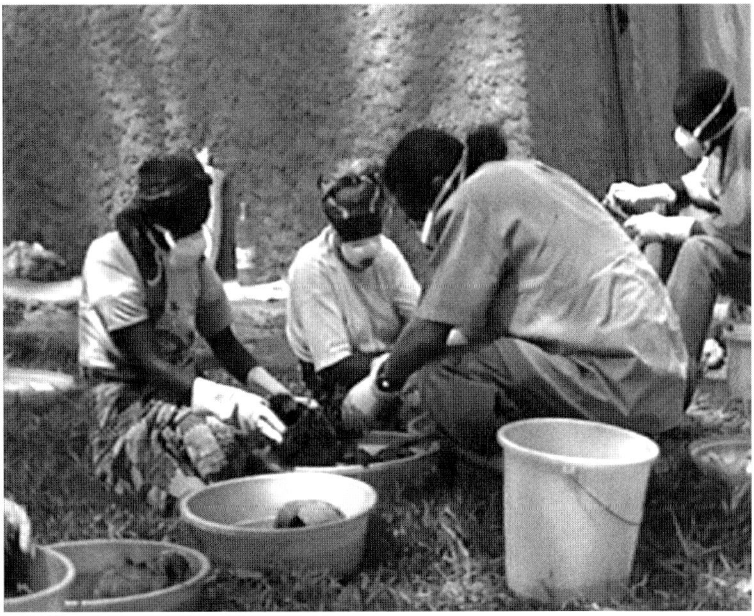

Figure 3. Video still showing Mario Ibarra reviewing efforts to conserve victims' bones with toothbrushes and soap (at Ruhashya near the Murambi Genocide Memorial). Image courtesy of Mario Ibarra, Chile.

approximates the exchange, telling Mario, "They want to take you to their house," referring to Rwandan customs of hospitality and friendship. Ibarra responds, "I could not possibly eat." They laugh as the camera zooms in to another woman as she uses one of the skulls to pour water into the other, flushing recent scrapings. The camera pans to an area behind the workers, where Dr. Kanimba and Mario discuss and inspect the cleaned remains that have been drying in the sun.

Far from irreverent to the tasks at hand, these scenes capture the mundane aspects of arduous and clinical conservation work. They also record the levity and humanity that individuals imparted to the work of "maintaining" memory of the genocide. This was not alienating labor, even if it was deeply painful for many. The intimacy of the work is palpable in the ways that conservation workers handled the remains of victims and connected with others in hopeful camaraderie. Many individuals were also struggling with significant losses and injuries on top of caring for others. Their memories of violence coexisted with their care for victims and each other in the hardest of times.

The views of conservation workers from this period are not well documented, and less so are their agency and humanity. Their perspectives demonstrate that early genocide memory work was not rigidly controlled by the government, even if that work required state authorization to occur. It developed from local initiatives motivated at least in part, as Vestine and her coworkers help to highlight, by care for those killed; by an ethics of non-erasure.

Domestic Refuge

Today, various sites of memory remain in tension with "authorized" genocide memorials, but not because they challenge the need and value of genocide remembrance. Rather, those other sites add to the history of violence in the country in ways that remain at odds with government priorities. An uneven landscape of officially recognized remembrance reflects differentials felt in citizenship, economic opportunity, psychological and physical health, and political power.

Genocide memorials are authorized in the sense that they are representative of state histories; are funded, maintained, and curated by government institutions; and are officially sanctioned sites of public education and commemoration.[11] They comprise what memory studies scholar Elizabeth Jelin has called, referring to similar phenomena in Latin America, the "master narrative" of the nation.[12] In Rwanda, genocide memorials have further regulatory function, forming part of a state legal-memory apparatus that manages national remembrance and regulates speech and citizenship with significant restrictions on civil liberties.[13] The result on public discourse is what anthropologist Jennie Burnet has called an "amplified silence."[14] Burnet advances this concept to describe the Rwandan government's sublimation of certain experiences of violence and survival that do not fit neatly into the binary logic of Hutu perpetrators and Tutsi victims.

"Unauthorized" trauma heritage exists among those silences in Rwanda.[15] Unauthorized sites of memory refer to genocide commemorative practices, places of memory, or narratives of experiences that are not sanctioned by the government. They include private burials of genocide victims that remain "under the radar" to thwart the forced relocation of bodies to nationally managed burial sites. They also include the more controversial memories held by Hutu wives and husbands of Tutsi genocide victims who are not officially recognized as genocide survivors because of their ethnicity. Those memories take discrete forms in the personal memory landscapes of "unauthorized" survivors and remembrance, and are rarely spoken about or have public presence.

For many older women in Rwanda today, especially those who survived children and husbands, traumatic experiences are kept close. They are felt more in the body than in open landscapes. Their embodied nature is common for officially recognized genocide memories, but there is often no other option for women whose grief has limited public reflection. In the absence of the public recognition of one's pain, the embodiment of trauma can feel very lonely.

I visited with Nkunzi in 2013 and 2018. She lives in a house downhill from the Murambi Genocide Memorial, where her vantage is primarily of the metal fencing that encircles the complex (Figure 4). She can also see the tops of the classroom buildings from her doorway. She had moved to the area in

Figure 4. A home on the periphery of the Murambi Genocide Memorial, within view. Author photo, 2018

the 1970s when she married in her early twenties. When I first spoke with her, she did not identify as a genocide survivor, but, she claimed, "We suffered too."[16] Her statement was cryptic, but in the context of our conversation, I understood it to refer to grief for the deaths of her close friends and neighbors. When I next spoke with her five years later, Nkunzi volunteered more, telling me that she lost a husband and a child to the genocide. She was reticent to talk about it because it was painful. But, also, as a Hutu, she is not officially considered a genocide survivor by the government. Yet, Nkunzi was married to a Tutsi husband and had a child and extended family who were killed in 1994. Her losses are just as real as those experienced by recognized survivors.

The Murambi Genocide Memorial does not tell Nkunzi's stories or those of others like her. She claimed not to have an opinion of what the memorial looks like. The choice to conserve bodies was not hers—it was the government's.[17] And yet, she sees the genocide all around her, both in the memorial and on paths and in houses across the hill. The ambivalence that Nkunzi expressed was common, especially among many Rwandans whose suffering remains unrecognized by authorities. On the one hand, the presence of the Murambi Genocide Memorial did not matter to Nkunzi because the deaths of her family were always with her; she carried the burden of their loss every day. Kept inside one's body, those memories feel, as another woman once told me, like ants at your throat, crawling over your heart.[18] And yet, the Murambi Memorial's proximity to Nkunzi's home was a constant reminder, pulling on her traumatic experiences and exposing them to view.

Between the isolation of memories felt only as bodily sensations and that of a landscape in which past traumas are everywhere, domestic spaces emerge as vital sites. A home can serve as a different type of memorial, a place that both symbolizes and enacts relationships with community, individual and family stories, and the struggles of everyday life. In many cases in Rwanda, unauthorized and prohibited accounts of the past find refuge in the homes and landscapes of domestic life—the very places that locate traumatic experiences. There, everyday trauma heritage stitches different times together. Those that remember are compelled to navigate the past in their present. When opened to view, those memories form stalwart resistance to authorized forgetting. Actively absent from collective memory landscapes, unauthorized trauma heritage is vigilant for change. It seeks to repair national narratives and edify self and kin.

Reparative Histories

From the beginning, the idea to conserve scenes and evidence of violence in public spaces was rife with controversy.[19] Most major massacre sites were located in living communities and surrounded by homes. The killing sites triggered sadness, grief, and anguish for residents that lived nearby. Many decried the objectification of relatives on display and related government prohibitions on traditional burial rituals. Still other residents believed that the display of bodies and bones were important to national remembrance; that the sites could educate future generations. The decision to open victims and massacres to view situated the memorials' value as evidence of crimes against concerns for the places' effects on the living.

That the approach gained traction at all in the development of Rwanda's genocide heritage derived in part from a linking of human rights to the conservation of genocide evidence. Mario Ibarra was critical to that effort. The first example of genocide heritage in the country, at Nyarubuye Church in the east, developed under his direction as head of the UN-HRFOR Kibungo Préfecture field office. There, the massacre of around three thousand people was preserved as it was found for over a year, in an initiative that preceded the state's institutionalization of related work. Nyarubuye provided material evidence in UN-HRFOR investigations and a reference for victims' advocacy in the context of international disregard. Its outsized impact on Rwanda's genocide heritage aesthetic came from its subsequent, and substantial, international attention. By July 1995, when UN Secretary General Boutros-Ghali visited, photographs of Nyarubuye had been frequently published in the international press.[20] Mario's early efforts to document and preserve conditions at Nyarubuye thus not only had a significant role in connecting human rights imperatives to preservation work; it stretched the time of the aftermath to permit "witnessing" to occur.[21]

Nyarubuye was only one of scores of genocide sites that Mario investigated as part of UN-HRFOR. In late 1995, he joined the newly formed Genocide Memorial Commission, leaving his post in the UN-HRFOR field office to work directly on the conservation of genocide evidence (including at the Murambi massacre site). In that role, he became, with the Commission's director Louis Kanamugire, a key partner in the development of Rwanda's genocide heritage. Through site investigations, testimony collection, and photographs, Louis and Mario created a Report and Map of the major genocide massacres in the country.[22] The Genocide Sites Map is an especially legible, and rare, early representation of the extent of mass violence in the country (Figure 5). Louis and Mario created it to show the world what happened. In 1997, Mario brought the map to his UN meetings in Geneva.[23] The Genocide Sites Map reveals countless markers of what Mario referred to as the "smell and the pain" associated with investigations of the genocide and conservation of related evidence. The map also represents nodes in an uneven political landscape where memory work enacts forms of empowerment.

In 2014, I interviewed Mario in his home in southern Chile about his work in Rwanda. With the Genocide Sites Map laid out on the table before us, I asked Mario why he thought that genocide memorials had become so politicized. I unwittingly provoked a strong reaction. He became immediately enraged, though I knew his anger was not directed at me. He was irate at the politicization of their work, and the subsequent distractions from the suffering and injustice that he witnessed. Adamant, he pointed to the map, responding:

> They said that there was a massacre here. The massacre was there, *MIRA*. IT WAS THERE. There, there, there, there, THERE. Look, here at the map. This serious crime of non-acknowledgment denies the *pueblo's* suffering. We are all, all, responsible in some part for this.[24]

For Mario, the Genocide Sites Map is both a visceral representation of his memory work in Rwanda and also of a greater geography of atrocity—one that links Rwanda to gross human rights violations throughout the world. Motivated by an ethics of non-erasure, their map and conservation of genocide sites and victims' remains call out for acknowledgment and recognition. "Look," he said, "the genocide took place there, THERE. Look, here at the map!" In doing so, Mario called on the Genocide Sites Map, and each of the places of massacre to which it refers, as visceral historical records. He claimed a role for historiography in repair.

Anthropologist David Scott has elaborated on what he and others have called "reparatory history." His view echoes the

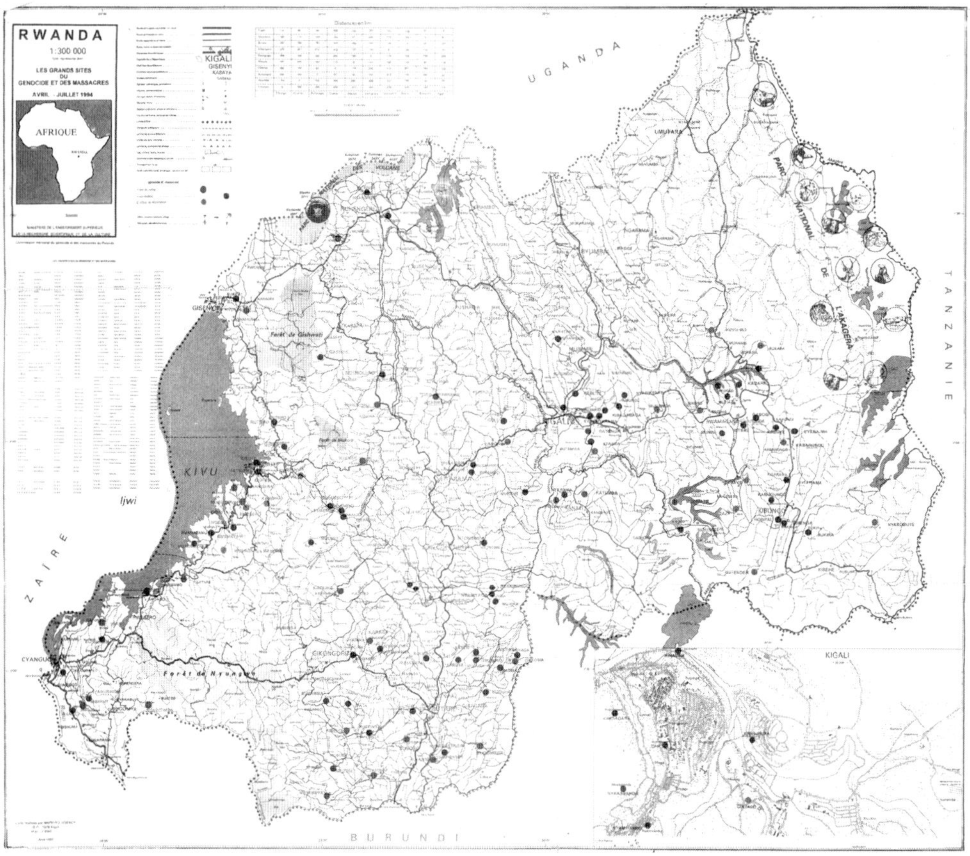

Figure 5. The 1997 Genocide Sites Map, developed by Louis Kanamugire and Mario Ibarra for the Genocide Memorial Commission. Courtesy Marc Bossuyt, Belgium.

representational work undertaken by Louis, Mario, and Vestine, and the aspirations of Nkunzi. Each of these individuals sought accountability for and recognition of crimes as forms of repair. Scott writes that within a category of "moral histories" that seek to recount histories of injustice, "reparatory histories" are distinct, concerned:

> with those historical evils and injustices that *remain* unrepaired in the present, [. . . and thus] to *reconstruct* these evil and unjust pasts in ways that potentially enable us to rethink the moral responsibility that the present owes in respect of them.[25]

Where Scott emphasizes the intentions and stakes of reparatory histories, scholars like Catherine Hall practice a reparatory history to emphasize the role that historical evidence and narratives have in correcting the omissions of slavery and colonialism in British national histories and social consciousness.[26] The resulting Legacies of British Slavery project is a database that follows material traces of racial capitalism in the wealth generated through the slave trade. Hall's practice of reparatory history underscores the importance of what Scott calls "reconstruction." Reparatory histories recover subaltern sources of knowledge, such as compiled in Hall's archival database, to narrate the minoritized experiences not represented in dominant or official histories.

Vestine, Mario, and Louis, too, are reparative historians. They conserved evidence of violent crimes—transforming it into heritage—to shape the writing of history. I use the term "reparative" to gently distinguish their commitments to histories established in landscapes, even while such work is aligned to Scott's and Hall's projects of moral realignment and truth-telling. Trauma heritage comprise an expanded historiography, "written" in place as strategic challenges to erasure, inattention, and obfuscating rhetoric. But trauma heritage is not merely historiographic. Its locations in communities and its ability to be experienced seek to enact forms of repair. By recognizing violence as part of the historical record, trauma heritage offers evidence for judicial processes, initiates processes of social acknowledgment and healing, and seeks to prevent recurrence.

An Era of Trauma Heritage

In Rwanda, the first genocide heritage sites emerged as fraught, if critical, strategies of repair. Those efforts developed from a larger memory justice and human rights movement, emerging from the mid-twentieth century, largely in the Global South, and continuing today. My Atlas of Trauma Heritage visualizes that "era of trauma heritage" (Figure 6).[27] It localizes phenomena arising from a need to mark the place where violence occurred—to *show* that people were disappeared, to claim that a crime happened *here,* to remember that people died *there*. That trauma heritage continues to be enacted today demonstrates the enduring and pivotal role that spatialized memory has in recognizing unacknowledged crimes.

Recognizing an era of trauma heritage in world history foregrounds the spatial and material forms of representation that were thought necessary, by diverse groups under siege, to bring attention to terror and mass death. As the Atlas shows, diverse efforts in remembering the Holocaust, Hiroshima, and racialized violence in the United States initiated this era. Holocaust memorialization, and especially the first efforts to open concentration camps and display the belongings and ashes of victims for public viewing, has been a major force in the era of trauma heritage.[28] But what the Atlas shows is that it is not the only center of such work. Sites of trauma heritage emerge with greater frequency in the 1970s. That increase corresponds with the second wave of human rights discourse and related liberation and social justice struggles. Diverse cases, including the activism of Las Madres de la Plaza de Mayo in Argentina and Mamie Till Mobley's decision to open her son's casket to

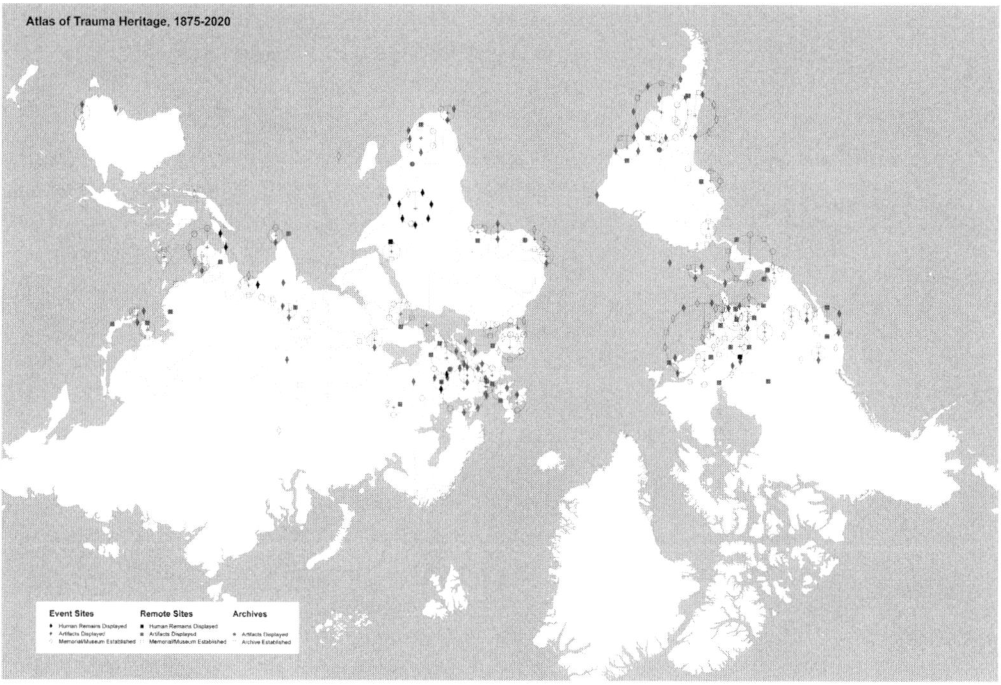

Figure 6. The Atlas of Trauma Heritage: Efforts to spatialize silenced and absenced violence, 1875-2020. Mapping by T. Rivera, Art by Z. DeGiulio, Wendel 2024.

a viewing public illustrate the independence of emblematic trauma heritage from experiments in Holocaust memorialization. The same is true of Rwanda's genocide heritage. The history of world trauma heritage demonstrates a rather more diffuse geography of parallel efforts.

Rwanda imparts a particular lens to this history. It situates similar efforts in spatializing hidden or normalized histories of violence within a global geography of memory justice activism. It also reads those sites as not merely commemorative, but also beset with intrinsic paradoxes to do with violence, politics, and empowerment. These are, moreover, efforts shaped by individual grief, rage, and care as much as by institutions and state interests. Situated thus, we see repair as unruly work.

The paradoxes inherent to rendering violent, traumatic experiences as heritage include the creation of a visceral historical record that needs to be seen in order to initiate repair. On the one hand, we see the powerful role of spatial representations in efforts in victim's advocacy and justice-seeking. As Mario and Vestine amply demonstrate, that process of historical reconstruction was not smooth, nor without personal costs. It is also incomplete and open to cooptation by powerful regimes. In Rwanda today, for example, the country's genocide memorial landscape represents efforts in memory justice alongside those of state sovereignty and sociopolitical control. As a result, unauthorized trauma heritage, including the memories held by Nkunzi, remain marginalized from public spaces. The individuals that remember them are not afforded the same pathways to repair; nor opportunities for full citizenship.

When understood as trauma heritage, and not only as symbolic memorials, we resist notions of repair as inevitable, immediately accessible, or achieved through techno-scientific acts of reconstruction. South African Psychologist Pumla Gobodo-Madikizela spent years listening to victims and witnesses of apartheid crimes as a former commissioner in South Africa's truth and reconciliation process. She claimed that those willing to represent their experiences in public create space and time for reparative processes. She described this as a "holding environment" that allows those responsible to face the violence and injustice that they perpetrate and benefit from.[29] I argue that sites of trauma heritage, in Rwanda and elsewhere in the world, perform similar roles as anticipatory holding environments for the work of repair. In this sense, reparative work is unsettling, part of an ongoing process. It is engaged in ongoing acts of witnessing that refuse closure and resist forgetting. It challenges dominant histories by holding contested memories, providing windows onto marginalized experiences.

Through the above vignettes I attempted three interventions. The first was to challenge the predominant assumption that genocide memorials are mere state symbols of power, that the display of bodies is solely in service of state aims. The second was to unsettle the hegemony of state genocide memorials by introducing an unauthorized memory of the genocide and the work that it does. Claiming each of these examples of trauma heritage as "unruly" situates the work of repair as both critique (a vigilance for contradiction) and active, reparative practice. The third was to make a case for trauma heritage as a reparative historiography, even while recognizing that the move that genocide heritage makes, from truth-telling to repair, is not equally available to all. Attention to these tensions and paradoxes does not dilute the significance of trauma heritage in the world. But they do suggest the need for more closely understanding the actors and contexts involved in such initiatives. Attention to Rwanda's early genocide heritage development along with its legacies three decades later provides a unique vantage of memory justice not as some romanticized effort, but one embedded in a messy politics of repair, searching for necessary, though near-impossible, redress for injustice.

Biography
Delia Duong Ba Wendel (she/her) is Assistant Professor in Urban Studies and International Development at MIT. Her interdisciplinary work explores peace-building after protracted violence. Current research builds from ten years of work in Rwanda and informs two book manuscripts. *Rwanda's Genocide Heritage* (forthcoming, Duke University Press) explores memory justice initiatives in Rwanda in the context of state control and human rights practices in the Global South. *The Ethics of Stability* analyzes peace-building as a sociospatial endeavor; one that is defined and challenged in the design of homes, settlements, and civic space. Wendel directs the Planning for Peace Research Collective and developed the "Memory Atlas for Repair" installation at MIT.

Notes

[1] A representative bibliography of significant work to advance understanding of the origins and dynamics of the 1994 genocide against Tutsi includes: Jennie Burnet, *To Save Heaven and Earth: Rescue in the Rwandan Genocide* (Ithaca: Cornell University Press, 2023); Alison Des Forges, *Leave None to Tell the Story: Genocide in Rwanda* (New York: Human Rights Watch, 1999); Lee Ann Fujii, *Killing Neighbors: Webs of Violence in Rwanda* (Ithaca: Cornell University Press, 2009); Catherine Newbury, "Ethnicity and the Politics of History in Rwanda," *Africa Today* 45, 1 (1998): 7–24; Scott Straus, *The Order of Genocide: Race, Power, and War in Rwanda* (Ithaca: Cornell University Press, 2006).

[2] Gretchen Baldwin, "Constructing Identity through Commemoration: *Kwibuka* and the Rise of Survivor Nationalism in Post-conflict Rwanda," *The Journal of Modern African Studies* 57, no. 3 (2019): 355–75; Annalisa Bolin, "On the Side of Light: Performing Morality at Rwanda's Genocide Memorials," *Journal of Conflict Archaeology* 7, no. 3 (2012): 199–207; Suzanne Buckley-Zistel, "Remembering to Forget: Chosen Amnesia as a Strategy for Local Coexistence in Post-Genocide Rwanda," *Journal of the International African Institute* 76, no. 2 (2006): 131–50; Jennie E. Burnet, *Genocide Lives in Us: Women, Memory, and Silence in Rwanda* (Madison: University of Wisconsin Press, 2012); Susan E. Cook, "The Politics of Preservation in Rwanda," in *Genocide in Cambodia and Rwanda: New Perspectives,* ed. Susan E. Cook (New Brunswick: Transaction Publishers, 2006), 281–99; Hélène Dumas and Rémi Korman, "Espaces de la mémoire du génocide des Tutsis au Rwanda: Mémoriaux et Lieux de Mémoire,"*Afrique Contemporaine* 2, no. 238 (2011): 11–27; Nigel Eltringham, "Bodies of Evidence: Remembering the Rwandan Genocide at Murambi," in *Remembering Genocide,* ed. Nigel Eltringham and Pam Maclean (London: Routledge, 2014), 200–18; Nicole Fox, *After Genocide: Memory and Reconciliation in Rwanda* (Madison: University of Wisconsin Press, 2021); Amanda Gryzb, "Unsettled Memory: Genocide Memorial Sites in Rwanda," *Brown Journal of World Affairs* 25, no. 2 (2019): 185–98; Sara Guyer, "Rwanda's Bones," *Boundary 2* 36, no. 2 (2009): 155–75; Rémi Korman, "La Politique de Mémoire du Génocide des Tutsi au Rwanda: Enjeux et Évolutions," *Droit et Culture* 66, no. 2 (2013): 87–101; Rémi Korman, "L'Etat Rwandais et la Mémoire du Génocide: Commémorer sur les ruines (1994–1996)," *Vingtieme Siècle: Revue d'histoire* 2, no. 122 (2014): 987–98; Rachel Ibreck, "The Politics of Mourning: Survivor Contributions to Memorials in Post-Genocide Rwanda," *Memory Studies* 3, no. 4 (2010): 330–43; Erin Jessee, *Negotiating Genocide in Rwanda: The Politics of History* (New York: Palgrave Macmillan, 2017); René Lemarchand, "The Politics of Memory in the Great Lakes Region," NIOD Lecture in Holocaust and Genocide Studies (Amsterdam: NIOD, 2013); Sarah Kenyon Lischer, "Narrating Atrocity: Genocide Memorials, Dark Tourism, and the Politics of Memory," *Review of International Studies* 45, no. 5 (2019): 805–27; Timothy Longman, *Memory and Justice in Post-Genocide Rwanda* (New York: Cambridge University Press, 2017); Laura Major, "Unearthing, Untangling and Re-articulating Genocide Corpses in Rwanda," *Critical African Studies* 7, no. 2 (2015): 164–81; Jens Meierhenrich, "Topographies of Remembering and Forgetting: The Transformation of Lieux de Mémoire in Rwanda," in *Remaking Rwanda: State Building and Human Rights After Mass Violence,* ed. Scott Straus and Lars Waldorf (Madison: University of Wisconsin Press, 2011): 283–96; David Mwambari, "*Agaciro,* Vernacular Memory, and the Politics of Memory in Post-Genocide Rwanda," *African Affairs* 120, no. 481 (2021): 611–28; Olivier Nyirubugara, *Complexities and Dangers of Remembering and Forgetting in Rwanda* (Leiden: Sidestone Press, 2013); Claudine Vidal, "La Commémoration du Génocide au Rwanda: Violence Symbolique, Mémorisation Forcée et Histoire Officielle," *Cahiers d'études Africaines* 3, no. 175 (2004): 575–92.

[3] Based on interviews with individuals who led and participated in the first genocide conservation efforts in 1994–98 along with photographs and videos of their work. See Delia Duong Ba Wendel, *Rwanda's Genocide Heritage: Between Justice and Sovereignty* (Durham: Duke University Press, forthcoming).

[4] Interview with Vestine Ndikuryayo, 23 July 2018, Murambi, trans. B.U. and author; Louis Kanamugire, 16 July 2018, Kigali, trans. by author.

[5] For a full treatment of my concept, "trauma heritage," see Wendel, *Rwanda's Genocide Heritage*, forthcoming.

[6] Maurice Halbwachs, *On Collective Memory,* trans. F. & V. Ditter (New York: Harper & Row Colophon, 1980 [1925]), 167.

[7] Pierre Nora, "Between Memory and History: Les Lieux de Mémoire," *Representations* 26 (1989): 7–24.

[8] Cathy Caruth, *Unclaimed Experience: Trauma, Narrative, and History* (Baltimore: Johns Hopkins University Press, 1996), 4. The concept of trauma heritage resonates with what Karen Till calls "wounded places" ("Artistic and Activist Memory-Work: Approaching Place-Based Practice," *Memory Studies* 1, no. 1 [2008]: 99–113).

[9] I elaborate on this method of seeing and listening, and its challenges, in the introduction to Wendel, *Rwanda's Genocide Heritage* (forthcoming).

[10] Interview with Vestine, July 23, 2018, Rwanda; trans. from Kinyarwanda by B.U. and D.W.

[11] I use the term "authorized" heritage following Laurajane Smith, *Uses of Heritage* (London: Routledge, 2006).

[12] Elizabeth Jelin, *State Repression and the Labors of Memory,* trans. Judy Rein and Marcial Godoy-Anativia (Minneapolis: University of Minnesota Press, 2003), 27–30.

[13] Erin Jessee and David Mwambari, "Memory Law and the Duty to Remember the '1994 Genocide Against the Tutsi' in Rwanda," in *Memory Laws and Historical Justice,* ed. Elazar Barkan and Ariella Lang (New York: Palgrave Macmillan, 2022), 291–319.

[14] Burnet, *Genocide Lives in Us,* 111.

[15] By my estimation, Rwanda's memory landscape comprises authorized sites of memory and a range of amplified absences, including those related to under-recognized, unauthorized, and prohibited memories.

[16] Interview with "Nkunzi" (pseudonym), 26 August 2013, Rwanda; trans. from Kinyarwanda by B.U. and D.W.

[17] Interview with Nkunzi, July 23, 2018, Rwanda.

[18] Interview with "Celeste" in central Rwanda, July 17, 2018.

[19] Several writers and human rights organizations interviewed residents in the first years after the genocide and those volumes include the first reactions to genocide sites in communities. See African Rights, *"Go. If You Die, Perhaps I Will Live": A Collective Account of Genocide and Survival in Murambi, Gikongoro, April-July 1994* (Kigali: African Rights, 2007); Burnet, *Genocide Lives in Us*; Martien Schotsmans, "A l'Écoute des Rescapés: Recherche sur la perception par les rescapés de leur Situation Actuelle" (Kigali: GTZ, 2000); Claudine Vidal, "Les Commémorations du Génocide au Rwanda," Les Temps Modernes 56, 613 (2001): 1-46.

[20] Including, most famously as the opening and closing images and vignettes in Philip Gourevitch's *New Yorker* article: Philip Gourevitch, "Letter from Rwanda: After the Genocide," *The New Yorker,* December 18, 1995, pp. 81–95.

[21] In trauma studies, the "secondary witness" is a spectator or bystander who sees and hears the testimonies of others; they are not a participant in the traumatic events, but in accounts of them. Shoshana Felman and Dori Laub, *Testimony: Crises of Witnessing in Literature, Psychoanalysis, and History* (New York: Routledge, 1991), 75–76; Dominick LaCapra, *Writing History, Writing Trauma* (Ithaca: Cornell University Press, 2001).

[22] Genocide Memorial Commission, *Rapport Preliminaire d'Identification des Sites du Génocide et Des Massacres d'Avril-Juillet 1994 au Rwanda* (Kigali: MINESUPRES, Feb 1996); Genocide Memorial Commission, "Rwanda: Les Grands Sites du Genocide et des Massacres, Avril-Juillet 1994" (Kigali: Rwandan Mapping Agency, April 1997).

[23] In tandem with his UN-HRFOR position and later work with the Rwandan Genocide Memorial Commission, Mario Ibarra was an elected alternate representative of Chile to the United Nations Sub-Commission on the Promotion and Protection of Human Rights, from 1994 to 1998. United Nations, Economic and Social Council, "Election of Members of the Sub-Commission on Prevention of Discrimination and Protection of Minorities," E/CN.4/1994/85/Add.2 (07 Feb 1994).

[24] Interview with Mario Ibarra, January 9, 2015, Chile.

[25] David Scott, "Preface: A Reparatory History of the Present," small axe 52 (2017): x.

[26] Catherine Hall, "Doing Reparatory History: Bringing 'Race' and Slavery Home," *Race & Class* 60, no. 1 (2018): 3–21. See also, in the same volume, Cathy Bergin and Anita Rupprecht, "Reparative Histories: Tracing Narratives of Black Resistance and White Entitlement," *Race & Class* 60, no. 1 (2018): 22–37.

[27] The "era of trauma heritage" is a subsequent development from what Holocaust studies scholars have called, variously, the "era of the witness" or the "era of testimony," referring to the proliferation and elevated significance of witness testimony to exposing and prosecuting the anti-Semitic violence that occurred during World War II. Dori Laub and Shoshana Felman, *Testimony: Crises of Witnessing in Literature, Psychoanalysis and History* (New York: Routledge, 1992); Annette Wieviorka, *The Era of the Witness,* trans. Jared Stark (Ithaca: Cornell University Press, 1998, 2006).

[28] James E. Young, *The Texture of Memory: Holocaust Memorials and Meaning* (New Haven: Yale University Press, 1993).

[29] Pumla Gobodo-Madikizela, "Aesthetics of Memory, Witness to Violence, and a Call to Repair," in *Post-Conflict Hauntings: Transforming Memories of Historical Trauma,* ed. K. Wale, P. Gobodo-Madikizela, J. Prager (London: Palgrave Macmillan, 2020), 136–38.

Figure 1. Snapshot of a video recording shot during the celebration of the Feast of the Crosses in Aynuqa Wila Kuntu, Ayllu Originario Huancollo (Tiahuanaco Municipality, La Paz, Bolivia), May 2018. Photo: Author.

Francesco Orlandi

Indigenous Heritage and Ontological Conflicts in the Southcentral Andes

Introduction

In her comprehensive ethnohistorical study of the Aymara people, Thérèse Bouysse-Castagne defines *taypi* as "a place where differences coexist."[1] Taypi is a relational principle structuring Andean epistemology, cosmology, and politics. It works by multiplying perspectives. Referring to the semantic multiplication generated by the modern era mining exploitation in Potosí, Silvia Rivera Cusicanqui found that *taypi* hosts a historical principle of hope in which the enduring anti-colonial struggles of Indigenous life-worlds in the Andes can be appreciated.[2] This working concept indicates the convergence of a plurality of temporalities, experiences, and other-than-human agencies toward a shared middle ground, which the Aymara-Bolivian sociologist elaborated in terms of "a zone of friction . . . that creates the magma enabling historical transformations, for better and worse."[3]

To locate this conceptual space in the actual geography and living experience of heritage in the southcentral Andes, it may be helpful a brief anecdote delivered by the sixteenth-century Spanish chronicler Pedro Cieza de León at the time of his first visit to Tiwanaku, in the Bolivian highlands.[4] He reported the laughter that his question about the builders of the site provoked in the native listeners, who associated it with the *Taypi Qala,* "the stone in the middle," mythological point of origin of the Andean cosmos. Cieza de León dismissed this reaction and complained about the absence of written records in the Americas capable of keeping memories and unveiling the mystery behind the monumental ruins that caught his admiration. He inscribed the ruins with a temporality in which things from time past are only known and remembered through writing, marking the beginning of the modern/colonial gaze on what would become the World Heritage Site of Tiwanaku: an outstanding example of architectural magnificence and state development in the region between the fifth and eleventh centuries.[5] However, drawing on the transformative potential of taypi, Cieza de León's unintended moment of hilarity allows us to visualize a space in which to disagree with a self-proclaimed universal perspective on Indigenous cosmopolitics, material histories and memory practices. In the gray areas that unsettle and blur a common order of heritage

Future Anterior
Volume XIX, Number 2
Winter 2022

relationships is found the affective power of taypi—an "arena of seduction and antagonism."[6]

The southcentral Andes region has been integrated since pre-Hispanic times through symbolic and economic circuits, which were disrupted by the Spanish conquest and colonial administration and the later fragmentation into nation-states. These colonial signatures continue to surface today, prompted by nationalist conceptions of cultural heritage in each country. The two main archaeological sites in the region—i.e., Tiwanaku (Bolivia) and Quilmes (Northwest Argentina)—are currently managed collaboratively by government agencies and Indigenous organizations in their respective territories, after decades of struggles to renegotiate values and strategies for community participation. Against the backdrop of the multicultural recognition of Indigenous peoples' rights and the intertwining of heritage with the global discourse of sustainable development, the shared management of these important sites for national and international prestige makes visible some fractures in the common understanding of what heritage is and how it affects the surrounding landscape. On the one hand, these fractures have emerged in the community takeover of the administration and re-signification of the ruins of Quilmes into the Sacred City of the Diaguita-Calchaquí people, the last bastion of Indigenous resistance to the Spanish colonization in the seventeenth century. On the other hand, the conflicts enacted by competitive understandings of Tiwanaku's heritage reached the dimension, at the same time paradoxical and transformative, of the symbolic and political construction of the plurinational state in Bolivia.

The ethnographic vignettes that follow draw on my fieldwork on the relations between heritage and rights of Indigenous peoples in the southcentral Andes.[7] Despite the particularity of each national context, these case studies showed a common field of political disputes around objects and sites of heritage desire. Combining oral histories and the social connections made possible by different engagements with materiality, the article emphasizes the multisited and multitemporal attributes of heritage and rights beyond the discourses that pigeonhole their relationships into the authorized frameworks of the modern (pluri)national states and international development cooperation.

Bringing to light the long memory of heritage-triggered conflicts over Indigenous peoples' land and property, this contribution underscores the unperceived coloniality of heritage-rights. This becomes palpable through the "ontological disagreements" that signaled the fractures in the consensus around indigenous heritage.[8] The articulation of cosmopolitical and decolonial thinking with archaeological and ethnographic sensibilities strengthens the collective endeavor of decentralizing heritage rights relationships from taken-for-granted anthropocentric and Western-based models and values.

The Land as a Social Participant

The kind of relatedness performed by taypi can be appreciated, for example, in politically charged community rituals—such as the case of the Feast of the Cross.[9] This is celebrated throughout the Andes at the end of the agricultural year on May 3 (Figure 1). The ritual cyclically inscribes the pact of reciprocity between the community households and authorities, the land as a social being and other beings of the landscape. At the same time, the celebration is a memory practice that is embedded in the historical consciousness of the *ayllu,* i.e., the Indigenous socio-territorial political unity articulated with, and opposed to, modern/colonial temporalities.

The contradictions of Tiwanaku's heritage politics are symptomatic of the fragile foundations of the plurinational regime consecrated by the 2009 Constitution.[10] While this innovative reform granted Indigenous peoples' right to self-determination, the government retained the centralizing prerogatives of defining and exploiting natural and cultural resources. Most people interviewed in the field referred to Tiwanaku as "*las ruinas de los gringos* [the foreigners' ruins]." The joke revealed the detachment of *ayllu's* social fabric from the values championed by the World Heritage designation. Attempts to conciliate the economic benefits generated by touristic exploitation and state-led decolonization converged into a participatory management plan, which set the principle of the harmonious coexistence between local institutions and communities with the research and conservation needs of Tiwanaku.[11]

The territory of the Ayllu Originario Huancollo has been especially affected by outsiders' centuries-long interest in the archaeological ruins of Tiwanaku. The metal fence around the reconstructed monumental core of the site is a constant reminder of the power dynamics at play in the definition of dominant heritage values.[12] Approaching community members and asking them about their relationship with the heritage of Tiwanaku inexorably overlapped with the *ayllu*'s recent history of dispossession and struggle for political recognition against state and supranational agents.

The polysemy of "heritage" and "community" disclosed unexpected connections. Alternative activators of heritage relationships became apparent in the animated hills to which was common to pay offerings, the dangerous water sources where people and cattle got lost, or the tangible memories attached to adobe houses as mnemonic markers of the population.

Moreover, farming practices and products, the rotation of community authorities and archaeological works shared the same reference system and decision-making processes as the official policies of conservation and rural development. In the uneven sedimentation of these interactions is found the nonverbal and contextual persistence of taypi relations. Through these silent flows of people, land and things, ayllu's subjectivity is constantly renewed, together with, and despite, the presence of the officially designed heritage areas.

Story-tracking Huancollo's community memories and territorial relatedness challenged what is worth addressing as indigenous heritage. The legal struggles to emancipate from the semi-slavery regime of the hacienda at the turn of the twentieth century were at the heart of the collected oral histories and memory places. The in-between space disclosed by authorized heritage-making practices reverberated in the compromises to reach the juridical status of peasant community in the aftermath of the 1953 Agrarian Reform. In those years, "a man sold his land to the ruins," as a research participant told me in her family plot at the edge of the archaeological area.

The ruined adobe houses bordering the perimeter of the site make apparent the conflicts between official heritage planning and ayllu's memories in which heritage-making is recalled as a loss of social bonds with the land (Figure 2). The importance of socio-territorial relatedness and ayllu's temporality emerged as the driving force during the "updating" of community land titles within the constitutional framework of local autonomy and affirmation of Indigenous peoples' rights.

The conflicts prompted by international standards of conservation and state regulations at Tiwanaku demonstrate ayllu's ability to resist assimilation by entwining people and territory in a pact of reciprocity and mutual commitments. In line with the current participatory management, a consensus was reached between the government heritage institution and the Indigenous authorities of Huancollo on the extension of the buffer zone around the monumental core of the archaeological site. However, informed consultation and shared decision-making cannot but reflect the irreducible disagreement on what is worth preserving as indigenous heritage.

Mullu Kuntu is the only nonfenced area of the three UNESCO designated conservation zones. It is also the only portion of the archaeological site whose land has not been expropriated by the state and it still belongs to the Ayllu Originario Huancollo. To maintain community ownership and prevent expropriation, the entire area of Mullu Kuntu was declared *aynuqa,* collectively own lands, by the General Assembly of the Ayllu. The aynuqas are usually dedicated to agriculture and social practices, such as the Feast of the Cross mentioned

Figure 2. Abandoned adobe house adjacent to the archaeological area, November 2018. Ayllu Originario Huancollo (Tiahuanaco Municipality, La Paz, Bolivia). Photo: Author.

at the beginning of the section. There are, however, other kinds of aynuqas that serve different community needs, such as the plots of land where the school, the church, the Natural Medicine Hospital and the community house are located. These areas are meant to preserve the common subjectivity of the ayllu as a social body in its historical evolution. In this case, the designation of Mullu Kuntu as aynuqa *with an archaeological reserve role* overlaps with the UNESCO buffer zone on the surface but implies a different orientation on how people, things, and places are held together as indigenous heritage and returned to the politics and memory of the ayllu.

The Ruination of Multiculturalism

The Sacred City of Quilmes is the main vortex around which indigeneity, heritage and rights converge in the Calchaquí Valleys in Northwest Argentina.[13] The site is an exceptional testimony of a fortified settlement of the Diaguita people, who flourished in the inter-Andean valleys since the ninth century. They were able to resist both Inka imperial expansion in the fifteenth century and later Spanish colonization. After 130 years of confrontation, Quilmes was the last Indigenous settlement to surrender to colonial forces in the Calchaqui Valleys. The aura of anti-colonial resistance converted the ruins of Quilmes into one of the most coveted treasures in the rush for Diaguita-Calchaquí antiquities. In the last quarter of the nineteenth century, the scientific development of archaeology well-fitted the needs of the early Argentine republic to legitimize its territorial borders and project itself as a modern nation, with a solid "indigenous" prehistory.[14]

The contemporary appearance of the archaeological site (Figure 3) bears witness to the spoliation committed by the

Figure 3. View from the top of the Sacred City of Quilmes, August 2018. The reconstruction works and the buildings of the museum and the abandoned hotel with swimming pool are visible in the foreground. Comunidad India Quilmes (Tucumán, Argentina). Photo: Author.

pioneers of nationalistic archaeology, such as Ambrosetti and Debenedetti—the latter confidently affirmed that "There will be no contenders in the distribution of indigenous heritage: science will be the only and universal heir."[15] Connivance between academic apparatus, landowning elites, and the military during the dictatorship in 1978 sponsored the tourist-driven reconstructions. The return to the democratic regime in the 1980s furthered the commercial exhibitionism of the "Ruins of Quilmes," which keep haunting the abandoned boutique hotel and the recently refurbished museum.

Since 2008 the management of the site is shared by the provincial government of Tucumán and the Quilmes Indian Community (Comunidad India Quilmes, CIQ). The recent history of struggles for juridical recognition and preservation of the territory has enhanced the significance of the site as the Sacred City of Quilmes. However, the anti-colonial foundations of this claim were firstly absorbed and then neutralized through mainstream multicultural propaganda. While the ancestral resistance became an object of celebration, other pathways through which indigenous heritage acts in the present have been rendered imperceptible.

Disputes over the heritage of the Sacred City involve the community governance of the CIQ and the provincial government of Tucumán, as well as the enduring consequences of colonization in the Calchaquí valleys. Indigenous rights on the site are supported by the 1716 Royal Deed, an official treaty in which the Spanish Crown recognized the possession of the land to the descendants of the Quilmes, Amaicha, and other partialities of the Diaguita people who resisted colonial occupation. Referring to the carob tree where this foundational piece of contemporary Diaguita-Calchaquí identity and land claims was carved, a late leader of the CIQ taught me about the mediation of territory in the fight for justice, cultural integrity, and dignity: "The Indio made the Royal Deed . . . he did not swear to God, he swore to the Tree, to the Place."

In his testimony, the activation of the ruins of Quilmes as indigenous heritage was not linked to the complicit scientific interest of outsiders, tourist pleasure or commercial investment, but rather stemmed from a legitimate desire for just compensation for a broken treaty. In the 1970s, he was among the first leaders of the CIQ to rise up against the landowners who had taken possession of the land a century earlier, benefiting from the dismantling of communal ownership. These large estates relied on the exploitation of local communities who were forced to work for the *padrones* (masters), to be educated by them as well as to pay them a tribute to live and take care of their own territory.

At the time of the multicultural reconfiguration of the nation state, the CIQ was granted the recognition of its Indigenous status but the territory is still disputed. In this context, the Sacred City is placed in "a government-private island located within the territory of the Quilmes Indigenous Community."[16] The elder's main concern during our conversation was that the younger generation of leaders would abandon "sympathy" to claim their rights as an Indigenous community. He argued that "the fight must be cherished," cracking the consensus on indigenous heritage as an instrument of multicultural reconciliation.

Performing the "good Indian" has turned into an essentialist strategic positioning for easy access to national recognition of Indigenous rights and international development funding, with the drawback of marginalizing the memories of struggles that connected heritage and territory.[17] An archaeological ethnography of heritage-rights in this context helped to notice the material connections that exceeded multicultural narratives and strategic essentialism. The counter-mapping of heritage-rights in the communities of Quilmes and Aimacha del Valle offered other readings on what is at stake when indigenous heritage is involved.

This is the case of the *apachetas* (Figure 4), the stone mounds that have proliferated as marks of authenticity and adaptation to the sociocultural context of the Argentinean Northwest. When I asked an elderly woman of the Indigenous Community of Amaicha del Valle about the significance of those artifacts for the collective memory of the community, she replied that "the apachetas always mark places where the paths diverge." In the same way, these objects have continued to warn about divergence and the precautions that must be observed to avoid getting lost in the multicultural landscape.

Figure 4. The apacheta, "shrine to pay offer to Pachamama (Mother Earth)," in the central plaza of the Indigenous Community of Amaicha del Valle (Tucumán, Argentina), August 2018. Photo: Author.

We can contrast the forking paths signaled by the apachetas with the elusive promises of international cooperation and ethnodevelopment projects. Grassroots aspirations for historical and political recognition partially connected with the trope of the "re-emergence" of peoples who were deemed obliterated by civilization and progress. The fragility of the consensus linking heritage, rights, and development practices lies in the uneven interplay between community governance and the regulation of neoliberal multiculturalism.

As a member of the Council of Elders of Amaicha del Valle told me on one occasion, "We have always been here, although they did not show us." Her words revealed the *taypi* zone that was hidden in plain sight. She considered how this underlying disagreement conceals the enduring trickery, "the colored balloons," the lures thrown up to confuse and dispossess. The ruins left by international development projects in the last three decades constellate the territories of Amaicha and Quilmes. These material debris act as mnemonic nodes in the socio-territorial fabric of the communities. As much as the *apachetas,* they served to mobilize indigenous heritage either as resistance or acceptance.

Paying attention to the ruination of multiculturalism entailed recomposing the entanglement between territory and heritage, so that if one is concerned, so is the other, and both constitute an integrated whole despite constant attempts of dissociation. An example of this recomposition is the abandoned high-pressure irrigation infrastructure built in Quilmes in the early 2000s thanks to a World Bank's loan channeled through the pilot "Indigenous Community Development Project" (Figure 5). This was intended to have an impact on the development of community governance and on the conversion

Figure 5. On the left, broken elements of the World Bank Indigenous Community Development Project. On the right, restoration of the ancient dam in the village of Talapazo (Quilmes Indian Community) funded through the touristic revenues of the Sacred City of Quilmes. October–November 2018. Photo: Author.

of subsistence farming into market products, especially by rationalizing water supplies and inducing the withdrawal of the customary cyclical rotation of shifts among community members.[18] Nonetheless, the unpredictable growth of the seasonal rivers, locally known as *volcán,* ended up destroying the tubes and made the promises of development vanish.

The World Bank's project brought suspicions of embezzlement and lack of transparency to the community leadership, which motivated the violent takeover of the administration of the Sacred City in November 2013 by a group of tour guides and families from the villages of Quilmes with the support of the Tourism Secretary of Tucumán. After five years of community governance and unsuccessful negotiations with the provincial government, the new administration fostered the touristic projection of the site and sponsored community-led initiatives, such as the restoration of old canals and dams to better preserve water, thereby increasing consensus through the integrated handling of heritage and territory.

The Coloniality of Heritage-rights

Through the fabric of taypi the link between heritage and rights is rooted in the encounter between partially connected worlds, couched in the long-standing memories of outsiders' interests in grabbing land and resources through lies and trickery. Indigenous peoples' logics, social and cultural institutions were condemned to remain on the margins of modern politics and science were it not for the intervention of the same structures subjugating them. The eruption of different perspectives on time, space, and materiality concurrently indicates the modern/colonial foundations of heritage-rights.

Upendra Baxi's distinction between "modern" and "contemporary" discursivities of human rights provided useful insights to bring light on the coloniality of contemporary heritage politics. He distinguished the 'modern' discursivity as that which regulates "who may speak," "how one may speak," and "what may not be named or conversed about."[19] This is the case of the nation-state, i.e., an undisputed entity holds the decision of who the right-holders are and embodies citizenship's memories and aspirations. By contrast, the “contemporaneity” of human rights brings to the fore the unbearable voices of suffering that stem from the “non-discursive order of reality, the materiality of human violations.”[20]

Baxi’s argument finds application in the analysis of Bartolomé de Las Casas’s *De Thesauris in Peru.*[21] The volume is an important source to think through heritage-rights outside the regulatory mechanisms of modern nation-states and transnational agencies. In this late work, Las Casas not only condemned the brutality of the Spanish conquest but also pledged to the restitution of the Indigenous sovereignty over their territories advocating for the “natural” right to remember and be remembered as part of a group and in communication with specific things, known as *wak’as,* animated sites or objects that actively partake of communities’ social life.

Las Casas’s plea was against the conquistadors who plundered the wak’as in the eager search for gold by invoking the legal justification that those findings were “treasures,” i.e., valuable belonging to none, which became owned by the first one who found them. He claimed against such an unlawful classification, demonstrating that those things were living shrines and graves to which every human being must pay due respect. Acknowledging the sacredness of the Andean *wak’as* as a crucial manifestation of Indigenous sovereignty, Las Casas was concerned with the physical harm as much as with the violation of the spiritual bonds between people and territory, collective memory and transgenerational communication.

While the “contemporaneity” of heritage rights can be appreciated through the political and affective relationships animating the wak’as, Las Casas’s *De Thesauris* also informed about the limitations of consensus-based approaches on which the “modern” regulation of heritage-rights leverages. Behind the radical critique of a colonial world built on the claim of something wak’a being a “treasure,” Las Casas foresaw a common world implanted in the alleged universal morality and legality of the Europeans. He went on with his argumentation claiming that the Spaniards had the obligation to recognize the legitimacy of Indigenous sovereignty, as well as the responsibility to provide guidance to those native people who had already embraced the colonizers’ faith.

Five centuries ago as it is now, the tension between obligation and responsibility in the disputed field of indigenous heritage assumes the shape of an ethical proposal for the correct engagement with local communities: a “notification,” in Las Casas’s view, which “must be timely, peaceful (that is, free of any disturbance that may affect the understanding and reason), gentle and friendly, very moderate and conciliatory of the minds of the listeners; finally it must be made slowly, in the course of a certain time and not suddenly (at the moment of the arrival of the Spaniards)."[22]

Slowing Down Heritage Studies

Seeking community consent and participatory management has increasingly become an institutionally regulated requirement for the democratization of heritage relationships. Further exploration of the frictional spaces engendered by the legal instrument of free, prior, and informed consultation (FPIC) is needed. This was first sanctioned to protect the physical and spiritual relationships of Indigenous peoples with their ancestral territories.[23] Since the early days of their participation in transnational arenas, Indigenous movements have strongly advocated for considering heritage and territory as interlinked forces in the reproduction of community life and self-determination according to local cosmologies and politics. The FPIC is the mechanism through which local values should articulate with national and global discourse, while keeping and strengthening the capacity "to reconnect the steps that link knowledge, globalization, citizenship and research."[24]

Nonetheless, ethics procedures and consent-seeking mechanisms have often become the gateway for the replication of the structural violence of coloniality over Indigenous bodies and territories. Particularly in South America,[25] Indigenous critics and ally researchers have shown that the uncritical implementation of collaborative strategies and participatory designs may replicate patterns of domination, silencing resistance and anti-colonial histories encoded with uncomfortable objects and sites. Looking at prior consultation procedures through the relational lens of taypi offered a vantage point to observe a diversity of social artifacts and interactions that are meant to last and guarantee consensus.

As everything that is culturally embedded, the frictional space of FPIC is made of "awkward, unequal, unstable, and creative qualities of interconnections across difference."[26] The materiality of prior consultation links social and territorial dimensions, situating consent-seeking procedures in a living space where trusting relationships can develop, as well as break down. This entanglement of things, places and people makes the silent struggles to stop the erosion of communal memories and territories perceptible. It is a task of identifying and caring for commons, which is, following Marisol De La Cadena, "the expression of a worlding of many worlds ecologically related across their constitutive divergence."[27]

Consultation—like hospitality[28]—is imbued with the inherent ambiguity of its co-constitutive relationships. These intermediate spaces help us scrutinize how Indigenous heritage-making overlaps and complements multicultural ethics and territorial ordering. Knowing how to walk in the animated landscape, to properly return greetings, and to share coca leaves before engaging in any kind of activity are mandatory requirements for a sustainable ground of collaboration in the southcentral Andes as much, and more than, academic consent forms and ethical guidelines. By calling absent subjects to participation, these materials and interactions have the power to "*slow down* reasoning" and widen taken-for-granted understandings of heritage-rights.[29]

Conclusions

The concept of taypi enabled the visualization of intercultural histories and practices that compose the heritage and rights nexus in the selected case studies while leaving room for people and things to disagree. Dwelling in the circumstance of taypi reconfigured audit procedures and heritage research in a cosmopolitical sense, as both an assemblage of social artifacts and a distinctive ecology of interrelated practices crisscrossed by human and other-than-human agencies. These encounters make the materiality of colonial suffering and the struggles for emancipation perceptible, revealing a critical standpoint to reassemble what matters to indigenous heritage.

Through this recomposition is possible to challenge univocal meanings of heritage and rights, echoing the cosmopolitical proposal for "a world in which many worlds fit."[30] Bringing to light voices, bodies, and histories that were considered an ontological barrier for the relentless march of progress or a transgression to the empty gestures of multicultural recognition, this contribution showed that thinking of heritage relationships through the fabric of taypi can be generative of new cultural forms that are not reduced to synthesis but allow differences to coexist. The difference, for better or worse, is the first thing everyone has in common with everyone else.

Biography
Francesco Orlandi holds a PhD in Archaeology from the University of Exeter (2022). His research interests intersect archaeological theory, critical heritage studies, and Indigenous peoples' rights. He was a visiting researcher at the Institute of Archaeology and Museum (National University of Tucumán, Argentina). Before his doctoral degree, he obtained an MA in Archaeology from the Universidad Complutense de Madrid and an MA in International Cooperation, Protection of Human Rights and Cultural Heritage from the University of Bologna. He is currently Adjunct Professor in Archaeology, Media and the Public at the Department of History and Cultures, University of Bologna, and Honorary Research Fellow at the Centre for the Archaeology of the Americas, University of Exeter.

Notes

[1] Thérèse Bouysse-Cassagne, *La identidad Aymara:* Aproximación histórica *(Siglo XV, Siglo XVI)* (Lima: IFEA, 1987), 195.

[2] Silvia Rivera Cusicanqui, "The Potosí Principle: Another View of Totality," *E-misférica* 11, no. 1 (2014), https://hemisphericinstitute.org/en/emisferica-11-1-decolonial-gesture/11-1-essays/the-potosi-principle-another-view-of-totality.html.

[3] Silvia Rivera Cusicanqui, *Un mundo ch'ixi es posible. Ensayos desde un presente en crisis* (Buenos Aires: Tinta Limón, 2018), 83–84.
[4] Pedro Cieza de León, *Travels of Pedro Cieza de* León *(AD 1532–50)*, trans. Clements R. Marckham (London: The Hackluyt Society, 1864 [1553]), Chapter CV, https://www.gutenberg.org/files/48770/48770-h/48770-h.htm.
[5] Alexei Vranich, "Visions of Tiwanaku," in *Visions of Tiwanaku*, ed. Alexei Vranich and Charles Stanish (Los Angeles: Cotsen Institute of Archaeology Press, 2013), 2.
[6] Rivera Cusicanqui, "The Potosí Principle."
[7] Francesco Orlandi, "Heritage Cosmopolitics: Archaeology, Indigeneity and Rights in Bolivia and Argentina" (PhD diss., University of Exeter, 2022), http://hdl.handle.net/10871/129335.
[8] Marisol De la Cadena, "Indigenous Cosmopolitics in the Andes: Conceptual Reflections beyond "Politics," *Cultural Anthropology* 25, no. 2 (April 2010): 360, https://doi.org/10.1111/j.1548-1360.2010.01061.x.
[9] Tristan Platt, "Liberalism and Ethnocide in the Southern Andes," *History Workshop Journal* 17, no. 1 (Spring 1984): 14.
[10] Michelle Bigenho and Henry Stobart, "The Devil in Nationalism: Indigenous Heritage and the Challenges of Decolonization," *International Journal of Cultural Property* 23, no. 2 (July 2016): 142, https://doi.org/10.1017/S0940739116000114; Donna Yates, "Archaeology and Autonomies: The Legal Framework of Heritage Management in a New Bolivia," *International Journal of Cultural Property* 18, no. 3 (December 2011): 298, https://doi.org/10.1017/S0940739111000257.
[11] Centro de Investigaciones Arqueológicas, Antropológicas y Administración de Tiwanaku—CIAAAT, "Plan de Manejo del Centro Espiritual y Político de la Cultura Tiwanaku (2015–20)," *El compromiso de todos para su preservación y conservación,"* World Heritage Committee (January 2015), 9, https://whc.unesco.org/en/list/567/documents/.
[12] Carlos Mamani Condori, "History and Prehistory in Bolivia: What about the Indians?," in *Conflict in the Archaeology of Living Traditions*, ed. Robert Layton (London: Routledge, 1994), 49.
[13] Marisa Lazzari and Alejandra Korstanje, "The Past as a Lived Space: Heritage Places, Re-emergent Aesthetics, and Hopeful Practices in NW Argentina," *Journal of Social Archaeology* 13, no. 3 (October 2013): 412, https://doi.org/10.1177/1469605313487616; Alejandra Korstanje, Jorgelina García-Azcárate, and Patricia Arenas, "Intercultural Processes of Territory-Heritage Recovery and Management in the Calchaquí Valleys, Tucumán, Argentina," *Nuevo MundoMundos Nuevos [en ligne]*, El pasado presente n. 2 (July 2013): 34, https://doi.org/10.4000/nuevomundo.65988.
[14] Christophe Giudicelli, "¡Bárbaros en Pompeya! La invención de una genealogía nacional y la invisibilización de los indígenas de los Valles Calchaquíes a finales del siglo XIX," in *Regímenes de alteridad: Estados-nación y alteridades indígenas en América Latina*, ed. Paula López Cabellero and Christophe Giudicelli (Bogotá: Universidad de Los Andes, 2018), 31.
[15] Salvador Debenedetti, "Ambrosetti y su obra científica," *Revista de filosofía*, 6, no. 5 (September 1917): 248.
[16] Korstanje, García-Azcárate, and Arenas, "Intercultural Processes," 58.
[17] Marina Weinberg, "From the Neoliberal State to a Neo-National Development in Northwestern Argentina," *Latin American Perspectives* 44, no. 4 (July 2017): 152, https://doi.org/10.1177/0094582X16648957; Axel Lazzari and Diana Lenton, "'The Indian' and 'Politics': Transgressive Indigeneities in Political Activism before and after State Terrorism in Argentina," *Journal of Intercultural Studies* 40, no. 6 (November 2019): 681, https://doi.org/10.1080/07256868.2019.1675617.
[18] World Bank, "Project appraisal document on a proposed Learning and Innovation Loan in the amount of US$ 5.00 million to the Government of Argentina for an Indigenous Community Development LIL," Report No: 20929-AR (September 2000), 19, http://documents.worldbank.org/curated/en/254371468238777067/pdf/350630BR.pdf.
[19] Upendra Baxi, *The Future of Human Rights* (Oxford: Oxford University Press, 2008), 23.
[20] Baxi, *Future of Human Rights*, 24.
[21] Bartolomé de Las Casas, *De Thesauris in Peru*, trans. Ángel Losada (Madrid: Alianza, 1992 [1563]).
[22] Las Casas, "De Thesauris," 179.
[23] Cathal Doyle, *Indigenous Peoples, Title to Territory, Rights and Resources: The Transformative Role of Free Prior and Informed Consent* (London: Routledge, 2014); Ana Filipa Vrdoljack, "Indigenous Peoples, World Heritage, and Human Rights," *International Journal of Cultural Property* 25, no. 3 (August 2018): 245, https://doi.org/10.1017/S0940739118000218.
[24] Arjun Appadurai, "The Right to Research," *Globalisation, Societies and Education* 4, no. 2 (August 2006): 175, https://doi.org/10.1080/14767720600750696.

[25] Carolina Crespo, "Processes of Heritagization of Indigenous Cultural Manifestations: Lines of Debate, Analytic axes, and Methodological Approaches," in *Entangled Heritages: Postcolonial Perspectives on the Uses of the Past in Latin America,* ed. Olaf Kaltmeier and Mario Rufer (London: Routledge, 2017), 153–74; Cristobal Gnecco and Patricial Ayala, eds., *Indigenous Peoples and Archaeology in Latin America* (New York: Routledge, 2016); Alejandro Haber, "Decolonizing Archaeological Thought in South America," *Annual Review of Anthropology* 45 (October 2016): 469–85, https://doi.org/10.1146/annurev-anthro-102215-095906.
[26] Anna Lowenhaupt Tsing, *Frictions: An Ethnography of Global Connections* (Princeton: Princeton University Press, 2005), 4.
[27] Marisol De La Cadena, "Uncommoning Nature: Stories from the Anthropo-not-seen," in *Anthropos and the Material,* ed. Penny Harvey, Christian Krohn-Hansen, and Knut G. Nustad (Durham: Duke University Press, 2019), 53.
[28] José Luis Grosso, "Excess of Hospitality: Critical Semiopraxis and Theoretical Risks in Postcolonial Justice," in *After Ethics: Ancestral Voices and Post-Disciplinary Worlds in Archaeology,* ed. Alejandro Haber and Nick Shepherd (New York: Springer, 2015), 79–101.
[29] Isabelle Stengers, "The Cosmopolitical Proposal," in *Making Things Public: Atmospheres of Democracy,* ed. Bruno Latour and Peter Weibel (Cambridge, MA: MIT Press, 2005), 994; Lesley Green, "Archaeologies of Intellectual Heritage?," in *Ethics and Archaeological Praxis,* ed. Cristobal Gnecco and Dorothy Lippert (New York: Springer, 2015), 229–43.
[30] Mario Blaser and Marisol De La Cadena, "Pluriverse: Proposals for a World of Many Worlds," in *A World of Many Worlds,* ed. Marisol De La Cadena and Mario Blaser (Durham: Duke University Press, 2018), 15.

Figure 1. Main façade of central ESMA building, 2018. Photo: Author.

Valentina Rozas-Krause

"Our Auschwitz is the ESMA"
Preservation and the Holocaust at the former Higher School of Mechanics of the Navy in Argentina

> *"Ole ole, ole olaa . . . como a los nazis les va a pasar, adonde vayan los iremos a buscar," [. . . like the Nazis it will happen to you, wherever you go we will find you].*
>
> —Common clamor directed at those responsible for State terrorism that can be heard during memory marches in Argentina

During the Argentine civic-military dictatorship (1976–1983), the Higher School of Mechanics of the Navy, ESMA for its Spanish initials, became one of the material symbols of the military human right violations (Figure 1).[1] Once the epitome of military power, the history of ESMA took a radical turn, when on March 24, 2004, during the commemoration of the twenty-eight years of the Argentine coup d'état, president Néstor Kirchner delivered his official apology speech at the infamous site. Kircher spoke form the exact site, where Emilio Massera, commander-in-chief of the Navy, co-plotted the 1976 coup d'état against the government of Isabel Martínez de Perón and became one of the three members of the military junta that ruled the country from 1976 to 1978. Standing in front of the large military education facility that ESMA was at the time, surrounded by crowds of cheering supporters, accompanied by his wife Cristina Fernández, a visibly emotional Kirchner apologized to the nation for the state's negligence in persecuting the crimes committed during the military dictatorship.[2] The apology came with a gift, Kirchner announced that the entire ESMA facility would be expropriated from the navy, and its use granted to human rights organizations. Beyond apology, the president's gesture was also an act of material preservation, which sought to defend the military site against demolition. In the years that followed this symbolic recovery, ESMA not only became a national historic monument and some of it a museum, but it was also the subject of a contentious debate about historic preservation—heightened by the application of the site to the UNESCO World Heritage List. What heritage can be built from the remains of crimes against humanity? What are the boundaries between the sacred and everyday life? Were the central questions that preoccupied the actors involved in this debate. Following these questions, this article explores how the efforts to preserve the memories of the victims of the civic-military

Future Anterior
Volume XIX, Number 2
Winter 2022

Figure 2. General Map of ESMA during its military use. Courtesy of Archivo Nacional de la Memoria.

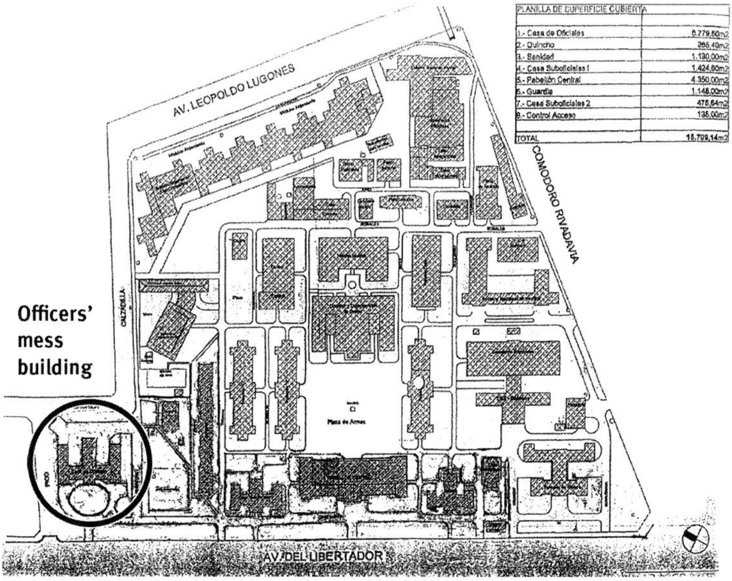

dictatorship were transmuted into the preservation of buildings, and how the local Argentine heritage discourse became entangled with global Holocaust tropes.

While the navy's educational institution dates back to 1897, the plot on which ESMA was located during the dictatorship was a forty-two-acre site in northern Buenos Aires donated to the navy by the city council of Buenos Aires in 1924.[3] Following the March 24, 1976, coup d'état, one of the many reinforced brick buildings of the complex, the officers' mess building, was transformed into the seat of Massera's Work Group 3.3.2, a terrorist military task force which was responsible for the capture and disappearance of an estimate of five thousand people and the appropriation of forty children born in its dreadful "maternity ward" (Figure 2).[4] While the building was adapted to fulfill the demands of Work Group 3.3.2, a clandestine detention, torture, and extermination center was housed in between the task force's offices; the residence of the director of ESMA known as Casa del Almirante; lodging rooms for officers; and various navy service areas. Testimonies of ESMA's former students who saw prisoners being moved around the building's staircases indicate that the makeshift torture center lacked a proper segregation of functions.[5] What these testimonies reveal is that the presence of prisoners was manifest not only to the residents of the officers' mess building, but to the occupants of the ESMA as a whole, as forced labor was used in various buildings and workshops throughout the military campus.[6]

Like most clandestine detention centers throughout Argentina, ESMA was a terrorist operation 'hidden' in plain sight. The location of ESMA within the capital reinforces this idea (Figure 3). The ESMA site was and is still located in an upper-

Figure 3. Map of the northern neighborhood of Nuñez in the city of Buenos Aires. Courtesy of the City of Buenos Aires Planning Department.

middle-class neighborhood. Its surroundings include a train station, residences, offices, sports facilities, and commercial as well as civic buildings. Especially the tall buildings along Avenida del Libertador, an avenue that divides the Núñez neighborhood from the ESMA complex to the west, had a privileged view into the movements in and out of ESMA, as well as into the front yard of the officers' mess building.[7]

Preserving ESMA

Only five years before Kirchner's 2004 reparation-and-return act at ESMA, the whole site had been slated for demolition. In January of 1998, president Carlos Menem signed an executive decree to move the Higher School of Mechanics of the Navy to a site in Puerto Belgrano, outside of Buenos Aires, and to demolish ESMA in order to build a "national reconciliation park." A national reconciliation monument was to take the center stage of this new park. According to the spokesperson of the Ministry of Defense, it would be a monument consisting of "a single great mast with a large but simple base, without bas-reliefs, on which a single Argentine flag would be hoisted as a symbol of national union."[8] Human rights organizations unanimously rejected Menem's proposal because they considered it an act of erasure and forgetting. Likewise, politicians from opposing parties and the city legislature manifested their discontent.[9] ESMA was ultimately saved in court after two human rights activists—Graciela Lois, from Relatives of the Disappeared (Familiares de Desaparecidos) and Laura Bonaparte, from Mothers of Plaza de Mayo-Founding Line (Madres de Plaza de Mayo Línea Fundadora)—presented an appeal to prevent its demolition.[10]

Although frustrated, Menem's gesture of reconciliation arose in the middle of a wider effort to unite and reconcile a divided Argentina, under what human rights organizations deemed as "politics of erasure and forgetting."[11] On an international level, Menem reconciled with the British after the loss of the Falkland Islands.[12] On a national level, as part of what he called a "Process of Reconciliation," between 1989 and 1990 Menem signed a series of ten decrees pardoning more than 1,200 convicted perpetrators of State terrorism, including the leaders of the Military Juntas, who had been convicted in the 1985 trial.[13] The transfer of ESMA to the outskirts of the city, in order to detach the institution from its criminal past, was another attempt of Menem's government to reconcile the country. Following this logic, the destruction of ESMA, as a symbol of military violence, would allow old wounds to heal and would build a new trust-based relationship between Argentine citizens and its military. One of the main consequences of this series of events during Menem's regime was that the tight relationship between a national rhetoric of reconciliation and amnesty was forged, along with an assumption that the built environment would play a vivid role in the process, either through presence or absence.

In response to Menem's proposal, representatives of the human rights organizations declared that to demolish ESMA was the equivalent of "demolishing memory" itself.[14] In their interpretation, the site became the equivalent of history itself.[15] It is in the blunt absence of justice that the rhetoric of pardon and amnesty was established, which found its parallel in the built environment. In this context, memory and justice—as well as truth as an outcome of both—were welded together with historic preservation as the only means capable of resisting the advance of the dual force of amnesty and amnesia.[16] The destruction of ESMA was intolerable, and its replacement with a monument unacceptable; because through this project Menem sought to materialize the idea of apology as erasure. In response to Menem's menace of physical erasure human rights organizations proclaimed historic preservation and archeology as the means to bring the sites marked by the civic-military dictatorship to life. This is why Kirchner's apology indicates a unique constellation of events that suggest an attempt to redefine the meaning of apology in Argentina. Instead of being equated with erasure, Kirchner's apology means preservation. When Kirchner apologized and acknowledged the State's responsibility for two decades of impunity while standing in front of ESMA, he was responding to Menem's rhetoric of reconciliation and his demolition threat.[17] In the case of ESMA, the act of preservation became a wedge that allowed an opening for verbal apology.

On March 24, 2004, Kirchner not only opened the doors of ESMA but also announced the creation of a Space for Memory and for the Promotion and Defense of Human Rights, formally marking the end of the site as ESMA and the beginning of a post-ESMA denomination of the complex (Figure 4).[18] In addition to his announcement to transform ESMA into a site of memory and museum, Kirchner also established a bipartisan commission to oversee the eviction process. Three years would pass until the navy effectively vacated the entire forty-two-acre of the site in November of 2007, and people could start visiting the entirety of the grounds freely.

The latency of this period provided a fruitful ground to debate the future of the former navy plot and discuss the impact of Kirchner's promise—to open a memory museum on the grounds of ESMA—for the site and for memory culture at large. The newspaper *Página12* provided a public forum to debate different proposals, as did publications like Marcelo Brodsky's *Memory Under Construction* and specialized journals including *Ramona*, *Punto de Vista,* and *Puentes*.[19] The debate boiled down to two main topics: what to do with the now empty thirty-two buildings and forty-two acres of the site and how to memorialize the most delicate building of the complex—the officers' mess—the former clandestine detention, torture, and extermination center. While there was general consensus among the human rights organizations to preserve and establish a site museum inside the former clandestine center, the proposed future uses of the entire complex turned out to be most controversial. As ESMA survivor Lila Pastoriza and Hugo Vezzetti suggest, the debate can be best represented by its two opposing positions: on the one hand the project of the Asociación de Ex Detenidos Desaparecidos, AEDD (Association of Former Detained Disappeared), and on the other hand,

Figure 4. Main Hall of the central building at ESMA dedicated to the Space for Memory and for the Promotion and Defense of Human Rights. Source: Author.

the proposals of human rights organizations like Centro de Estudios Legales y Sociales, CELS (Center for Legal and Social Studies), Servicio Paz y Justicia, SERPAJ (Peace and Justice Service), and Buena Memoria (Good Memory).[20] Most of these human rights organizations proposed a mixed use for the site, hosting the ESMA Site Museum alongside other art and justice museums, together with the offices of human rights organizations and public institutions at the city and national level, including the newly created Institute Space for Memory and the National Memory Archive. Perhaps the most drastic of this group of proposals was that of CELS, which advocating for austerity and long-term management argued that only two buildings should be dedicated to the specific history of the site: the officers' mess and the four-columned central building. According to CELS, the future use of the rest of the buildings should be decided by the state, without ruling out the permanence of the main educational building of the navy school. The suggestion to co-inhabit the site with the institution of the perpetrators aroused strong resistance among survivors and activists; however, the members of CELS argued that only the coexistence of the memory site and the navy school would secure a future human-rights-abiding military and would we able to build consensus around the history of the site.[21]

AEDD's idea for the site was radically different. The Association of former Detained Disappeared proposed to preserve the complete forty-two-acre lot, based on its role as evidence in ongoing trials, and to dedicate it in its entirety to the representation and reconstruction of the former clandestine center. The project explicitly rejected the incorporation of any new uses, including the newly created public memorial institutions and future educational organizations, with the intention to seal off the site from everyday life. For AEDD, "[At ESMA] there should be no room for a routine movement of staff or public that could allow the naturalization of the space and an emptying of its content to displace its significance as a clandestine center of disappearance and extermination."[22] One of the recurring phrases that the government and the city repeated during ESMA's recovery and later conversion into a site of memory was "Where there was death, today there is life."[23] The group of survivors of the civic-military dictatorship represented by AEDD strongly reacted against the idea of bringing life into a place of horror. They argued that "Where there was death it must be marked, remembered, evidenced, and known that there was death, who were those who died, why they died and who killed them. It should not be pretended that there is now life."[24] Vezzetti maintains that, by excluding any complementary uses and future visitors, AEDD's project of complete preservation and partial reconstruction seeks an impossible endeavor: to return a sacralized and intangible site to the past and keep it there.[25] The only function of ESMA, the AEDD states, should be "its role as material testimony of the genocide."[26] This, they add, should be secured based on the principles of cultural heritage.[27] Despite their differing positions, it was a foregone conclusion—for all parties involved—that the built environment was an indispensable part of how Argentina would work through the future not only of ESMA but of the memory landscape at large.

Once the navy moved out of ESMA, it was time to make a decision. The Space for Memory and for the Promotion and Defense of Human Rights, the public entity created to manage the site, decided to privilege mixed use, which led to the distribution of ESMA's existing buildings among human rights organizations and public institutions (Figure 5).[28] As a consequence of this decision, AEDD, alongside other human rights organizations opposed the project and decided to renounce their right to move into the complex. However, their struggle against the intrusion of everyday life at ESMA continues. Two recent events brought the original debates around the use of ESMA back to the forefront. A holiday party (2016) and a barbecue (2013) hosted by the National Human Rights and Cultural Pluralism Secretary (Ministry of Justice and Human Rights), which occupies a building on the site, aroused an outcry by the members of AEDD. They considered these acts an offense to the dead, and extremely inappropriate activities to be hosted in a place of horror.[29] "Who would dance at Auschwitz?," ESMA survivor Carlos Lordkipanidse asks rhetorically? In his opinion, quotidian activities are a menace to the site's sacredness,

Figure 5. Map of former ESMA transformed into the Space for Memory and for the Promotion and Defense of Human Rights, 2013. Source: Wikimedia.

because everyday uses threaten to resignify and overpower ESMA's historical meaning. Put differently, quotidian activities allow the banality of evil to seep in. It is simply too difficult to "work at Auschwitz," he adds.[30] Here again conservation conjures the fears of erasure. The threat this time is not that of a total erasure as proposed by Menem, but an erasure through resignification stirred by a thousand tiny everyday acts. Against this position, Hijas e Hijos por la Identidad y la Justicia contra el Olvido y el Silencio (HIJOS)—the organizations of sons and daughters of the disappeared—argued that Argentina's sites of memory were no cemeteries, and that there was no privileged way to remember the dead, nor a single authoritative voice to guide those memories.[31] The debate about the uses of the ESMA is a good reminder of the unsteady boundaries between two dimensions thought to be incommensurable and mutually exclusive: the extraordinary circumstances of state terrorism and the mundane inhabiting of a place. The entanglement between these two dimensions of life, which writers like Henri Lefebvre have tried to separate, affects not only the meaning of a place, but also its preservation.[32] What is at stake in this debate is the sacredness of the ESMA, and the status of the Argentine State's terrorism in a global stage shaped by memories of and repentance for the Holocaust.

Our Auschwitz

The *Nunca Más* (1984) report, in combination with the Trial of the Military Juntas (1985), had an unexpected effect: it catapulted the local Argentine experience with state terrorism into a global discourse shaped by the Holocaust. Vezzetti argues that these two related post-dictatorial events universalized the local experience. ESMA played a central role in the Argentine terror machine, most of the prisoners who were "disappeared" from the Navy Officers' Mess Hall were thrown into the La Plata River alive and drugged, or dead, in what came to be known as the 'death flights.'[33] This practice followed the terrorist plan that the Argentine military had learned in the infamous US School of the Americas: to leave no traces of their victims and render them forever disappeared.[34] Thus, the genocide perpetrated by the Argentine military is more than a national event, it was one of the grounds of the Cold War in Latin America. As a culmination of the US National Security Doctrine, the systematic annihilation of political enemies in Argentina was replicated across the continent.[35] Consequently, Argentina's state terrorism was inscribed within a broader narrative of genocide, human rights defense, and memory culture that emerged in response to the 'limit event' of the Holocaust, as well as Cold War imperialism.[36] In particular, the *Trial of the Military Juntas*, which was seen through the lens of the Nazi trials in Nürnberg and Adolf Eichmann's trial in Jerusalem, transformed Argentina's approach to its past into a model for international transitional justice.[37] Thus, not only did the Argentine dictatorship become one of the great twentieth-century planned massacres; but also, the nation's response to it put Argentina in what Vezzetti calls "the western path of moral repudiation" of racially, politically, religiously, and ethnically driven genocide.[38]

Against the dominant notion of incomparability of the Holocaust, Argentina's latest dictatorship is constantly being compared to the Third Reich. Likewise, ESMA is defined through the lens of Auschwitz. Like Vezzetti, numerous local authors have addressed the entanglement between the Argentine dictatorship, its aftermath, and the Holocaust. This relationship has been discussed on many different levels: on the level of memory, Leonor Arfuch describes how the figure of the *desaparecido* plays a central role in both Argentina's state terrorism and the Shoa. Further, she argues that the Shoa, as the representation of the ultimate horror, allows Argentine human rights activists to uncover the ethical potential of memories in Argentina and elsewhere to stand against violence.[39] On the level of the Jewish experience, Emmauel Kahan analyzes the Argentine military regime's anti-Semitism, and together with Laura Schenquer he examines the uses of the Holocaust during the dictatorship.[40] On the level of the *dispositifs* of violence, survivor Pilar Calveiro describes Argentine clandestine detention centers as concentration camps.[41] On the level of the perpetrators, Daniel Feierstein maintains that the motivations behind the Nazi and Argentine killings are similar.[42] And on the level of aesthetics Ana Longoni and Gustavo Bruzzone discuss the influence of Holocaust memory activism in the artistic artifacts produced by the Argentine human rights movement and its supporters. For example, the main symbol for the post-dictatorship justice and recognition campaign—the silhouette of the disappeared—was inspired by a Polish artist's poster of Auschwitz.[43] This brief overview of some of these debates illustrates that the Holocaust as an historical event, trope, and imaginary has had multiple effects on the memorial landscape of Argentina. ESMA is no exception; in fact, it is often referred to as "our Auschwitz."[44]

In a newspaper editorial published in 2000, Argentine philosopher José Pablo Feinmann discussed Theodor Adorno's famous dictum, "writing poetry after Auschwitz is barbaric."[45] Stressing the need to write after Auschwitz and the impossibility to do so from the position of cultural production or outside of it, he writes: "Adorno's challenge includes us. Not only because we are part of humanity, but because we are Argentines and we have our own Auschwitz. Its victims were fewer, but its horror was not. *Our Auschwitz is the ESMA*."[46] Like ESMA, the concentration, forced labor, and extermination camps known as Auschwitz-Birkenau are meaningful not only because, against Holocaust denials, they serve as material evidence of the systematic murder of human bodies and spontaneity, but also because, beyond their materiality, they have become an emblem for the twentieth-century slogan "Never Again."[47] Auschwitz is a reminder of Europe's fragility in the wake of the dangers of fascism, nationalism, racism, xenophobia, and homophobia. Pointing toward the darkest aspects of the human condition, Auschwitz has been preserved as a site of World Heritage to shape future behavior: to never let genocide occur again.[48] As such, it has become *the* icon of the Holocaust.[49] Auschwitz does not only denote Auschwitz, but refers to all Nazi concentration and killing camps. Similarly, ESMA has become a symbol for all clandestine centers in Argentina through a process of metonymic transference.

Regarding ESMA as "our Auschwitz" is not a scholarly peculiarity, but a widespread phenomenon ingrained in the local perception of the Argentine site. Speaking on the radio show "Otras Voces" (Other Voices), in May 2015, in the context of the inauguration of the ESMA Site Museum, ESMA survivor Enrique Fukman talked about the process of re-signification of the site—particularly through new naming policies—which in his opinion were a mode of erasure. He argued:

> Are the effects of the dictatorship still present today? Does this present have to do with that past? If it has to do with that past, it is the ESMA. Saying 'former ESMA' [ex-ESMA]

> is like saying that it is something that has nothing to do with us. But it has a lot to do with our present. [. . .] So, it's the ESMA, it's not the former ESMA. As we always say, has anyone ever heard of a '*former Auschwitz*' or is it always called *Auschwitz*? Why? Because its consequences are in the present. And it might have been 70 years, like Auschwitz, however the consequences are still with us.[50]

Why does an ESMA survivor need to reinforce this argument with a comparison to the Holocaust? On the one hand, it universalizes his experience; on the other hand, it forecloses any eventual argumentative retorts. Auschwitz shields his argument: there is nothing beyond Auschwitz, nor are there any argumentative resources that could counter it, and thus by invoking the limit of the limit event, Fukman also establishes the paradigm to be imitated.

World Heritage

In 2017, the Space for Memory and for the Promotion and Defense of Human Rights deployed a similar argument in a request—submitted by the Permanent Delegation of the Republic of Argentina to UNESCO—to include both the ESMA Site Museum and the entire former Higher School of the Navy as part of the World Heritage List.[51] Auschwitz plays a central role in the request to grant the site global recognition. According to the nomination's narrative, it is because five other sites of the most gruesome human crimes—Auschwitz-Birkenau (Poland); the Hiroshima Peace Memorial (Japan); Robben Island (South Africa); the Island of Goreé (Senegal); and the Old Bridge Area of the Old City of Mostar (Bosnia and Herzegovina)—have been preserved for the world to learn from them, that ESMA, as a symbol for Latin American Cold War dictatorships, deserves to be incorporated into UNESCO's World Heritage List.[52] UNESCO's preservation policy in regard to sites of mass murder and atrocity, as well as how it has changed over time, deserves a detailed analysis that exceeds the scope of this article.[53] However, the nomination provides further evidence for ESMA's claim to universalism through the use of the Holocaust as a point of comparison.

A close reading of the World Heritage List nomination reveals that both material and historical aspects are stressed as part of ESMA's distinctiveness. ESMA's integrity and authenticity (the original building structure remains), representativeness (ESMA's clandestine camp was part of a broad networks of more than seven hundred detention, torture, and extermination centers across the nation), and uniqueness (it was the largest, most deadly camp, and the only that included a maternity ward and forced labor program) are the main characteristics said to make the site an ideal candidate for the list.[54]

The story of one of the babies born in captivity, in the basement of the officers' mess—Rodolfo Fernando Pérez Roisinblit—illuminates the intention of the 2018 nomination of combining material and immaterial dimensions of the site. Members of the Air Force kidnapped both of Rodolfo's parents and his fifteen-month-old sister in October of 1978. His mother, Patricia, was eight months pregnant with him. While his sister was released a few days later, his parents, both members of the left-wing organization Montoneros and Jewish, were detained and tortured in an unidentified residence in Buenos Aires. Shortly before giving birth in November of 1978, Patricia was transferred first to ESMA's basement infirmary and later to a poorly ventilated storeroom next to the upstairs maternity ward. Three days after his birth, Rodolfo and his mother disappeared from the navy officers' mess hall.[55] While his parents remain disappeared, Rodolfo was found in the year 2000, living under a different name—Guillermo Gómez—with the family of an Air Force intelligence agent.[56] Patricia's fate was unfortunately that of most women who gave birth at ESMA: they remain disappeared. Rodrigo's story of appropriation by a military family is also no exception: of an estimated five hundred children born in captivity during the Argentine civic-military dictatorship, to date (October 2023) only 133 have been found.[57]

Rodolfo recovered his identity thanks to the tireless efforts of his maternal and paternal grandmothers, Rosa Tarlovsky de Roisinblit and Argentina Rojo de Pérez, both members of Abuelas de Plaza de Mayo (Grandmothers of Plaza de Mayo), an organization established by the grandmothers of the disappeared to find their grandchildren (Figure 6).[58] Rosa was, for many years, the vice president of Abuelas de Plaza de Mayo, and continued her search for more kidnapped children even after finding her grandson Rodolfo. Likewise, his sister, Mariana, searched for him for years, until she convinced him to take a DNA test.[59] These women, alongside the female prisoners who built a network of support around his mother, and those who survived to give testimony to his birth, allowed him to recover his first name—Rodolfo— usurped by his "military appropriators" together with his identity. This meant not only to recover the name that his parents had chosen for him as an adult but also to rediscover his Jewish identity captured in his mother's family name.

The story of Rodolfo is not part of the UNESCO application, at least not explicitly. However, I argue, that through the incorporation of those networks of female activism, grandmothers, and survivors into its argumentation, the 2017 application tries to bridge the material with the immaterial, suggesting that the heritage value of the site lies somewhere in this relationship. The existence of the building that was used as a camp

Figure 6. Guillermo Rodolfo Fernando Pérez Roisinblit and his maternal grandmother, Rosa Tarlovsky de Roisinblit. Photography by Hernán Churba, part of his photographic portrait series "Retratos Recuperados." Courtesy of Hernán Churba.

makes ESMA preservation worthy, but beyond materiality, what the nomination stresses are human experiences that are interwoven into the materiality as testimony of past events. Argentina's Permanent UNESCO Delegation based its nomination on two of the ten possible criteria defined by UNESCO for determining Outstanding Universal Value:

> (iii) Bear a unique or at least exceptional testimony to a cultural tradition or to a civilization which is living or which has disappeared.
> (vi) Be directly or tangibly associated with events or living traditions, with ideas, or with beliefs, or with artistic and literary works of outstanding universal significance.[60]

Criterion (iii) is addressed briefly, most likely in response to UNESCO's rule that criterion (vi), which justifies Auschwitz-Birkenau's preservation, cannot be used in isolation. Here, the nomination makes two important claims that would be reinforced by the justification for the second criterion. First, it states that the survivors of the systematic plan of disappearance, their testimonies, and their search for justice, alongside the human rights organizations that emerged in response to State terrorism, are a living "cultural tradition" that has become an example for the rest of the world and deserves to be recognized as such. While UNESCO uses the word "testimony" as a synonym for evidence in its definition of criterion (iii), within ESMA's submission the word gets charged with a different meaning. Echoing the testimonial turn in Argentine post-dictatorial memory, *testimonio* is the key word that binds the building with the voices of those who survived the tortures they underwent in its interior.[61] Material and immaterial testimony are united in a circular motion in which survivors' testimonies confirm the authenticity of the clandestine detention, forced labor, torture, and extermination center at ESMA, while at the same time the material evidence of the site confirms the veracity of the survivors' testimonies. What is implied in this exercise is that a survivor's testimony is not enough to prove a crime. Put differently, when words are not enough, space—as a signifier for both location and material evidence—plays the role of secondary witness.[62] The reciprocity between space and speech is reinforced by the uniqueness of ESMA: with more than two hundred survivors, it has the highest survival rate across clandestine camps in Argentina. This high rate of survival is attributed to the "Prisoner Recovery Process" program that Task Force 3.3.2 implemented within ESMA to reform prisoners through forced labor.[63]

The second claim made in the justification for criterion (iii) is that the exceptional memorial culture that emerged out of the military oppression is under threat. Argentina's Permanent UNESCO Delegation presents the 2017 demand to preserve ESMA as a pressing issue by describing the navy's intention to transform the interior spaces of the officers' mess building through architectural interventions, and President Carlos Menem's attempt to erase the entire site to build a "reconciliation park."

The explanation for criterion (vi) is divided into five paragraphs that each stress one dimension in which the Argentine experience embodied in ESMA is of outstanding universal value. Interestingly, without mentioning any individual names, these arguments carefully balance the universal with the very local embodied experience of survivors and activists.

The first paragraph highlights the contribution of the human rights struggles of Argentine activists to the global field of memory, democracy, and human rights. The second one mentions the creation of the Argentine Forensic Anthropology Team, EAAF for its Spanish initials (Equipo Argentino de Antropología Forense), which, in 2005 first produced scientific evidence to prove the "death flights" and has been a key nongovernmental organization in the identification of victims remains. In continuity with the previous section, the third paragraph underlines the scientific breakthroughs that emerged out of the search for the identities of the victims. In this regard, the text mentions the Abuelas de Plaza de Mayo's search for stolen and appropriated babies, highlighting the work of Rosa and Argentina, and so many others. The quest to find the children of the *desaparecidos* led to the creation of the Grandparenthood Index, which determined blood relationships without the parents' genetic material, and later, after the introduction of DNA testing, the creation of a National Genetic Data Bank. Rodolfo's genetic material was identified in this context, after both his grandmothers and sister had provided their own DNA to the data bank. Paragraph four presents the court procedures against the perpetrators, and argues that Argentina is an ideal model to study the ongoing prosecution of the crimes against humanity before local courts of justice. Also here, Rodolfo's experience is echoed. In 2014 Rodolfo and his grandmother Rosa testified in court in the context of the *ESMA megacausa*, a collective trial against sixty-eight perpetrators of the ESMA.[64]

While these four paragraphs analyze the innovations that emerged out of the Argentine human rights struggle, the last paragraph hones in on the ESMA site, revealing what has been achieved so far: its recovery in 2004 and its transformation into a museum in 2015 (Figure 7). Rodolfo himself, has stressed the importance that visiting the ESMA basement had on his recovery (Figure 8). In 2005, when it was not yet a museum, he visited the officers' mess building with Miriam Lewin, who had been imprisoned with his mother, and had cared for them after his birth.[65] In his words:

> I accepted myself as Rodolfo in 2005 for the first time, in the basement of the former ESMA. Miriam told me: "Look, Rodolfo, this is the place where you were born." And I turned around. I had never responded to that name before, and it was happening there, where I'd been called Rodolfo for the first time. I think this was a beautiful way to close the circle.[66]

To read the nomination to UNESCO's World Heritage List alongside Rodolfo's story, allows to see the human experiences and traumas that inevitable get abstracted in a preservation regime that values the meaning of a particular site to the whole world. What is remarkable about this nomination is that, besides the mention of Nestor Kirchner's act of returning the site to the city, the State is either absent or antagonistic to the main actors of the nomination: human rights organizations. They are the protagonists of ESMA's preservation story, and this document is an attempt to preserve their voices, names, experiences, and memories. How do stories like Rodolfo's fit into buildings that, although materially preserved, could be rendered meaningless without them? I argue that this nomination is an attempt to answer this puzzling question.

Figure 7. Main access to the ESMA Site Museum, located inside the former Navy Officers' Mess Hall, 2018. Photo: Author.

Conclusion

As I was editing the final version of this article, on September 19, 2023, ESMA received its global recognition, and was added to the World Heritage List.[67] Finally, ESMA's value is considered universally outstanding, the UNESCO statement says:

> The ESMA Museum and Site of Memory—Former Clandestine Centre of Detention, Torture and Extermination is closely and tangibly associated with, and highly representative of, the illegal repression of armed and non-armed opponents and dissenters carried out and coordinated by the dictatorships of Latin America in the 1970s-1980s on the grounds of the enforced disappearance of persons, in a climate of global geopolitical tensions between opposing worldviews about the world's socio-political order.[68]

While the effects of this recognition are unfolding, and too recent to analyze, it is important to note that the official 2023 UNESCO documentation differs from the 2017 nomination.[69] While the early nomination proposed to include both the ESMA Site Museum and the entire former Higher School of the Navy as part of the World Heritage List, the UNESCO designation is focused only on the Navy officers' mess hall, the museum. Further, the immaterial dimensions emphasized by the early document—human rights activism, Grandmother Index, forensic science development—are, although present, secondary to the material building, which is framed to fit into the three World Heritage categories: integrity, authenticity, and protection

Figure 8. Basement of the Navy Officers' Mess Hall, now part of the ESMA Site Museum, 2018. Photo: Author.

management. The comparison with Auschwitz however remains firmly embedded in the justification to preserve ESMA.

Even before the UNESCO recognition was granted, the preservation efforts of ESMA discussed in this article, reveal the labors behind the construction of sacredness on the grounds of the former navy school. Survivors' groups, such as AEDD, tend to use Holocaust analogies in combination with a global preservation rhetoric to return the site to the past, in an attempt to make the violence and horror of ESMA its central and only meaning. Preservation thus becomes another mechanism to defend the site against the menace of apology and amnesty, symbolized most clearly by Menem's reconciliation park. Conservation conjures the fears of erasure. Perhaps then, it is not a coincidence that the inclusion of the ESMA Site Museum into the World Heritage List, comes at a time of growing far-right negationism about the last Argentine civic-military dictatorship.[70]

Biography

Valentina Rozas-Krause is Assistant Professor in Design and Architecture at Universidad Adolfo Ibáñez in Chile. She is the 2024–25 Keith Haring Chair at Bard College and was the Frieda L. Miller Fellow at the Harvard Radcliffe Institute for Advanced Study in 2023–24. Valentina holds a PhD in Architectural History from the University of California, Berkeley, as well as a Master's Degree in Urban Planning, a professional degree, and a B\Arch, from Pontificia Universidad Católica de Chile. Valentina has published *Ni Tan Elefante, Ni Tan Blanco* (Ril, 2014), and co-edited *Disputar la Ciudad* (Bifurcaciones, 2018). These books join peer-reviewed articles in *History & Memory, e-flux, Latin American Perspectives, Anos 90, ARQ, Revista 180, Cuadernos de Antropología Social, Memory Studies,* and *Bifurcaciones,* alongside a chapter in *Neocolonialism and Built Heritage* (Routledge, 2020). Her most recent publications include *Decolonization*, a special issue of journal *ARQ* (2022), and the collective volume *Breaking the Bronze Ceiling: Women, Memory and Public Space* (Fordham, 2024).

Acknowledgments
I would like to thank the staff and director of the ESMA Site Museum. Alejandra Naftal provided invaluable insights, and resources to this research. Friends and colleagues including Martín Bergel, Adrián Gorelik, Daniel Herwitz, and Francisca Márquez, as well as my dissertation advisors Andrew M. Shanken, Julia Bryan-Wilson and the late Paul Rabinow, have been invaluable interlocutors, and I thank them wholeheartedly. I am also grateful for the thoughtful comments and suggestions provided by the two anonymous reviewers and Tao DuFour. This research was supported by ANID Becas Chile (72150057), Institute of International Studies at UC Berkeley, Center for Latin American Studies at UC Berkeley, UC Berkeley Global Urban Humanities, Doreen B. Townsend Center for the Humanities, the Mellon/ American Council of Learned Societies, and the University of Michigan National Center for Institutional Diversity.

Notes

[1] An ongoing debate exists around naming and thus the type of dictatorship that ruled Argentina between 1976 and 1983. There are three strands of definitions, those who talk about military dictatorship, those who talk about civic-military dictatorship, and those who talk about civic-military-religious dictatorship. The debate reflects not only the need to name the perpetrators and their collaborators but to distinguish this particular dictatorship from previous military dictatorships. I have chosen the term civic-military dictatorship, based on the twofold model it implanted: political repression and economic reform. This is not to dismiss the role that the Catholic religion played for the military officers in charge, or the complacency of the Catholic Church. See Felipe Pigna, "La Historia de Todos," in *Memoria En Construcción: El Debate Sobre La ESMA*, ed. Marcelo Brodsky (Buenos Aires: La Marca, 2005), 57–66.

[2] "Kirchner en la ESMA: 'En nombre del Estado, vengo a pedir perdón,'" *Clarín*, March 25, 2004, https://www.clarin.com/ediciones-anteriores/kirchner-esma-nombre-vengo-pedir-perdon_0_H1aZQ9pyAKg.html.

[3] Marcelo Brodsky, ed., *Memoria En Construcción: El Debate Sobre La ESMA* (Buenos Aires: La Marca, 2005).

[4] Espacio Memoria website: https://www.espaciomemoria.ar/.

[5] Narrative presented at the official guided tour through ESMA 2018. Permanent Delegation of the Republic of Argentina to UNESCO, "World Heritage List Nomination: ESMA Site Museum—Former Clandestine Centre of Detention, Torture, and Extermination" (UNESCO World Heritage—Tentative List, April 25, 2017), Ref. 6248, https://whc.unesco.org/en/tentativelists/6248/.

[6] Víctor Basterra, "Testimonio de Víctor Basterra Para El Juicio a Las Juntas," § Dr. López, Dr. Ledesma, Dr. Moreno Ocampo, Dr. Buero, Dr. Aguirre Obarrio, Dr. Goldaracena et. al. (1985), http://www.desaparecidos.org/nuncamas/web/testimon/basterra.htm.

[7] For an analysis of the role of neighborhood communities around former clandestine detention centers in Buenos Aires, see Estela Schindel, "'Ahora los Vecinos Van Perdiendo el Temor' La Apertura de Ex Centros de Detención y la Restauración del Tejido Social en Argentina," in *Disputar la Ciudad: Sometimiento, Resistencia, Memorialización, Reparación*, ed. Pía Montealegre and Valentina Rozas-Krause, Cuervos en Casa (Santiago: Bifurcaciones, 2018), 177–99.

[8] La Nación, "Insiste el Gobierno en mudar la ESMA," *La Nación*, January 9, 1998, sec. Politica, 3, https://www.lanacion.com.ar/84973-insiste-el-gobierno-en-mudar-la-esma.

[9] El Clarín, "Demolerán la ESMA y colocarán un monumento por la unión nacional," *El Clarín*, January 8, 1998, https://www.clarin.com/politica/demoleran-esma-colocaran-monumento-union-nacional_0_rJklVnbyU2l.html; El Clarín, "ESMA: el Gobierno salió a rechazar las críticas," *El Clarín*, January 9, 1998, https://www.clarin.com/politica/esma-gobierno-salio-rechazar-criticas_0_r1NgFS1-RYl.html; La Nación, "Insiste el Gobierno en mudar la ESMA."

[10] Victoria Ginzberg, "La Corte Suprema Dispuso Que La ESMA No Se Demoliera. El Emblema Del Horror, En Pie," *Página/12*, February 1, 2001, https://www.pagina12.com.ar/2001/01-02/01-02-14/pag11.htm.

[11] El Clarín, "Demolerán la ESMA y colocarán un monumento por la unión nacional"; Ginzberg, "La Corte Suprema Dispuso Que La ESMA No Se Demoliera. El Emblema Del Horror, En Pie."

[12] Ediciones El País, "Menem y Major sellan la reconciliacion de argentinos y británicos," *El País*, October 24, 1995, sec. Internacional, https://elpais.com/diario/1995/10/24/internacional/814489204_850215.html.

[13] Ricardo Luis Lorenzetti and Alfredo Jorge Kraut, *Derechos Humanos, Justicia y Reparación: La Experiencia de Los Juicios En La Argentina: Crímenes de Lesa Humanidad* (Buenos Aires: Sudamericana, 2011).

[14] La Nación, "Insiste el Gobierno en mudar la ESMA."

15 Dell Upton observes a similar phenomenon in the US south, in which publics conflate a selective symbol of a deed, event, or person with its full memory. Dell Upton, *What Can and Can't Be Said: Race, Uplift, and Monument Building in the Contemporary South* (New Haven: Yale University Press, 2015).
16 Paul Ricoeur, *Memory, History, Forgetting* (Chicago: University of Chicago Press, 2004).
17 Hugo Vezzetti, *Sobre La Violencia Revolucionaria: Memorias y Olvidos, Sociología y Política* (Buenos Aires: Siglo Veintiuno, 2009), 222.
18 For more information, see the site's official webpage: http://www.espaciomemoria.ar/english.php.
19 José Pablo Feinmann, "Pensar y Escribir Después de La ESMA," *Página 12*, March 25, 2000, https://www.pagina12.com.ar/2000/00-03/00-03-25/contrata.htm; José Pablo Feinmann, "Auschwitz y La Filosofía," *Página/12*, January 29, 2000, https://www.pagina12.com.ar/2000/00-01/00-01-29/contrata.htm; Brodsky, *Memoria En Construcción*. See in particular "Dossier Museo de la Memoria," in *Ramona*, 42, July 2004; *Punto de Vista*, 68, December 2000; *Puentes*, 11, May 2004.
20 Lila Pastoriza, "La Memoria Como Política Pública: Los Ejes de La Discusión," in *Memoria En Construcción*, ed. Marcelo Brodsky, 85–94; Vezzetti, *Sobre La Violencia Revolucionaria*. For a summary of the different proposals for ESMA, see the annex of Brodsky, *Memoria En Construcción*.
21 To CELS's credit, the current website of the now called ESSA—Escuela de Suboficiales de la Armada Argentina—does no mention its role during the civic-military dictatorship and argues that the justification for moving into the new site in Puerto Belgrano was based on the spatial demands of a growing institution. See http://www.essa.ara.mil.ar/Historia.html (accessed December 12, 2018). Hugo Vezzetti examines the CELS proposal in Vezzetti, *Sobre La Violencia Revolucionaria*.
22 Summary of AEDD proposal included in Brodsky, *Memoria En Construcción*, 224. Original quote in Spanish: "no debe establecerse allí un movimiento rutinario de personal o de público que permita la naturalización y vaciamiento de contenido del espacio y desplace su significación como centro clandestino de desaparición y exterminio."
23 For example, this phrase is the title for one of the oficial catalogs of the site: Espacio Memoria y Derechos Humanos, ed., *Donde Hubo Muerte, Hoy Hay Vida* (Buenos Aires: Espacio Memoria y Derechos Humanos, ex ESMA, 2016).
24 AEDD cited in Pastoriza, "La Memoria Como Política Pública," 93. Original quote in Spanish: "donde hubo muerte debe señalarse, recordarse, mostrarse, saberse que hubo muerte, quiénes fueron los que murieron, por qué murieron y quiénes los mataron. No debe pretenderse que ahora haya vida."
25 Vezzetti, *Sobre La Violencia Revolucionaria*, 250.
26 AEDD cited in Pastoriza, "La Memoria Como Política Pública," 93.
27 Vezzetti, *Sobre La Violencia Revolucionaria*.
28 Vezzetti, *Sobre La Violencia Revolucionaria*.
29 Daniel Feierstein and Fernando Tebele, "#FiestaEnLaESMA: 'Debemos Centrar Nuevamente El Eje En Qué Hacer Con Los Espacios de Memoria,'" *La Retaguardia* (blog), January 15, 2017, http://www.laretaguardia.com.ar/2017/01/feierstein-ESMA.html; La Retaguardia, "Denuncian Una Fiesta En La ESMA," *La Retaguardia* (blog), January 9, 2017, http://www.laretaguardia.com.ar/2017/01/denuncia-una-fiesta-en-la-esma.html; La Nación, "Denuncian nuevos "asados" de funcionarios del Gobierno en la ex ESMA," *La Nación*, September 2, 2013, sec. Politica, https://www.lanacion.com.ar/1616295-denuncian-indignacion-y-lagrimas-por-nuevos-asados-de-funcionarios-en-la-ex-esma; RNMA, "El Debate Sobre La ESMA, ¿recordar o Resignificar?," *La Retaguardia* (blog), June 4, 2013, http://www.laretaguardia.com.ar/2013/06/el-debate-sobre-la-esma-recordar-o.html; Enrique Fukman and La Retaguardia, "Enrique Fukman: 'Están Intentando Desaparecer La ESMA,'" *La Retaguardia* (blog), May 20, 2015, http://www.laretaguardia.com.ar/2015/05/enrique-fukman-estan-intentando.html.
30 La Retaguardia, "Denuncian Una Fiesta En La ESMA."
31 HIJOS, "Basta de Mentiras Sobre La Ex ESMA," September 3, 2013, http://www.agenciapacourondo.com.ar/ddhh/hijos-basta-de-mentiras-sobre-la-ex-esma.
32 Henri Lefebvre, *Critique of Everyday Life* (London: Verso, 2008).
33 Horacio Verbitsky, *The Flight: Confessions of an Argentine Dirty Warrior* (New York: New Press, 1996).
34 Luis Ignacio García and Ana Longoni, "Imágenes Invisibles. Acerca de las fotos de desaparecidos," Revista Grumo, April 2012; J. Patrice McSherry, "Operation Condor as a Hemispheric 'Counterterror' Organization," in *When States Kill: Latin America, the U.S., and Technologies of Terror*, ed. Cecilia Menjívar and Néstor Rodriguez, 1st ed. (Austin: University of Texas Press, 2005).
35 J. Patrice McSherry, "Operation Condor as a Hemispheric 'Counterterror' Organization," in *When States Kill: Latin America, the U.S., and Technologies of Terror*, ed. Cecilia Menjívar and Néstor Rodriguez, 1st ed. (Austin: University of Texas Press,

2005); Daniel Feierstein, *Genocide as Social Practice: Reorganizing Society under the Nazis and Argentina's Military Juntas*, Genocide, Political Violence, Human Rights Series (New Brunswick, NJ: Rutgers University Press, 2014), https://muse.jhu.edu/book/30821; Daniel Feierstein, "National Security Doctrine in Latin America: The Genocide Question," in *The Oxford Handbook of Genocide Studies*, ed. Donald Bloxham and A. Dirk Moses (Oxford: Oxford University Press, 2010), 489–508, https://doi.org/10.1093/oxfordhb/9780199232116.013.0025.

[36] Hugo Vezzetti, *Pasado y Presente: Guerra, Dictadura y Sociedad En La Argentina, Sociología y Política* (Buenos Aires: Siglo XXI, 2002), 111–12. On the emergence of the human rights discourse in Argentina, see Silvia R. Tandeciarz, *Citizens of Memory: Affect, Representation, and Human Rights in Postdictatorship Argentina* (Lewisburg, PA: Bucknell University Press, 2017); Andreas Huyssen, "Memory Studies and Human Rights," *MLA Profession*, May 2014, online. As a limit event, the Holocaust has not only been conceived as the most radical rupture with the Western Enlightenment tradition and human kind in general, but it has also shaped post-Holocaust politics and identities across the world. See Simone Gigliotti, "Unspeakable Pasts as Limit Events: The Holocaust, Genocide, and the Stolen Generations," *Australian Journal of Politics & History* 49, no. 2 (2003): 164–81; A. Dirk Moses, "Conceptual Blockages and Definitional Dilemmas in the 'Racial Century': Genocides of Indigenous Peoples and the Holocaust," in *Colonialism and Genocide*, ed. A. Dirk Moses and Dan Stone (New York: Routledge, 2007), 149–80.

[37] Mark Osiel, *Mass Atrocity, Collective Memory, and the Law* (New Brunswick, N.J.: Transaction Publishers, 1997); Hannah Arendt, *Eichmann in Jerusalem: A Report on the Banality of Evil*, Penguin Classics (New York,: Penguin Books, 2006); Mark Osiel, *Mass Atrocity, Ordinary Evil, and Hannah Arendt: Criminal Consciousness in Argentina's Dirty War* (New Haven: Yale University Press, 2001).

[38] Vezzetti, *Pasado y Presente*, 111–12.

[39] Leonor Arfuch, "Arte, Memoria y Archivo," *Punto de Vista. Revista de Cultura* XXIII, no. 68 (December 2000): 34–37.

[40] Emmanuel Nicolás Kahan, *Recuerdos Que Mienten Un Poco: Vida y Memoria de La Experiencia Judía Durante La Última Dictadura Militar (1973–2007)*, Prometeo Bicentenario (Buenos Aires: Prometeo Libros, 2014); Emmanuel Nicolás Kahan and Laura Schenquer, "The Use of the Past During the Last Military Dictatorship and Post-Dictatorship: The Holocaust as the Horizon of Identification, Alienation and Negotiation for the Jewish Community," *Temas de Nuestra América. Revista de Estudios Latinoamericanos* 32, no. 60 (December 11, 2016): 131–48, https://doi.org/10.15359/tdna.32-60.7.

[41] Pilar Calveiro, *Poder y Desaparición: Los Campos de Concentración En Argentina*, Puñaladas (Buenos Aires: Colihue, 1998).

[42] Feierstein, *Genocide as Social Practice*.

[43] Ana Longoni, Gustavo A. Bruzzone, and R. Aguerreberry, eds., *El Siluetazo* (Sentidos. Artes Visuales) (Buenos Aires: Adriana Hidalgo Editora, 2008).

[44] Feinmann, "Pensar y Escribir Después de La ESMA"; La Retaguardia, "La Corte reabrió la discusión acerca del museo en la ESMA," *La tinta: periodismo hasta mancharse* (blog), June 5, 2018, https://latinta.com.ar/2018/06/la-corte-reabrio-la-discusion-acerca-del-museo-en-la-esma/.

[45] Theodor W. Adorno, *Kulturkritik Und Gesellschaft*, ed. Rolf Tiedemann, 2. Aufl, Gesammelte Schriften; Bd. 10 (Frankfurt am Main: Suhrkamp, 1996).

[46] Feinmann, "Auschwitz y La Filosofía," 2. The original quote in Spanish is: "El desafío de Adorno nos incluye. No sólo porque somos parte de la humanidad, sino porque somos argentinos y tenemos nuestro Auschwitz. Sus víctimas fueron menos, pero no fue menor su horror. Nuestro Auschwitz es la ESMA."

[47] Hannah Arendt, *The Origins of Totalitarianism* (San Diego: Harcourt Brace, 1979); Promotional Video for the ESMA's World Heritage Nomination.

[48] ICOMOS—International Council on Monuments and Sites, "World Heritage List: Auschwitz Birkenau. German Nazi Concentration and Extermination Camp (1940–1945)" (UNESCO World Heritage Centre, 1978), Ref. 31, https://whc.unesco.org/en/list/31/documents/.

[49] Oren Baruch Stier, *Holocaust Icons: Symbolizing the Shoah in History and Memory* (New Brunswick, NJ: Rutgers University Press, 2015).

[50] Fukman and La Retaguardia, "Enrique Fukman," 2. The original statement in Spanish: "¿Los efectos de la Dictadura siguen vigentes al presente? ¿Este presente tiene que ver con ese pasado? Si tiene que ver con ese pasado, es la ESMA. Decir ex ESMA es como decir que es algo que no tiene que ver con nosotros. Pero tiene mucho que ver con nuestro presente. [. . .] Entonces, es la ESMA, no es la ex ESMA. Como nosotros siempre decimos, ¿alguien escuchó alguna vez hablar de un ex Auschwitz o siempre se dice Auschwitz? ¿Por qué? Porque sus consecuencias están en el presente. Y puede haber pasado 70 años, como Auschwitz, y todavía las consecuencias están."

[51] Space for Memory and for the Promotion and Defense of Human Rights is composed of a tripartite executive board integrated by a representative of the national government, a representative of city of Buenos Aires and a representative of the directory of human rights organizations. See http://www.espaciomemoria.ar/prensa.php (accessed November 30, 2018).
[52] Permanent Delegation of the Republic of Argentina to UNESCO, "ESMA's World Heritage List Nomination;" video for the ESMA's World Heritage Nomination https://www.youtube.com/watch?v=3AKeerlUFI4 (accessed November 16, 2018).
[53] UNESCO World Heritage Centre, "18 EXT.COM 4—Decision. Outcomes of the Open-Ended Working Group on Sites of Memory Associated with Recent Conflicts," 2023, https://whc.unesco.org/en/decisions/8046/.
[54] Permanent Delegation of the Republic of Argentina to UNESCO.
[55] Munú Actis et al., *That Inferno: Conversations of Five Women Survivors of an Argentine Torture Camp*, 1st ed. (Nashville, TN: Vanderbilt University Press, 2006), 244–47.
[56] "Guillermo Rodolfo Pérez Roisinblit. Nieto restituido por las Abuelas de la Plaza de Mayo," Educación y Memoria, n.d., https://www.educacionymemoria.com.ar/guillermo-rodolfo-perez-roisinblit; n.d., "PÉREZ ROISINBLIT, Guillermo Rodolfo Fernando," Abuelas de Plaza de Mayo, n.d., https://www.abuelas.org.ar/caso/perez-roisinblit-guillermo-rodolfo-fernando-284?orden=c.
[57] Abuelas de la Plaza de Mayo Website, https://www.abuelas.org.ar/caso/buscar?tipo=3 (accessed January 4, 2021). "Abuelas de Plaza de Mayo confirmó el hallazgo y restitución de la identidad del nieto 133," *infobae*, August 28, 2023, sec. Sociedad, https://www.infobae.com/sociedad/2023/07/28/abuelas-de-plaza-de-mayo-confirmo-el-hallazgo-y-restitucion-de-la-identidad-del-nieto-133/.
[58] n.d., "Rosa Roisinblit: 'Me llevó 15 años conquistar el cariño de mi nieto,'" *Infobae*, May 21, 2016, sec. Argentina, https://www.infobae.com/2016/05/22/1813308-rosa-roisinblit-me-llevo-15-anos-conquistar-el-carino-mi-nieto/.
[59] n.d., "Guillermo Rodolfo Pérez Roisinblit."
[60] Vezzetti, *Pasado y Presente*; UNITED NATIONS EDUCATIONAL, SCIENTIFIC AND CULTURAL ORGANIZATION and INTERGOVERNMENTAL COMMITTEE FOR THE PROTECTION OF THE WORLD CULTURAL AND NATURAL HERITAGE, "Operational Guidelines for the Implementation of the World Heritage Convention" (UNESCO, World Heritage Convention, July 12, 2017), http://whc.unesco.org/en/guidelines.
[61] For a critical analysis of what she calls subjective turn, see Beatriz Sarlo, *Tiempo Pasado: Cultura de La Memoria y Giro Subjetivo: Una Discusión*, Sociología y Política (Buenos Aires: Siglo Veintiuno Editores Argentina, 2005).
[62] Valentina Rozas-Krause, "Neither Words nor Materiality Are Enough: The Role of Testimony in the Preservation of an Argentine Clandestine Detention Center," *Memory Studies,* May 8, 2024, https://doi.org/10.1177/17506980241247273.
[63] Permanent Delegation of the Republic of Argentina to UNESCO, "ESMA's World Heritage List Nomination."
[64] Diario Pagina12, "Rosa Roisinblit y Guillermo Rodolfo Pérez Declararon En El Juicio Por Los Crímenes de La ESMA," Museo de la Memoria de la Argentina, May 29, 2014, http://museodelamemoria.gob.ar/page/noticias/id/1393/title/Rosa-Roisinblit-y-Guillermo-Rodolfo-P%C3%A9rez-declararon-en-el-juicio-por-los-cr%C3%ADmenes-de-la-ESMA; Mar Centenera, "Argentina cerró 2017 con 198 nuevas condenas por delitos de lesa humanidad," *El País*, January 4, 2018, sec. Argentina, https://elpais.com/internacional/2018/01/03/argentina/1515006341_328707.html.
[65] Actis et al., *That Inferno*.
[66] This quote has been widely published, see an English version here: https://issuu.com/pablostorino/docs/identity_-_a_pedagogy_on_collective_memory/s/12177899 (accessed October 26, 2023).
[67] In 2008 ESMA had already been declared a National Historic Monument by Argentina's National Monuments Council (ESMA file, Archive Comisión Nacional de Monumentos, de Lugares y de Bienes Históricos. Ministerio de Cultura, República Argentina). Daniel Politi, "Argentina's Former Detention and Torture Site Added to UNESCO World Heritage List," *AP News*, September 19, 2023, sec. World News, https://apnews.com/article/argentina-esma-unesco-memory-heritage-20d563addf91113e07adce1e64dba35a.
[68] UNESCO World Heritage Centre, "ESMA Museum and Site of Memory; Former Clandestine Center of Detention, Torture and Extermination," World Heritage List, 2023, https://whc.unesco.org/en/list/1681/.
[69] Permanent Delegation of the Republic of Argentina to UNESCO, "ESMA's World Heritage List Nomination."
[70] Constanza Lambertucci and Mar Centenera, "La ultraderecha de Javier Milei ataca el consenso contra la dictadura en Argentina," *El País Argentina*, September 5, 2023, sec. Argentina, https://elpais.com/argentina/2023-09-05/la-ultraderecha-de-javier-milei-pone-a-prueba-el-consenso-contra-la-dictadura-en-argentina.html.

Figure 1. The view from inside the tunnels of the bunker. Children can be seen running in the distance where skylights illuminate the ground below every few meters. Still from *The Bunker, the Barracks, and the Base*, a short film by Batoul Faour, 2023.

Batoul Faour and Meriam Soltan

The Bunker, the Barracks, the Base, and the Border

Preservation as Resistance in South Lebanon

Rods of steel reinforcement jut out of a massive chunk of concrete that cleaves the pathway before us. The tangled mess of metal and aggregate makes it difficult to forge a direct route to the underground entrance ahead. Other remnants of the destroyed slab—blasted apart in an airstrike years ago—litter the entirety of the field around us. The children I follow toward the entrance step deftly around the wreckage. They brush past sun-bleached grass and overgrown weeds, upset ting gravel that skitters into fractures in the cement underfoot. The pebbles and dust softly ricochet around in the darkness of the void below. I catch myself, nearly slipping into the cavity of an open skylight. The sun overhead reveals a maze of rooms and corridors. My grandmother has told me of these rooms, many carved so deep into the earth, they have never seen the daylight. Like the kids leading us into the bunker, she too had played here with her friends as a child. The game has not changed much in the decades since. Still children run through the bunker's many tunnels, and still they attempt to make their way out the other side without getting lost in the darkness.

Up here, above the labyrinth of ruined rooms and corridors, the abandoned bunker camouflages neatly into the fields and farmland that extend around it in every direction. At a distance, the rubble is not unlike the rocky hills and outcroppings that emerge around Sahel El Khiam.[1] The fertile plain and its surrounding village share borders with occupied Palestine to the South and Syria in the East. Its proximity to both has placed it at the forefront of incessant regional turmoil. Israeli military operations, armed invasions, and occupations have threatened border towns like Khiam since the establishment of the State of Israel in 1948.[2] The flat expanse of the Khiam-Marjaayoun Valley has made it an advantageous point of entry for invading Israeli forces in recent years. So strategic is this visual corridor that it would take just seven days for Israeli Forces to sweep across the plains and claim most of South Lebanon during its second invasion of the country in 1982.[3] Khiam, along with the other villages included in the Israeli administered South Lebanon Security Belt, would remain occupied for eighteen years until liberation could be won in 2000.[4]

In that time, Khiam was chosen to host one of Israel's most notorious detention centers, a hilltop facility built upon the site of colonial French military barracks and used to detain

Future Anterior
Volume XIX, Number 2
Winter 2022

more than five thousand prisoners throughout the occupation. In more recent years, the village has had to help absorb the fallout of civil war in Syria.[5] The influx of refugees is ongoing, with many settling and taking up agricultural work in the village's reclaimed flatlands. Today, they join the Palestinians that sought refuge in these lands before them, neighbors and family members that fled north to Lebanon in the wake of the *Nakba,* or catastrophe, and who too now tend to land on the other side of the border.

Of this land, that which is plowed, sown, and harvested within the bounds of Khiam's decommissioned airbase is sited but half a kilometer (0.31 miles) from the Israeli border wall. Also a colonial-era remnant, also bombarded in the wars fought since, the base—like the bunker and the barracks—are of the oldest surviving structures in the region. They have outlived the regimes responsible for their existence and have since been evolved by generations of villagers beyond their intended purposes. The bunker, a playground; the barracks, a memorial to victims of torture; the base, reclaimed for farmland: all are recalibrated to fulfill the diverse imperatives of those making a life in and around these sites today.

At the heart of each of these undertakings are various forms of preservation—concerted efforts made to salvage the ruins of the built and natural environment, but also, and perhaps more critically, unfailing commitments made to safeguarding the right to childhood, the right to remember, the right to a future beyond occupation. This is a heritage preserved only when it is itself performed, realized only when it is lived. In the face of protracted local and regional turmoil, the very act of preservation in South Lebanon is thus, also, one of resistance. In this essay, we look to Munira Khayyat's theorization of resistance as summoned in the everyday practices of villagers at the frontlines. Together, we search beyond militaristic and ideological conceptions of resistance in South Lebanon to also embrace it as "humbly and variously rooted in life ongoing—and oriented toward life defiant."[6]

We also here borrow Hoda El Shakry's theorizations of *sumud,* or steadfastness, which she defines in her own research on Palestine as "the strive to preserve the knowledge practices and lifeworlds of Palestinians against the forces of cultural, historical, and territorial erasure."[7] Similarly and in solidarity, sumud as practiced across South Lebanon is read here not only as an impulse to preserve the past, but as also being an "investment in the future."[8] That which spans this spatiotemporal spectrum are the oral histories, narrated elder to youth, that have, for generations, safeguarded the lifeworlds of southern villagers in the face of colonial dispossession. Among the great and varied discourse on this knowledge practice, we look to Lucine Taminian's research on oral history as a multigenre that centers community voices, wherein remembering together through play, poetry, songs, and stories becomes a means of upholding the rights and dignity of each narrator.[9]

The encounters that follow trace a few such histories across Khiam's colonial-era structures—the bunker, the barracks, the base, and the border that mediates them. The relationship of these sites to the land and to each other is rife with contradiction, and yet what binds them are the oral histories—memories, spirits, outlooks—of those that have learned to make a life through, with, and despite them. When read in tandem, these relationships make legible an intergenerational desire to nurture what it is we have together inherited beyond the mere materiality of these structures. The oral histories that inform this research reveal how the work of preservation in South Lebanon is a means of resistance in the wake of occupation and colonial violence, and that to receive and carry forth this work is also to collectively defy the lingering vestiges of these power structures.

The Bunker

Military violence and borderland aggression far predate the Israeli occupation of South Lebanon (1982–2000), their ongoing occupation of Palestine (1948–), and even the invention of modern Lebanon (1943).[10] Mandates established in the region between the world wars apportioned the Levant into territories ruled by various Western powers. Prior to its independence and the establishment of its republic, Lebanon was ruled by France under a mandate that lasted twenty-three years (1923–1946). In that same time, Palestine fell under British rule. But with administration of the Lebanese mandate having been overtaken by Vichy French forces in 1941 after the fall of Paris to Nazi Germany,[11] British armies were mobilized northward, from Palestine and into Lebanese territory, to ensure Allies-led authority was maintained across the region. The Vichy-French and the British clashed in a brief series of military operations over the Khiam-Marjayoun territories, the longest battle of which was fought over the barracks where the French had made a stronghold of what they came to call the Khiam Fort.[12] In the end, British forces won that battle and claimed the barracks and unrestricted hilltop views it offered for themselves. Following that victory and under their extended tenure in South Lebanon, the British built a series of defensive fortifications across Khiam, among them a military airbase, a series of mountainside trenches, and, as it happens, the bunker my grandmother frequented as a child.

Just before World War II took a turn in their favor, British forces buried what they had managed to build of the bunker beneath five meters (16.4 feet) of soil. The olive grove planted atop the mound was meant to both camouflage and fortify it against German airstrikes. And although intended to function as a military hospital bunker to treat the wounded in case of an invasion, any attacks the British anticipated while building this structure never actually came to pass. Nazi-allied forces did not carry out any attacks across the region in the final years of World War II, and the conclusion of the war by 1945 saw the Allies largely withdraw their military presence from Palestine, Syria, and Lebanon shortly thereafter.

While that retreat marked the conclusion of colonial mandates across the region, authority was not retracted without significant deliberation on border demarcations. There was intense dispute among French and British forces regarding whether land south of the Litani River would be attributed to Lebanon or Palestine. That Khiam, at the edge of either, was eventually designated as Lebanese territory was a matter of safeguarding Western geopolitical interests. With the establishment of the State of Israel on the horizon, lands south of the Litani River were identified as prime territory for the creation of an oil pipeline that Iraqi officials refused to channel through occupied Palestinian territory.[13]

My grandmother was born in the wake of these deliberations and, as children often do, found extraordinary ways to live and play amidst the chaos. In between shifts harvesting olives,[14] she and her cousins eventually spied the bunker's entrance hidden within the dense grove of olive trees. By then, wild grass had woven its way across skylights, and olive roots had burrowed deep into the earth, fracturing even the densest slabs and retaining walls. Returned to nature, the structure sparked the imaginations of children who played in the safety and shade of its fortified, underground labyrinth. But peace would not last, and the child that had already escaped the city for the South with the outbreak of the Lebanese Civil War in 1975, would again flee the South for the city during the Israeli invasion of 1982.

The children that invite me to explore the bunker with them today made it here by chance, as refugees displaced by a new generation of wars, just across the border in Syria. A few of them are young enough to have no memory of their home country. The oldest though, a girl named Rodayna, runs a small, calloused hand across a bit of tangled rebar, the sight of ruined concrete all too familiar.

I met Rodayna and her friends on my first visit to document the bunker. What I thought was an abandoned colonial-era war structure was really more of a playground teeming with children sliding down caved-in ceilings and running through gravel-strewn hallways. Intrigued by my camera, she and her friends invited me into the tunnels below. With temperatures across the valley exceeding well over 35 °C (95 °F) in the summer months, the cool, fortified underground was a much welcome respite from the sun above. The mornings they are not helping their parents pick, water, and prune crops in the surrounding fields, they meet here and play until it is time to attend school in the afternoon. As is the case across most of Lebanon and its overwhelmed and underfunded public-school systems, Syrian children attend school in the afternoon, with classes extending well into the evenings during exam times. In villages like Khiam, any time spent outside beyond that is restricted by discriminatory curfews.[15]

Rodayna, her friends, and their families live in nearby fields, just west of the bunker. For most of them, home is a tent supplied by the United Nations. The rest live in accommodations provided by the owners of the grounds they tend. Modest though their living quarters are, the children and their families are generous enough to invite me over for tea. Rodayna and her parents explain to me what it has been like to neighbor the bunker for ten years now—how strange, disconcerting sounds sometimes carry over to their field in the nighttime. The following mornings, says Rodayna, they will notice some of the bunker's amenities missing here and there: looted steel vents and outdated wall fixtures, probably to be sold for scraps at market. Other times, litters of stray cats and dogs will turn up, nested in the cool shade of the maze below. The band of friends are happy to have me tag along for their games whenever I manage to turn up at the bunker for photos and videos over the following weeks. As my guides, they unknowingly inherit a tradition of stewardship from those tasked with ushering visitors around the grounds before them.

When families like my own returned home to their villages in the wake of the liberation of South Lebanon in 2000, the bunker had once again become a point of interest in Khiam. By 2004, the municipality had plans drawn up to renovate the structure into a museum dedicated to the region's World War–era history. Also included in the plans were visions for an expansion, for a fairground of sorts where locals could sell crafts and produce.[16] The project, funded by American humanitarian aid organization, Mercy Corps, was part of a larger vision dedicated to reviving the town post-occupation.[17] In the space of a year, tunnels were renovated, paving stones were laid, exhibits were organized, and guides were trained in preparation of the opening events.

With primary funding provided by the United States, US ambassador to Lebanon, Jeffrey Feltman, attended the museum's inauguration in 2005. His presence, however, proved less than welcome.[18] Coverage of the event at the time by

As-Safir newspaper details a massive interruption to the opening ceremony incited by the father of a local martyr. "You are not welcome here," shouted the man on behalf of his son, killed in resistance operations during the Israeli occupation of their village. "We will not let you come here again. You represent George Bush, and he supports Israel!"[19]

Although animosity toward the renovation's funders lingered, the museum was frequented by crowds of visitors from across Lebanon for the few months that it was in operation. Despite its success though, this era of the bunker, like those before it, was short lived. The following year, it was all but decimated by Israeli shelling during Lebanon's 2006 war. With the onset of yet another Israeli invasion, the uniforms, maps, and artifacts on display in delicate glass casings were cleared to make room for weaponry. Where tour guides had once walked and children played, armed men ran for shelter. The bright paving stones installed during the renovation to guide visitors around the site instead came to direct planes in the sky to their target. Bunkers, as the ultimate military surface architecture, marked the sky's arrival in war.[20] It was with this arrival that visibility became synonymous with destruction—the function of the arms and the function of the all-seeing eye one and the same.[21]

Throughout the month of armed conflict, missiles struck the bunker in quick succession, destroying access to the maze of underground rooms and tunnels. The ceiling collapsed, and the earth held in by its retaining walls caved in, relegating most of the restored rooms, once again, to total darkness. In the span of a few weeks, a local attempt to preserve history had dared render the invisible visible. And in so doing, the traces of one occupier were again swiftly rewritten by another. To live and nurture lifeworlds in the shadows of armed occupation—whether British, French, or Israeli—is not so much to dwell as it is to "take on," or consistently resist, the forces for which the casemate (fortress) is the instrument.[22]

The airstrikes had blasted three large pits in the ground and blocked off many of the original access points. Navigating the site today requires knowing how to traverse both the tunnels designed by the British and the wreckage wrought by the Israelis. Rodayna and her friends show me how to do both. With her in the lead, the children guide me through the parts of the tunnels that remain accessible, show me where it is safe to step, and warn me away from where it is too dark to see.

At the northernmost entry point—one of the few still intact—converging stone retaining walls emerge from the ground at an angle, a hint that earth has been excavated for the tunneling of hallways below. The passage, a primary axis stretching from North to South, occasionally branches into secondary rooms and pathways (Figure 1).[23] Earth fills the spaces in between, a common practice in military bunker construction.[24] The compacted earth acts as a protective layer to isolate any explosions from setting off a chain reaction across the structure. Destruction here is an act of controlled preservation, one where the earth is made to contain the power of the impact. When the airstrikes hit, these mounds collapsed into the rooms, creating hills that the children now step down onto through breaks in the uppermost slab (Figure 2). In some rooms, the earth is piled high enough for them to climb down through the skylights themselves—originally five meters from the ground—and land safely in the tunnels below.

Here, now, planimetric relationships are reordered by the chaos of destruction, and destruction transformed by the typologies of play (Figure 3). Ephemeral and effervescent, they overwrite the militaristic ambitions imposed by those who will never value people and land beyond that which can be (forcefully) taken from them.

The Barracks

In between speed limit warnings, welcome signs, and political flags and paraphernalia local to South Lebanon, the occasional road sign staked into the ground will direct drivers on across the hills toward Khiam Prison.[25] Up the Khiam-Marjaayoun Valley, past the main square, and beyond the municipality is a bend in the road around which, some 750 meters (2460 feet) above sea level, the structure has been carved into the hilltop. It is the highest point for miles around, popular with those looking to visit both for the site's history and for the unobstructed views it offers south, onto Palestine.

In the distance, I spot Abo Ali. Today, on liberation day, he guides crowds across the ground's many prison blocks. Children dip in and out of the smallest cells, while parents linger in the courtyards, hesitant to step any further in. Many of these visitors are relatives of former prisoners. Others have made the trip out from cities further up north in celebration of the occasion. Present too are a handful of foreigners—journalists perhaps. They are the visitors that Abo Ali takes special care of. "They have an image of us in the West, that we're violent savages, terrorists even," explains Abo Ali on a later visit. "I recount for them exactly what has happened here, so that they leave knowing what violence and injustice has been committed against us." *Us* meaning that Abo Ali was himself imprisoned here for seven torturous years during the occupation. It was not until villagers stormed the barracks on May 23, 2000, overtook the remaining guards, and ripped the locks off his shared cell that he was able to again walk free. Today, he makes a home of the guardhouse and guides visitors across the grounds in memory of everything he first lost here.[26]

Figure 2. Children are seen playing aboveground through a break in the bunker's ceiling slab. Still from *The Bunker, the Barracks, the Base, and the Border,* a short film by Batoul Faour, 2023.

Figure 3. Skylights, which have been blasted out of the ground, are overturned in the field above the bunker. Still from *The Bunker, the Barracks, and the Base,* a short film by Batoul Faour, 2023.

The Khiam Prison, also identified in historical records as the Khiam Detention Center, was founded in 1985 on an underlying structure of abandoned colonial-era barracks. Under Israeli occupation, the South Lebanon Army (SLA), known locally as Jesh Lahed,[27] was tasked with overseeing administration of the prison on behalf of the Israeli Forces until their withdrawal in 2000. The State of Israel has repeatedly denied any connection to administration of the prison throughout the fifteen years that it was operational. Regardless—and beyond the countless eyewitness reports and personal testimonies offered by former prisoners[28]—an extensive report published by Amnesty International in 1992 details irrefutable evidence of human rights abuses, unlawful detainment and interrogation of civilians, and torture carried out by the Israeli soldiers and their allied forces at the prison throughout the occupation.[29] Of the many abuses committed by Israeli Forces across Lebanon, these are among the most indisputable—a microcosm of the occupation in its entirety. “As I was inside this small cell,” recalls a former prisoner on tape in 1993, “I started to think . . . it’s strange how this place’s history encapsulates the history and suffering of a nation, one whose sovereignty has been infringed upon by so many—both friend and foe, neighbor and foreigner. The history of the Khiam Prison,” he reflects, “is a condensed version of the history of this country.”[30]

As with the bunker hidden in the valley below, the municipality worked to convert the prison into a museum of that history post-occupation. Also like the bunker, the prison was destroyed in a series of targeted airstrikes during the war in 2006. Locals are convinced that those missiles were dropped to destroy any material evidence of the war crimes that played out within those walls. Still, what remains of the prison blocks today is considerable. And those that have walked its grounds since will attest to the destruction having only further heightened their experience of the site and its history, that which, in so many ways, remains ever-present. Plans for a second renovation will write the craters in the central courtyard into this living heritage.[31]

At the prison’s northern block, Abo Ali pauses to recite a few introductory remarks to visitors on his special tour. Such is his daily speech, one he has known by heart for some time now. The northern block is one of four longitudinal single-story buildings that ring the site’s central courtyard. A single door on either end of the northern block leads into a narrow corridor that mediates between a succession of windowless cells. The hall is tight enough that we have to make our way through single file. Abo Ali limps ahead of us, and continues to narrate softly in the darkness, the weight of what has happened to him here settling heavily around us.

He points to a rusted metal door punctured by a grate at eye level. A sliding panel welded into the metal below it is notched open, revealing a cavity just large enough for a hand or two to slip through. We have seen this door before[32]—seen the grasping hands that clung desperately to those of family and friends that smashed rocks and heaved crowbars against steel locks until their hands bled; heard the joyous cries that echoed across the hilltop, out of the televisions, and into our own homes as prisoners, one after the other, tumbled out of cells and into the arms of their loved ones. Abo Ali pushes the door open for us to peer inside. The cells are no larger than 2.5 × 10 meters (8 × 32 feet), though the rotting mattresses and bunk beds attest to their having hosted up to fifteen prisoners at a time (Figure 4).

Figure 4. The view from inside one of the cells in the Khiam Detention Center. Up to fifteen prisoners would share a room of this size, with an exposed urinal on the opposite end. Still from *The Bunker, the Barracks, and the Base,* a short film by Batoul Faour, 2023.

Outside again, Abo Ali pauses by a utility pole—standard enough—but points out some extra wiring rigged between it and the building opposite (Figure 5). With the power disconnected now, he gathers some of it into his hands and demonstrates how prisoners—fellow men, friends, comrades—were once stripped and strung up, doused in cold water, and electrocuted. They—he—were then left to hang there, sometimes for days at a time. Cell after cell, he looks to the haphazardly scattered remains to resurface these memories for us, with us.

In lieu of any historical records or formal archives, Abo Ali's guided tours are of the few preservationist practices preventing this history from being lost to time. His personal testimony is living documentation of what has happened here, by whom, and at what cost. These memories are not ones we inherit from him passively. It is work to sort through this past, to carry it forward in absence of a repository available to bear it, to safeguard it, to hold it on our behalf. And yet we do it because in places and homes like our own, where material heritage is constantly blasted to pieces, to learn of our past is to remember together, through each other, for one another. To sort through this inheritance is to survive it.

The Base

My great-grandfather, like so many from across Khiam and Marjaayoun, was enlisted to help build the airbase, bunker, and other miscellaneous fortifications carved into the earth under British control. His eldest son—my grandfather—would walk down into the heart of the valley to deliver his lunch for the day, one he ate in between laborious shifts digging, sculpting, and stacking sandstone into walls and foundations across each site.[33] Many friends and relatives recount similar stories of their fathers from that era of occupation. One elder, a friend of

Figure 5. Abo Ali walks down the corridor through one of the buildings of the barracks. To the left is the relief of one of the cell doors. The utility pole he refers to is seen in the distance ahead. Still from *The Bunker, the Barracks, and the Base,* a short film by Batoul Faour, 2023.

the family, jokes about how his father would make an appearance at the trenches, rub some dirt into his face, and return to collect his wages from unsuspecting British officers at the end of the day. Locals were paid between 25 and 60 *qirsh,* or piastres,[34] for their daily labor.[35]

The airbase is today located at the southernmost edge of the Khiam-Marjaayoun Valley, a peripheral point just 500 meters (0.31 miles) away from an Israeli settlement called Metula. Known in Arabic as El Mtolleh, meaning "the overlook," it is named for its hilltop perch that provides uninterrupted views of the surrounding valleys. The settlement is plugged into the hill in large, calculated modules, all of which ring a central surveillance tower installed at the very top. The western half of this periphery is marked by the border wall, a 9-meter-high (30 feet) barrier of prefabricated concrete and barbed wire equipped with surveillance cameras every few meters. The wall, however, abruptly ends at the settlement's eastern edge (Figure 6).[36] Beyond that, the only thing separating our lands is a short chain-link fence or, at times, nothing at all. This area is known as El Shareet El Hodoudy, or the border strip, and is one of the most heavily surveilled portions of land in the entire region. It is officially demarcated and yet endlessly contested, both in life and on paper. Its porosity has allowed for a number of incidents over the years, with news reports citing the occasional shepherd chasing a wandering flock into Israeli controlled territory, and the warning shots fired in retaliation because of them.[37] "Nature does not answer to the systems of control instituted by man," these shepherds will say upon their return. "Sheep will graze where they please."

The airbase, like the bunker, was never operated as intended. Known locally as Matar El Mtolleh—the Mtolleh Airport—it was built to host fighter planes and coordinate

Figure 6. A view from barracks shows the border wall cutting through the landscape and the airbase running through the valley below. Still from *The Bunker, the Barracks, and the Base*, a short film by Batoul Faour, 2023.

airstrikes during World War II. When the anticipated combat never broke out, it was abandoned. The runway, today fractured and overgrown with weeds, is encircled from end to end by twelve identical hangars and their adjacent storage rooms.[38] The hangars themselves, cobbled together by my great-grandfather and his friends, are curved to accommodate the cockpit and wingspan of British-allied warplanes that never arrived.

Today, the soft mooing of cattle is carried over to us by the wind. We smell and hear them before we see them, dairy cows grazing in the fenced-off expanse of a stone hangar (Figure 7). Their herder, a farmer named Maher, undoes the makeshift fence and leads the cattle to a nearby watering hole before settling them into an adjacent hangar enclosed with corrugated steel sheets for the evening. Maher is originally from Kfarkela, another border town a few villages over where colonial-era ambitions also rend the land apart in certain areas.

He offers to tour us around the airbase, pointing out the complex network of infrastructure built into the land around us. The trenches that cut into the mountainside, he explains, were meant to block the passage of incoming tanks, while the adjacent ditches were used to position targets and carry out surveillance. Resistance forces adapted them for use in their defensive strategies during combat under the occupation. The craters in the mountainside today are evidence of the airstrikes that blasted these same defenses apart in 2006. Running between them are exposed lengths of pipes and wells designed to carry water to the airbase. Today, they have been re-rigged to irrigate crops across the site.

While Maher and his cows make use of two of the twelve hangars, other farmers raise chickens and goats, store their tractors and farming equipment, and collect water for irrigation in the remaining ten (Figure 8). The hangars' original design

Figure 7. Cows grazing inside an adapted airplane hangar. Still from *The Bunker, the Barracks, and the Base,* a short film by Batoul Faour, 2023.

Figure 8. A hangar that is now used to store water. Still from *The Bunker, the Barracks, and the Base*, a short film by Batoul Faour, 2023.

helps naturally delimit the boundaries between each farmer's crops—wheat, corn, other seasonal vegetables—with the runway accommodating the cars and tractors that traverse the land between them. With harvest season nearly upon us, the wheat blazes, golden in the sunlight for miles around (Figure 9). What was once built for military aviation is now commandeered in service of local agricultural infrastructure.

Most days we were out with Maher, he would request that my camera be left behind in the car. Ours is a tenuous peace, and these lands, especially by the border, are still actively surveilled—so much so, he laughed the first time around, when I went to lock the car door. "You don't have to do that," he said. "I can bet you an arm and a leg that no one will touch

Figure 9. Maher walking through the sunlit wheat field. Still from *The Bunker, the Barracks, and the Base*, a short film by Batoul Faour, 2023.

that camera or your car. Nothing happens here—and when I tell you nothing, I mean you can't take a piss without knowing that someone," he gestures around "is watching and ready to intervene. It's the safest, most secure place on Earth." Strange, how something can be both so true and yet so incredibly false, at the same time.

In his truck, as close to the border and Metulla as we dare, we are reminded of the daily journeys our families made by foot, between each other's fields, into Palestine, and back again. We remember when olives were harvested and carried from Khiam to be sold at market all the way in Jerusalem. Together, we remember a time when the wall did not exist.

Life Along the Border

We have inherited the aforementioned cycles of displacement from our parents, just as they have inherited them from theirs. Alongside knowledge of when to pick our olives—after the first rain—and how to press and brine them—with a firm hand, slices of lemon, and a red chili or two;[39] in tandem with how to tell time with the sun and track the months by moonlight; along with the southern dialect they have, word by word, passed down to us, there is also this: an instinct for when to stay and defend, when to flee, and when—perhaps—it is safe enough to come home. Such is our inheritance: complex and contradictory, born of defiance, but also of necessity.

This living heritage, shaped both by occupation and the resistance we levy against it, is anchored in the collective memory of those who survive each armed invasion. That which survives colonial violence and emerges as resistance are the oral histories performed and preserved despite this brutality. Together, they animate what is today little more than rubble and rebar. These memories, shared and inherited, together resist the vestiges of occupation in ways that material history alone can rarely manage.

It is within our overlooked, underrepresented landscapes that the most valuable forms of knowledge come from those who inhabit, experience, and inherit it. To compile the histories of this borderland—for there are many—is to read beyond the cycles of destruction mandated by occupation and instead look to the multiplicity of lived experiences that its people safeguard amidst it all. To do so is to transform this built inheritance from ruins to sites and spaces of intergenerational resistance, ones where playing, tending to land, and remembering together are of the most revolutionary, justice-seeking acts imaginable.

Biographies

Batoul Faour is a visual artist and architect working between Beirut and Toronto. Her work operates at the intersection of politics, spatial histories, and media—blending a journalistic, documentary approach with the empirical and the architectural. She is a recipient of the 2021 *Avery Review* Essay Prize at Columbia University. Her work has been screened and exhibited at Arquiteturas Film festival (Porto), Images festival (Toronto), Bureau Europa (Maastricht), and most recently a solo exhibition at the MINA Image Centre (Beirut). She holds a BArch from the American University of Beirut (2019) and a MArch from the University of Toronto (2021).

Meriam Soltan is a writer and architect interested in how political, artistic, and cultural production intersect across the Middle East. She currently edits for Columbia Books on Architecture and the City and is a graduate of both the Massachusetts Institute of Technology (SMArchs 2022) and the American University of Beirut (BArch 2019). Meriam is the recipient of the MIT Architecture Thesis Award and the Berkeley Essay Prize, and has had her writing featured in *Postmedieval, The Funambulist, Rusted Radishes: Beirut Literary and Art Journal, Thresholds,* and Arab Urbanism. She is the author of the book *Lebanon and the Split of Life: Bearing Witness through the Art of Nabil Kanso* and is currently working on writing a people's history of South Lebanon.

Notes

While the encounters that follow are written in the first person as a record of Batoul's experiences on site, the work of this essay is a result of our shared writing and reflection in the months that followed this fieldwork. The images in this essay are excerpted from Batoul's *The Bunker, the Barracks, and the Base*, a three-channel video that premiered in Beirut at the Mina Image Center in 2023. This year-long research project was made possible by funding awarded to the project by the Canada Council for the Arts and the Toronto Arts Council. Earlier iterations of this project include Batoul's "The Memory Bunker," published in *Thresholds* in 2021.

[1] Sahel El Khiam, or the Khiam Valley, are the plains and farmland that surround the denser heart of Khiam proper, a hilltop village that sits 750m above sea-level at its highest point. It is also often referred to as Sahel El Khiam-Marjayoun, since the valley is delimited by Khiam to the East and the town of Marjayoun to the West.

[2] The establishment of the State of Israel in 1948 is marked by the *Nakba*, or catastrophe—the displacement and dispossession of Palestinians from their homelands. For bordering towns like Khiam in South Lebanon, it marks the beginning of a series of recurring cycles of militarized conflict with the State, leading up to two major Israeli invasions in 1978 and 1982. For oral testimonies from Palestinians who witnessed and survived the Nakba, see "The Palestinian Oral History Archive," AUB Libraries, accessed Oct. 11, 2023, https://libraries.aub.edu.lb/poha/; "Nakba Archive," accessed Oct. 11, 2023, https://www.nakba-archive.org/new/.

[3] For personal accounts of the siege, see Chris Giannou, "Eyewitness: The Battle for South Lebanon. Interview by Helena Cobban," *Journal of Palestine Studies* 11–12, nos. 4 & 1 (1982): 69–84, https://doi.org/10.2307/2538335.

[4] By 1985, around 150 villages fell under administration of the Security Belt. While the civil war north of the Security Belt ended with a ceasefire and the signing of the Taif agreement in 1990, and as rebuilding efforts commenced, villages in the South remained under Israeli control for another ten years. For research on the implications of this disparity in liberation, see Munira Khayyat, *A Landscape of War:*

Ecologies of Resistance and Survival in South Lebanon (Oakland: University of California Press, 2022). For coverage of liberation in 2000, see “الجنوب يحرر الوطن / The South Liberates the Homeland,” *As-Safir,* May 24, 2000, https://archive.assafir.com/#/articles?pageSize=16&pageNumber=1&order=DESC&sortBy=relevance&searchWithin=title&searchWithin=keywords&value=230484#الجنوب%20يحرر%20الوطن.

[5] Syrian refugees officially account for over 20 percent of Lebanon’s population. According to the UNHCR, “Lebanon currently hosts approximately 1.5 million refugees from Syria, including approximately 815,000 registered with UNHCR.” With how unreliable reporting mechanisms have become in recent years, these numbers are likely much higher. Data is updated annually with the most recent numbers being from the year 2023, at the time of this writing. See “Syria Regional Refugee Response,” UNHCR, last modified Oct 10, 2023, https://data2.unhcr.org/en/situations/syria/location/71.

[6] Khayyat, “Introduction,” *A Landscape of War,* 9.

[7] Hoda El Shakry, “Palestine and the Aesthetics of the Future Impossible,” *Interventions,* no. 5 (2021): 669–90.

[8] Alexandra Rijke and Toine Van Teeffelen, “To Exist is to Resist: Sumud, Heroism, and the Everyday,” *Jerusalem Quarterly* 59 (2014): 93, quoted in El Shakry, “Palestine and the Aesthetics of the Future Impossible,” 673.

[9] Lucine Taminian, “Documenting the Oral History of Iraqis in Times of Conflict: Challenges, Ethics, and Standards of Practice,” in *Oral History in Times of Change: Gender, Documentation, and the Making of Archives: Cairo Papers in Social Science,* ed. Hoda Elsadda and Hanan Sabea (Cairo: The American University in Cairo Press, 2018), 121.

[10] The history of modern Lebanon is a tenuous one, with the republic founded largely on sectarian lines and anachronistic colonial-era narratives. For more on this history and others written to counter it, see: Ussama Makdisi, “The Modernity of Sectarianism in Lebanon: Reconstructing the Nation-State,” *Middle East Research and Information Project* 200 (Fall 1996), https://merip.org/1996/09/the-modernity-of-sectarianism-in-lebanon/; Mohamad Nahleh, “Umm Kamel’s Affair: How Infidelity Liberated the Night Sky in Jabal ‘Amil,” *Journal of Architectural Education* 78, no. 1 (2024): 14–25.

[11] During World War II, and with the invasion of Paris by the Nazi regime, French allegiance was split between Vichy French and Free French authorities. Vichy France operated as a government sympathetic to the Nazi regime, while Free France remained allied with the British against the Germans. It was through this alliance that British and Free French forces invaded Lebanon through Palestine in the summer of 1941. For more on this history, see David Sutton, *Syria and Lebanon 1941: The Allied Fight against the Vichy French* (Oxford: Osprey Publishing, 2022).

[12] War diaries of the campaign at the time were compiled based on interviews with surviving infantry and cavalry members and are available for review at the Kew National Archives, London. See “Syrian Narratives—25 BDE at Khiam, Merdjayoun and Jezzine—to 14 June 41,” Reference nb: CAB 106/897.

[13] “Iraq: Oil Pipelines,” Encyclopedia Britannica, accessed Oct. 11, 2023, https://www.britannica.com/place/Iraq/Oil-pipelines.

[14] The olive harvest is so cherished in these lands that families will brave even enemy fire to see it through. See Khayyat, “Introduction,” *A Landscape of War*, 12.

[15] See “Lebanon: At Least 45 Local Curfews Imposed on Syrian Refugees,” Human Rights Watch, October 3, 2014, https://www.hrw.org/news/2014/10/03/lebanon-least-45-local-curfews-imposed-syrian-refugees; “Measures Impacting Refugees in Lebanon Curfews,” UNHCR, January 2020, https://data.unhcr.org/en/documents/details/75104.

[16] “The Renovation of the ‘English Hospital’ in Al-Khiam to become a museum and fairground for local activity,” *As-Safir,* December 16, 2004. See https://archive.assafir.com/#/articles?pageSize=16&pageNumber=1&order=DESC&sortBy=relevance&searchWithin=title&searchWithin=keywords&value=%D8%A7%D9%84%D9%85%D8%B3%D8%AA%D8%B4%D9%81%D9%89%20%D8%A7%D9%84%D8%A5%D9%86%D9%83%D9%84%D9%8A%D8%B2%D9%8A#703816.

[17] Kamil Faour, former mayor of Khiam, also mentions other intended projects including the construction of a local resort as part of a vision for attracting new waves of tourism to the South and shaking the stigma purveyed by its war-torn history. Faour oversaw the renovation and opening of the bunker. Kamil Faour, interview by Batoul Faour, December 21, 2022.

[18] “The Father of a Martyr to Feltman in El-Khiam: ‘You are not welcome here!’” *As-Safir,* October 24, 2005. See https://archive.assafir.com/#/articles?pageSize=16&pageNumber=1&order=DESC&sortBy=relevance&searchWithin=title&searchWithin=keywords&value=%D8%A7%D9%84%D9%85%D8%B3%D8%AA%D8%B4%D9%81%D9%89%20%D8%A7%D9%84%D8%A5%D9%86%D9%83%D9%84%D9%8A%D8%B2%D9%8A#744054.

[19] This interruption was echoed by the crowd and led to the swift retreat of Feltman and his security team. Some locals speculate that this encounter also contributed to the subsequent targeting of the site. Faour interview.

[20] Paul Virilio, *Bunker Archeology,* trans. George R Collins (New York: Princeton Architectural Press, 1994), 12.

[21] Virilio, *Bunker Archeology,* 17.

[22] Virilio, *Bunker Archeology,* 43.

[23] The structure is sited within an olive orchard, spanning a total area of around 8,770 square meters. It comprises a series of 30 rooms of various sizes connected by 4 long spanning tunnels (ranging between 37 to 95 meters) and is lit by 65 skylights. It has a total of 13 different entry/exit points, only 5 of which are currently accessible due to the wreckage. The overhead clearance of the tunnel is around 2.7 meters, covered by a 1-meter-thick slab and a 1.5-meter-deep layer of soil above. This is based on both local observations and renovation drawings of the bunker acquired from the Khiam Municipality.

[24] Jean-Louis Cohen, *Architecture in Uniform: Designing and Building for the Second World War* (Montréal: Canadian Centre for Architecture, 2011).

[25] Although we formally identify the site as a prison for the purposes of this essay, we recognize and underwrite former prisoner and survivor Suha Bchara's refusal to call it the Khiam "prison," stressing the illegitimacy of the site and the means of its operation outside of any legal authority or rule. Souha Béchara, *Resistance: My Life for Lebanon* (New York: Soft Skull Press, 2003), 198–99.

[26] For the testimony of former prisoners and rehabilitation efforts, see "The Liberation of Khiam, the Liberation of South Lebanon: Memories and struggle continue!" *Samidoun,* May 25, 2022, https://samidoun.net/2022/05/the-liberation-of-khiam-the-liberation-of-south-lebanon-memories-and-struggle-continue/; Khiam Rehabilitation Center for Victims of Torture, accessed Oct. 11, 2023, https://www.khiamcenter.org/en/p.php?lang=en&aid=2.

[27] For more on the SLA, the circumstances of its formation, and its administration of the South Lebanon Security Belt, see Ahmad Beydoun, "The South Lebanon Border Zone: A Local Perspective," *Journal of Palestine Studies* 21, no. 3 (1992): 35–53, https://doi.org/10.2307/2537518.

[28] See Stephanie Khouri, "Khiam Prison: Unpublished Archival Documents Reveal the Extent of Shin Bet Involvement," *L'Orient Today,* March 25, 2022, https://today.lorientlejour.com/article/1294808/khiam-prison-unpublished-archival-documents-reveal-the-extent-of-shin-bet-involvement.html.

[29] "Israel/South Lebanon: The Khiam Detainees: Torture and Ill-Treatment," Amnesty International, May 1992, accessed October 11, 2023, https://www.amnesty.org/en/wp-content/uploads/2021/06/mde150081992en.pdf.

[30] From an interview with a former prisoner in *Talaeen a Junuub* (Up to the South), directed by Jayce Salloum and Walid Raad (1993), 00:08:34 to 00:10:06, https://vimeo.com/81763753.

[31] According to municipality officials, plans to renovate the prison-turned-museum were set to begin during the summer of 2024.They have since been indefinitely postponed given the latest outbreak of war with Israel in South Lebanon and Gaza, ongoing at the time of this writing.

[32] News footage of the liberation of the Khiam prison is symbolic of and synonymous with the liberation of the South. For live footage from that day, see الشيخ فادي حيدر, "The liberation of Khiam Year 2000/ تحرير بلدة الخيام سنة 2000," YouTube, 12:33–27:41, https://www.youtube.com/watch?v=gRKzGwwSnoE&t=807s&pp=ygUy2KrYrdix2YrYsSDZhdi52KrZgtmElNin2YTYrtmK2KfZhSDYudin2YUg2aLZoNmg2aA%3D.

[33] Stone was extracted from the nearby Hamames hills, east of the site, and carried down into the valley.

[34] A single Lebanese lira comprises 100 piastres. For comparison, the US dollar is today currently valued at 93,000 lira.

[35] "The English Hospital in Khiam to Return as a Touristic Site," *As-Safir,* April 16, 2003, https://archive.assafir.com/#/articles?pageSize=16&pageNumber=1&order=DESC&sortBy=relevance&searchWithin=title&searchWithin=keywords&value=%D8%A7%D9%84%D9%85%D8%B3%D8%AA%D8%B4%D9%81%D9%89%20%D8%A7%D9%84%D8%A5%D9%86%D9%83%D9%84%D9%8A%D8%B2%D9%8A#607712.

[36] The wall, still a work in progress, is built and funded completely by the State of Israel. Continued efforts to erect walls on and along Lebanese territory in villages like Kfarshouba has incited protests and standoffs between Israeli Forces and local Lebanese farmers. See Ahmad Mantash, "Israeli Troops Fire Tear Gas to Disperse Protesters along Lebanon Border," *AP News*, June 9, 2023, https://apnews.com/article/lebanon-israel-border-tear-gas-protesters-eb3c3459c8f7a77267f6e6ad69714455.

[37] Raja Abdulrahim, "The Disputed Border Where Every Shepherd is Seen as a Potential Spy," *The New York Times,* November 3, 2022, https://www.nytimes.com/2022/11/23/world/middleeast/israel-border-shepherds-spies.html; Richard Hall and Oliver Holmes, "Shepherds without Borders, Israel's War with Lebanese Herders," *The Guardian,* August 5, 2018, https://www.theguardian.com/world/2018/aug/05/shepherds-without-borders-israels-war-with-lebanese-herders.
[38] Original plans of the airbase show evidence of two runway strips, between 1000 to 1100 meters in length each. One of these strips has been preserved as a road for access but the second has since been reworked as farmland.
[39] Jarred olive recipe from Meriam's grandmother, Em Abbas: 1 kilogram green olives (handpicked and thoroughly washed), one lemon, thinly sliced, 3–4 dried red chilis, 1 tablespoon of coarse salt, fill to the rim with extra virgin olive oil.

Figure 1. Deqa Abshir, *Fragmented II*.

Anooradha Iyer Siddiqi

The Intimacies of Restitution

Reinscribing the Dadaab Refugee Camps

This article centers a significant aspect of the research I conducted for the book *Architecture of Migration: The Dadaab Refugee Camps and Humanitarian Settlement,* involving experimental acts of restitution.[1] Although *Architecture of Migration* is a scholarly, historical work, it became a progenitor for works by practitioners engaged in creative artistic and architectural practices. These artistic experiments emerged from my twelve years of historical research and scholarly intimacy with refugee contexts: especially a place called Dadaab. During this process, I turned to nonacademic forms of intellectual intimacy that a study of Dadaab might scaffold, thinking on how scholarship might open onto critical heritage practices. I initiated the production of a critical archive of works—exercises in drawing Dadaab. I argue that they enable forms of restitution, perhaps, as W. E. B. Du Bois posits in *The Souls of Black Folk,* forms of communing across time, so that we may bear sorrows across generations, struggling alongside our elders as well as those yet to arrive.[2] I will come to this critical archive after first acknowledging a place and a text, each a site of theory.

Dadaab

By way of introduction, let us immerse ourselves in the Dadaab refugee camps, in northern Kenya near the border of Somalia, an environment and ecology that represents a devastating politics and aesthetics of ephemerality. My work in Dadaab began in 2011, when I had the privilege of visiting this place. In interviews with hundreds of people who lived and worked in Dadaab, I helped to develop research and report on gender based violence (under the aegis of the Women's Refugee Commission, an organization affiliated with the International Rescue Committee, one of the nongovernmental humanitarian service providers in the camps). Many people I interviewed discussed matters related to the architectural and environmental studies at the core of my scholarship.

This massive complex of settlements at Dadaab has been for much of its existence the largest ever refugee-hosting site administered by the United Nations High Commissioner for Refugees (UNHCR), the designated international agency responsible for the protection of refugees. The UNHCR is mandated to provide protection to people fleeing across a border due to political persecution. It administers many sites in Africa, where refugees are also protected by the legal terms established by the Organization of African Unity (OAU). This international body extended the foundation of the UNHCR legal instruments by providing for people who were fleeing a host of other insecurities and instabilities in the milieux of regime change and superpower interference in the 1960s.

At Dadaab, the UNHCR and the Kenyan government established relief operations in a region that has been both an artifact of a past colonial frontier and a postcolonial theater of war between the Kenyan government and a pastoralist minority. It thus carries with it a memory of architectures of detention and an imaginary of territorial instability. These invisible and violent intimacies are heightened by Dadaab's location in the bush: semi-arid hyena country where marabou storks loom against plains peppered with low-growth scrub.

The first humanitarian settlement was established at Dadaab in 1991. It hosts approximately a quarter of a million registered refugees in multiple settlements, with unregistered migrants bringing the total to nearly half a million, the third largest population grouping in Kenya after Nairobi and Mombasa. It only began to appear on common maps with the advent of Google Earth in 2005. The scale of this camp complex resulted from a Kenyan government policy to contain refugees and curtail their mobility. People who sought refuge in Dadaab have remained entirely dependent upon aid, and the trade in humanitarian food and nonfood items has become integral to the local economy. Yet, the bustling markets in Dadaab suggest more. The site has accommodated a diverse international humanitarian labor force and facilitated considerable financial flows, with investment in refugee-related operations reaching $100 million and overall trade volume at $25 million USD in 2010; between 1989 and 2010, the surrounding host population had grown tenfold.

The refugee camps around the town of Dadaab form a space that has been bounded, yet accessible to outsiders, which has occasioned frequent study by academic and policy researchers in a range of disciplines, compared to other UNHCR sites. Three generations of people have been born in the camps, all subject to legal restrictions on education, work, mobility, and migration. Intended as a legal and political point of transit, the camp complex has entrenched itself in various ways, suspending refugees in a prolonged liminal state, and creating a sociopolitical and built form that might persist even if the UNHCR removed itself or the Kenyan government decommissioned the camps.

Such a possibility has not been unimaginable. Very recently as of this writing, in 2024, in cooperation with international bodies such as the World Bank and International

Monetary Fund (IMF), the refugee settlements at Dadaab moved toward incorporation as a municipality within Kenya, a transition in process as of this writing. Earlier, in May 2016, the government of Kenya announced the intent to decommission the settlements before the end of the year, citing security threats and a lack of international support, and dismantling the Department of Refugee Affairs: a closure that was stayed by a ruling of Kenya's High Court in February 2017. Such a political move, confronting the asymmetries of international support for countries stemming a sudden mass migration that many narrated as throwing the borders of Europe into "crisis," also produced leverage within the voting constituencies in Kenya. At such politically charged moments, Dadaab's durable ephemerality has come into sharp relief: demonstrating that its political ephemerality has also been architectural.

The paradox of permanent impermanence under which the Dadaab settlements have endured for over three decades must be understood through an architecture of lightweight, additive elements, built of found, recycled, and remnant material. This architecture signals transience even as it anchors hard infrastructures in the earth and sky. Dadaab has indeed produced a heavy infrastructural footprint, in contrast to the lighter touch of most UNHCR camps. The central compound, where humanitarian organization and international agency staff members reside and from which they distribute food and water, administer medical aid and social service operations, is composed of buildings and structures designed for durability: an architecture of masonry rather than textiles. The presence of common technologies and those specific to humanitarian activity have enabled long-range transportation and wireless communications outside regular mapped networks, which support aid operations in this undeveloped region. Its body of artifacts include telecom masts planted in the desert, ground vehicles adapted as mobile antennae, and satellite hardware connecting field offices with headquarters in capitals worldwide. The prolonged existence of the settlements, regularly framed only in terms of protracted political crisis, results from the continuous yield of the freshwater Merti aquifer, a relic of a Jurassic-era rift. Borewells penetrating the sedimentary layers to consume the aquifer have breached its envelope through saltwater layers surrounding it, which introduced salinity into the groundwater over time. However, even as the intensity of inhabitation above compromised the aquifer, they did not put it at risk of depletion. In spite of permanent structures from the surface of the land to beyond the earth's atmospheric borders, the prolonged humanitarian intervention has instantiated a persisting and changing body of architectural ephemera, including mobile dwellings and repurposed materials and goods that have imprinted into the landscape the economic and technological flows of the international agencies and local traders. In spite of empirical signs of impermanence, concrete infrastructure has engaged with the surrounding ecosystem: figured as much by the visual frailty of dwellings clad in recovered textile fragments as by an array of satellites, aeronautic and all-terrain vehicular fleets, aluminum and polyvinyl chloride water storage towers, hydraulic extraction machinery, and the large settlements themselves. This materiality and aesthetics is cloaked in an architecture that appears as little more than shanties and huts in the bush.

To speak of Dadaab is to speak of several paradoxes. It performs ephemerality in many registers. Due to its political and social complexity, scale, and yet prolonged impermanence, it approaches yet resists common characterizations of the urban. Its relationship to the tenuous architectures that signify a camp is equally ambivalent. Its incipient urbanity grows unexpectedly out of emergency and unsettlement. The shocking ephemerality of this massive complex of settlements is regularly framed in the most pejorative of terms, which undermine the lives of people—mostly women and unaccompanied minors—who have run for their lives, in the words of the poet Warsan Shire, "when home is the mouth of a shark."[3] What is almost never narrated is that the instability and crisis behind this running, if not from 1991, then at least from 1992, stems almost purely from climate-based insecurity around essentials: food, water, shelter. If the industrialized and globalized "North" has imposed this insecurity so that states have so concretely failed these refugees, how can we imagine restitution? What forms of restitution can attend to this arresting ephemerality?

The Intimacies of Restitution

To resolve this question of restitution and come to the heritage practices—the exercises in drawing Dadaab that form the critical archive at the center of this article—let us turn to a text by Edward Said. It is a special privilege to think about Said's work, which remains pressing, over forty-five years since *Orientalism* was published and over twenty since his own passing. The text, titled "Identity, Authority, and Freedom," is from a talk he delivered in Cape Town just prior to Nelson Mandela's election in 1994 (in the years immediately following the establishment of refugee camps at Dadaab).[4] The moment and the place were perhaps impregnated with thought on restitution. The talk takes the reader on a contradictory path toward academic freedom. Said first thinks through the North American university's will to remain apart, to self-isolate in order to avoid collusion with political forces. He walks the reader through the reactionary counterproposal of some to not only admit worldly concerns into the academy but particularly to seek relevance for it. He contrasts these vicissitudes with those in the Arab world, in which the calls to decolonize and Arabize the curriculum, he noted, fell to nationalistic forms, not of freedom but of fear: "not the advancement of knowledge but self-preservation." In this reflection, he recognizes that "every society has its Other."[5] However, he lays out the foundation that the academic precinct is ultimately intellectual. Academic freedom, he says, is the freedom to be critical. Of the irony of being a Palestinian invited as an American to speak to South Africans at a South African university, he writes that, when "well over two-thirds of the population in Occupied Palestine is made up of people under the age of 18, the sheer massive brutality of denying them school and college or university by systematic edict is extraordinary."[6] This leads him to a different question, namely, "what kind of identity do we then allow to lead us, to guide our study, to dictate our educational processes?"[7] His essay concludes on two figures. The first is of the king, the "potentate," for whom academic freedom rests upon authority and power, mastery and detachment. The second is the traveler, who need not defend the frontiers of the university, but who "*crosses over,* traverses territory, and abandons fixed positions, all the time."[8] Which identity does Said choose?

To imagine the field for such a decision, it helps me to think concretely about what restitution looks and feels like. When entering a state of restitution, what is the first book to be read? What is the first song to be heard? What would a restituted terrain be? I believe, with Said, it would not be the domain of the potentate, but of the traveler, one who may migrate with the greatest intellectual freedom, free of the need for either self-protection or self-adulation, free of dogma, open to play and to joy. "To do this with dedication and love as well as a realistic sense of the terrain," Said writes, "is, I believe, a kind of academic freedom at its highest."[9] To follow Said into academic freedom and to think concretely on restitution, I argue that this question of identity, authority, and freedom in the university is mirrored in refugee worlds. The problem of restitution lives specifically in the question of humanitarian promise, and the restored world it is to represent. The conundrum is that the refugee camp forecloses this promise. In writing *Architecture of Migration,* I became interested in stepping outside humanitarian forms of restitution and thinking with new languages, new ways of speaking about a camp.

Reinscribing the Dadaab Refugee Camps

My arguments in *Architecture of Migration* center on a land politics, asking what we learn from close looking at a refugee camp.[10] I find in the refugee camp an embodiment of partitions, a history of sedentarization of pastoralists and migrants, the construction of domesticities in emergency, and the creation of infrastructures through design. Perhaps most surprising, I find that the refugee camp *holds an archive.* My research counters the argument that architectural history must be predicated on fixity—whether of buildings or of landed archives—and instead argues that it opens onto the messier and more elusive problem of heritage.

Following these findings, I initiated an experiment. First, I struggled with whether the book's arguments could inhabit a land politics beyond the word on the page; I thought, if my arguments held true, they might be tested through artistic experiments. Second, I aimed to create new forms of academic freedom with people working out of a sense of solidarity: not with any investment in the humanitarian promise, nor in the security state that executes it in Dadaab.[11] I worked with concerned people who labored to draw Dadaab in its myriad forms, and thereby to renarrate and reinscribe it. Through their experimentation and commitment, the project resolved in crafting material intimacies with the past and the future.

I worked with artists and architects who conceived works that used Dadaab and humanitarian settlement as referents to test the arguments proposed in the book. This creative experiment in knowledge production demonstrates ways that Dadaab, as an object lesson and basis for intellectual history, offers a springboard for theory. These concerned artists developed new languages, counter-maps, critical heritage practices, and a critical archive.[12] Their work supplanted the authority of the UNHCR map. I thank all of these artists. Their work will be shared at the exhibition "Dadaab Commons" at the GoDown Arts Centre in Nairobi in 2025.

I was inspired to undertake this iterative process on learning of the work of artist Deqa Abshir, who applied her graduate study in art and social work to a practice of trauma therapy for former residents of Dadaab living in the Eastleigh neighborhood of Nairobi—"the Nairobi home of Somalis even before it had been named Eastleigh," as anthropologist Neil Carrier writes of "Little Mogadishu."[13] Abshir's double-canvas painting *Fragmented II* centers a heritage of migration through the tuqul, an object that has transformed from a symbol of tradition to one of refugee life. She splits the painting into two "fragments," which purposely misalign the image, offsetting the geometric lines and planes just as the canvas edges are arranged in alignment. The aligned canvases produce a series of shifted, broken lines and planes, disrupting the compositional narrative across the break between canvases. This small move sows just enough visual discord. Her fragmented rendering of the domed tuqul dwelling translates her perspective of home-making in the bush, built over years of being raised in Nairobi in a refugee family in diaspora, positioned as a foreigner when returning to Somalia. In the lower painting, she excerpts and reinterprets text from the poem "Gold" by her sister Idil Abshir, writing by hand on the canvas:

> cultures like liquid gold
> stories that were never
> told, this is our africa
> our children will be born
> with golden glitter on
> their faces never knowing why

Deqa Abshir's work reckons with visits to her relatives in Somalia and the alienation from her grandmothers' building traditions as they were imposed upon her. "Will we conserve, restore and rebuild traditions honouring forgotten principles," she asks, "or will we keep creating a new city and culture, pressing our foundations ever further into the earth?"[14] Through its lenses on gender and memory, her painting demonstrates how architecture performs critical heritage work, keeping custody of histories and laying foundations for futures.

That theorization sparked my foray into the construction of a critical archive, as I began to explore a creative process with other artists. I turned next to AbdulFatah Adam, a rare East African: a University of Nairobi–trained architect who practices professionally in Nairobi and Mogadishu, a Kenyan citizen from Somali, Boran, and other communities in Kibera (a Nairobi neighborhood often described as the largest "informal" settlement in the world), and a descendant of dissenters in Kenya's Northeast whose history lies behind Dadaab's segregation from the rest of the country. Through a counter-mapping exercise comprising four works, he draws Dadaab from his situated and embodied perspective. The works, titled "Origins," "Partitions," "Borders," and "Migrations," tell a serial story through the rich materialities of mixed media. Each appropriates techniques of abstraction in drawing and mapping to tell new grounded stories about places made universal and fungible on colonial maps. "Origins" is a watercolor rendering on heavy paper of the contemporary African and Middle Eastern states that represent a wider region of relationships for many people in the Dadaab refugee camps. The subtle watery gradation in color saturation, which distinguishes one place concretely from another, is overwritten by his overlay of abstract Cartesian coordinates locating Dadaab. Adam writes: *Origins. Some historians claim Somalis are descendants of the Pharaohs. Geologists have also claimed the oil deposits in Somalia are greater than any other country in the region, even the Arabian Peninsula. The existence of Dadaab could be attributed to this gift, or curse.* "Partitions" gestures to Soomaliweyn, the area of Greater Somalia that was partitioned by European colonial powers. He writes: *Partitions. Colonialist and neo-Colonialist policies have divided the Somali nation over the years affecting their integration and identity. The business acumen of Somalis is however putting these divisions to test with their emergence as an economic force.* "Borders" speaks of the distance and roughness of fleeing from one border town to another, Dhobey in Somalia to Liboi in Kenya. This traversal is made across terrain modeled in crumpled paper and conceptualized as a steep climb in the work's vertical orientation, representing the path of a person's flight to the east. He writes: *Borders. Border towns are typically developed and integrated urban areas, with local people's mobility unaffected by administrations on either side. Kenya's borders with Somalia demonstrate intentional separations of otherwise connected communities across the administrative lines.* "Migrations" punctuates the series, using the Morpholio Trace computer program over a Google Earth map of Ifo camp, overwriting a surveillance image with his own. The drawing suggests the primacy of the livestock grazing trails made by the hands and feet of people and animals over the foreign vehicular routes. Together, these paths suggest the multiple infrastructures scaffolding the camp, some "hard," some "soft." He writes: *Migrations. The networks for migration and circulation highlight the contrast between natural and man-made processes. Footpaths leading into the centre of Dadaab are organic like the homesteads and tuquls, weaving around trees and landscapes. The planning of Dadaab is artificial like the roads designed for vehicle access, making false boundaries and territories. Somalis' migration patterns are as contingent as their circulation paths, leading them to settle all over the world and in most unexpected places.* Adam's body of small sculptural works quietly describe ways of seeing Dadaab from outside the humanitarian perspective, from the ground of Somalia.

Just as these works offer local emplaced histories, they open onto planetary ecological intimacies, setting the Dadaab refugee camps into wider ecosystems. Architect Elsa MH Mäki (Anishinaabe and Finnish), a founder of the Indigenous Design Collective and the only artist in this group based outside of Africa, directly confronts the act of gazing upon refugee camps from afar by provincializing the surveillance technology of the particular satellite, the Landsat-7, which captures visual data on East Africa. Her intervention positions the Dadaab refugee camps within a global Indigenous politics of resistance. The spare line and color patterns in her digital drawing examine a satellite's survey and process of image production, while her text comments on the conditions of artistry and authorship. Mäki developed her image using information from UNHCR maps and Google Earth's satellite imagery of Hagadera from approximately 2003 to 2021. While she investigates Dadaab's relation to the sky, Nairobi architecture studio Cave Bureau, led by principals Kabage Karanja and Stella Mutegi, examines Dadaab's relation to the earth, studying the infrastructure of the Dadaab settlements in relation to the Merti Aquifer, a remnant of the Jurassic era. Through diagrams of settlements, hardware, and stone, readings of geohydrology reports, and imaginaries of borewells, the architects narrate the camps' connection to the prehistoric interlocking underground cave system. Their text explains the impact of borewell drilling on the aquifer, and, conversely, the occasion of its eruption above ground, the water tap stand in the camps. The drawings that Elsa MH Mäki and Cave Bureau created as part of this exercise offer ways to critically restore the Dadaab refugee camps from emergency subjecthood to a different ecological belonging.

To acknowledge those larger forms of ecological, social, and political belonging, I return to my argument that Dadaab uniquely teaches us about restitution. Global architectural and planning practices carried out in response to contemporary humanitarian crises were systematized in Dadaab in the 1990s. Yet, Dadaab's ways of knowing and building are uniquely African. They tie into generations of migratory building and craft practices, including ancient connections with the landscape and ecology, particularly that of a Jurassic-era aquifer; the spatial politics and historical particularities of a region connected to Swahili coast and Indian Ocean relations and ways of life; song and oral traditions of knowledge sharing; and socialities around land that supersede proprietary approaches. Understanding Dadaab—through the critical archive of art and architecture presented here and the framework it establishes for reinscription as a practice of knowledge formation—allows us to move beyond reductive interpretations of refugee camps into cohabitations undertaken by people living through extraordinary conditions. These "drawings" refuse representations of exigency, impoverishment, and vagrancy in camps, and give us instead a way to theorize the processes, material practices, and long colonial traditions of humanitarian settlement, foregrounding uniquely African environments that conserve intellectual and political resources as a critical heritage practice. This approach to the Dadaab refugee camps enables us together to experience and build an intellectual and political commons, our own intimate act of collective restitution.

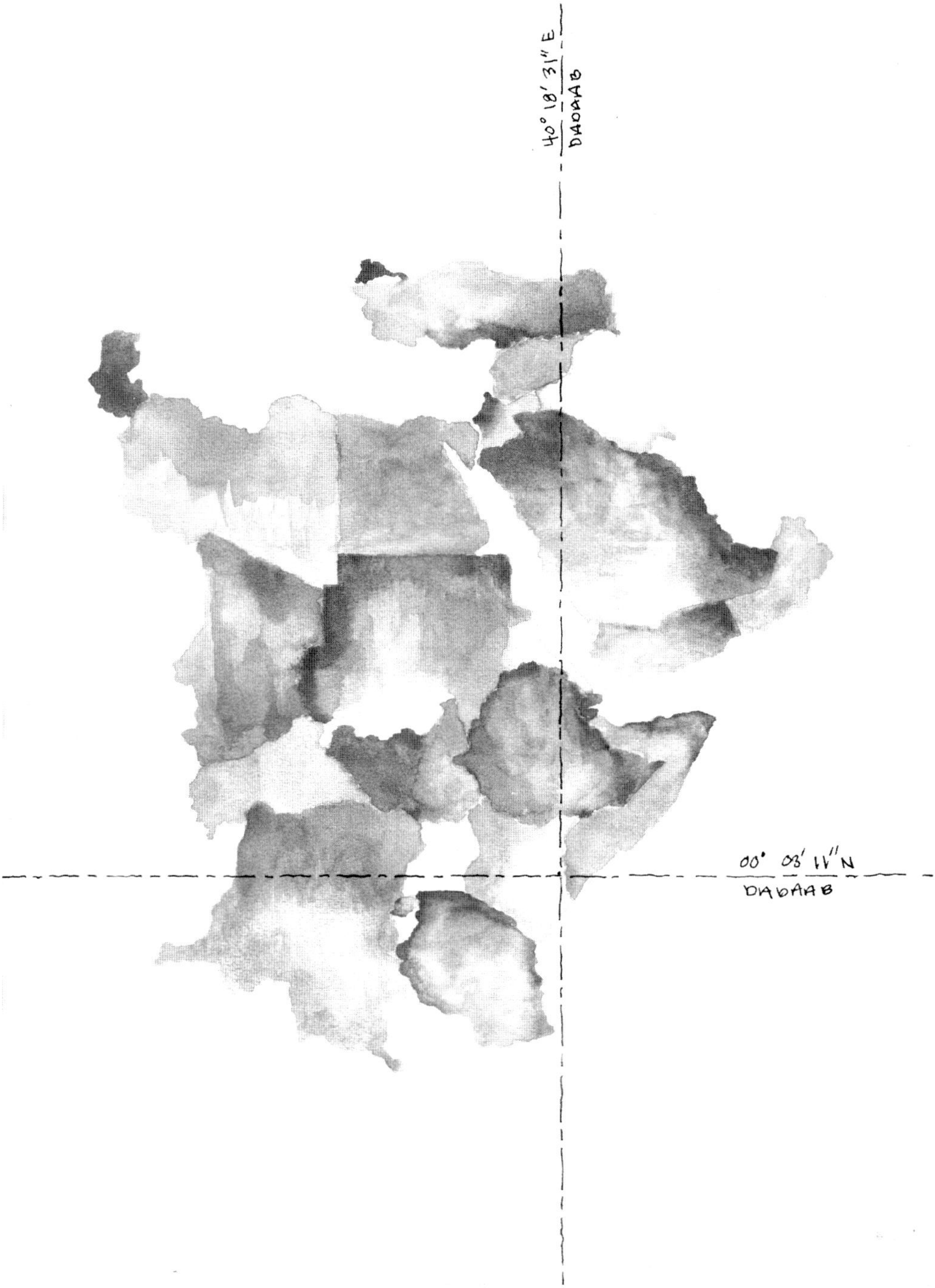

Figure 2. AbdulFatah Adam, *Origins*.

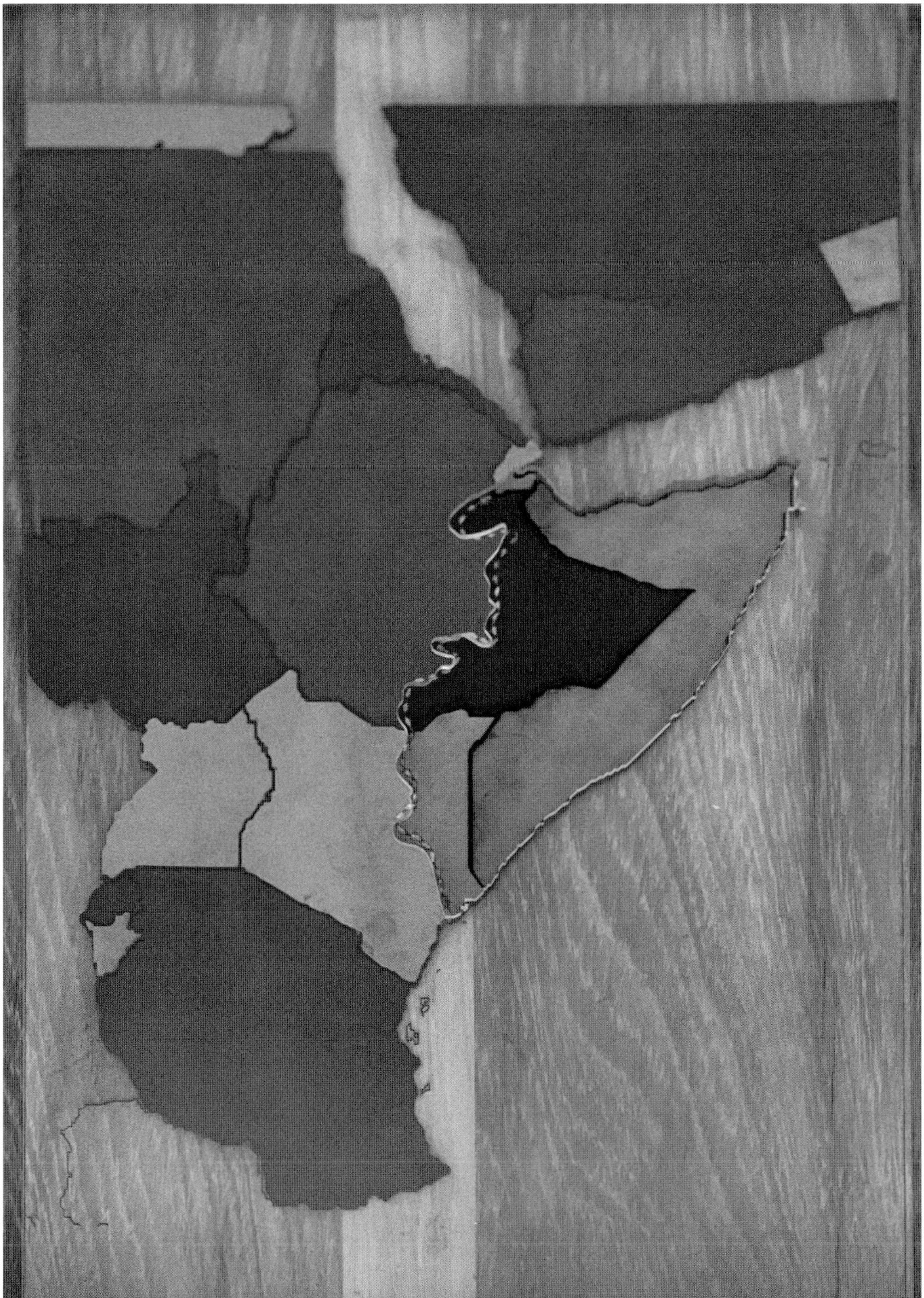

Figure 3. AbdulFatah Adam, *Partitions*.

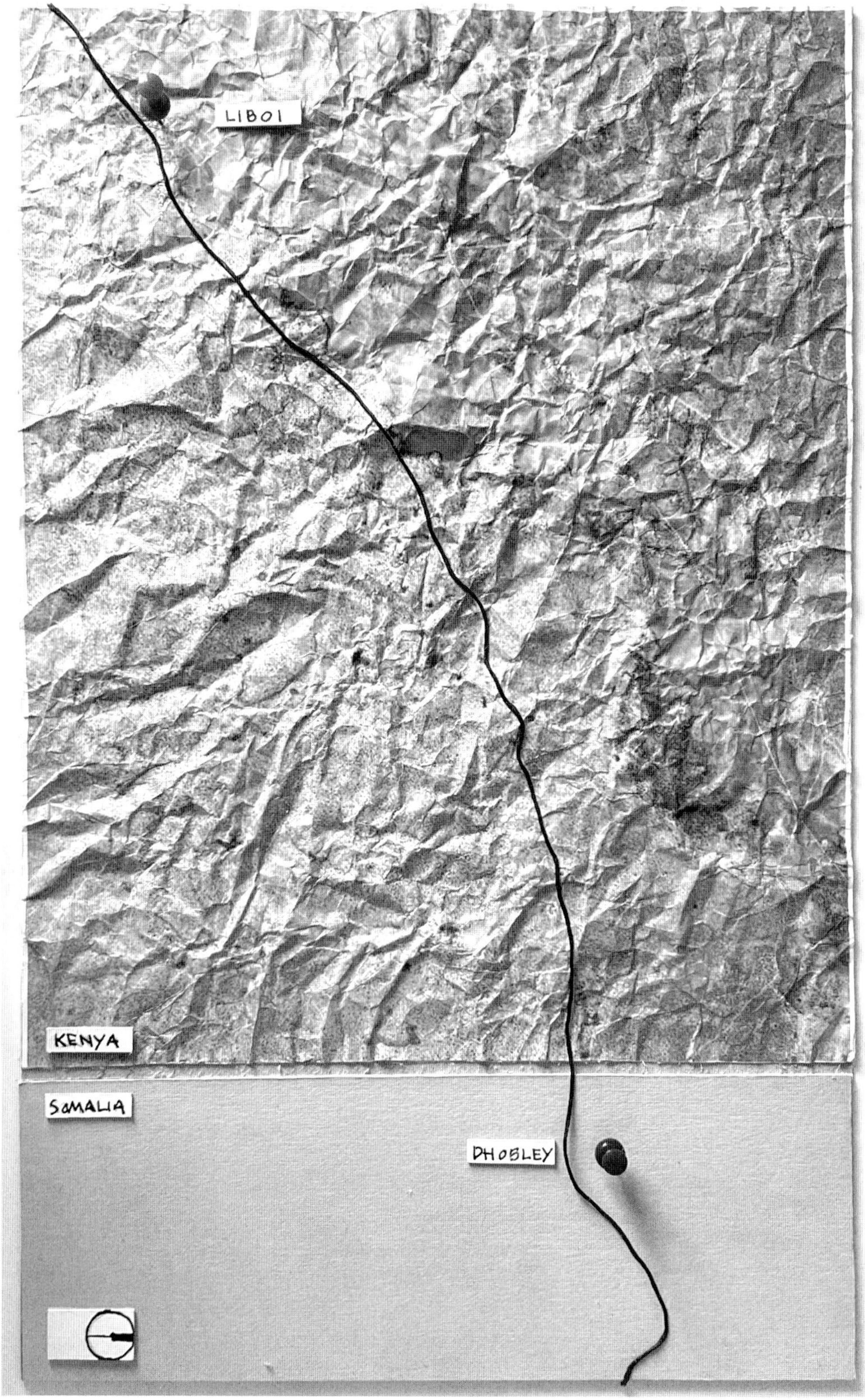

Figure 4. AbdulFatah Adam, *Borders*.

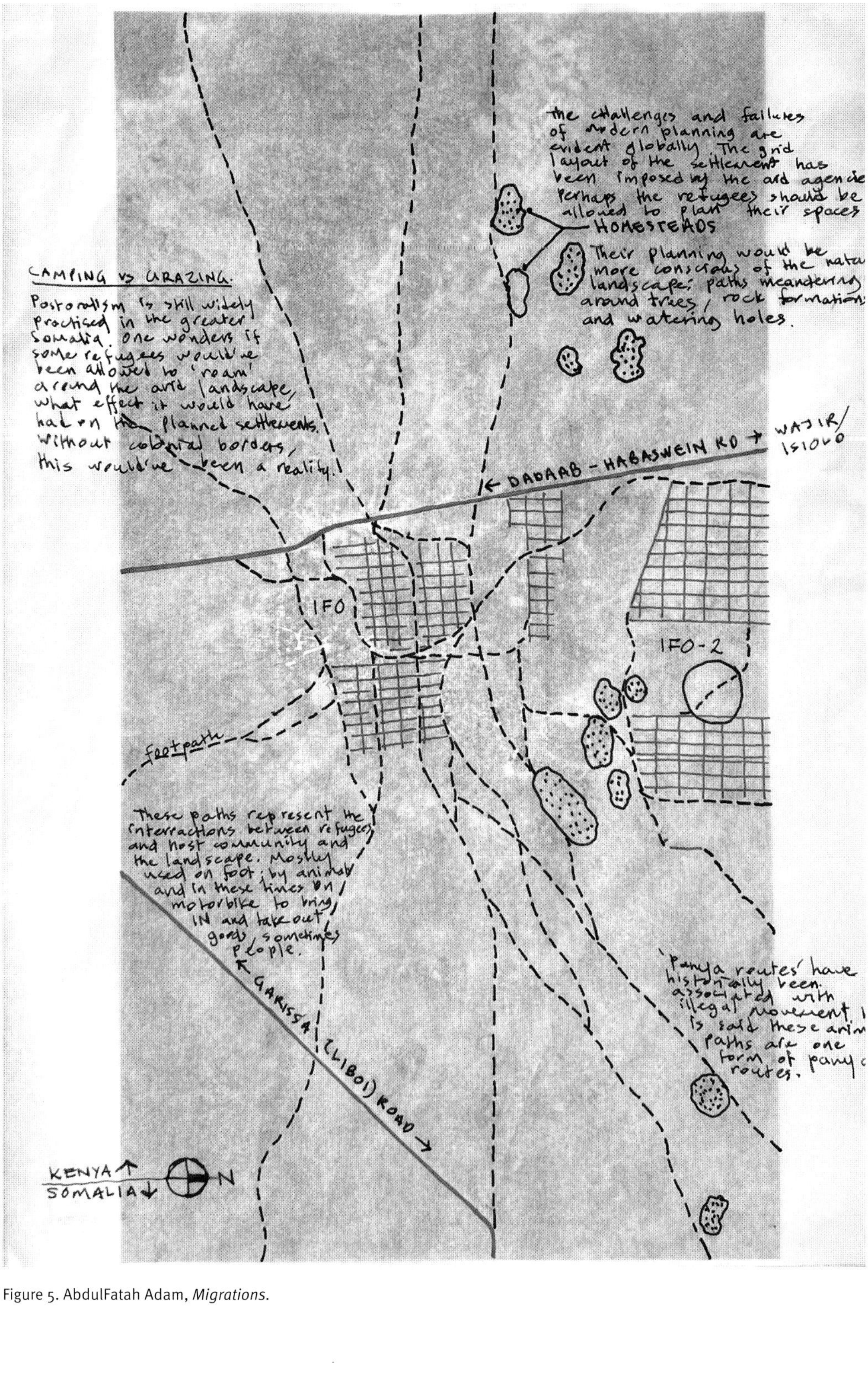

Figure 5. AbdulFatah Adam, *Migrations*.

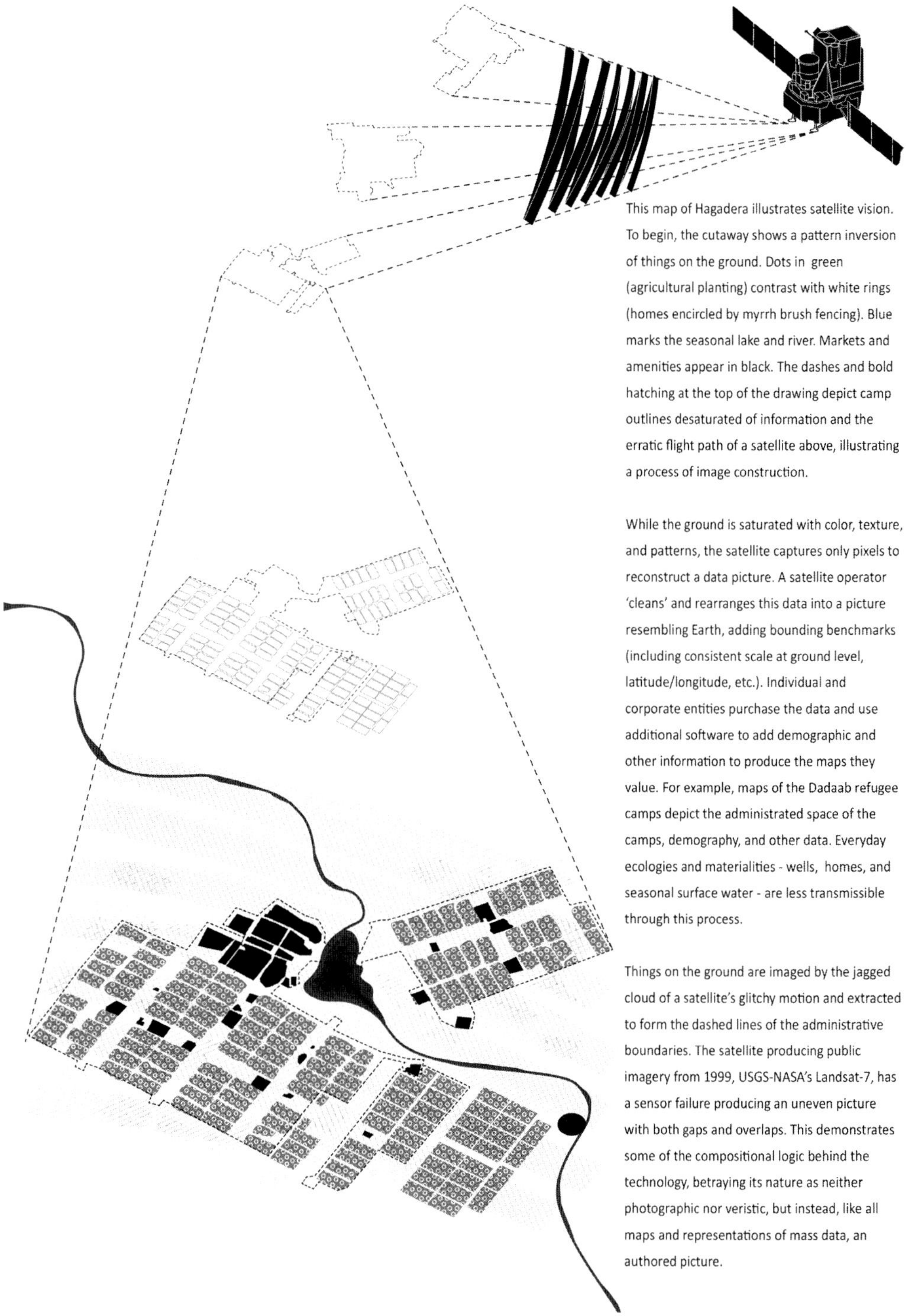

This map of Hagadera illustrates satellite vision. To begin, the cutaway shows a pattern inversion of things on the ground. Dots in green (agricultural planting) contrast with white rings (homes encircled by myrrh brush fencing). Blue marks the seasonal lake and river. Markets and amenities appear in black. The dashes and bold hatching at the top of the drawing depict camp outlines desaturated of information and the erratic flight path of a satellite above, illustrating a process of image construction.

While the ground is saturated with color, texture, and patterns, the satellite captures only pixels to reconstruct a data picture. A satellite operator 'cleans' and rearranges this data into a picture resembling Earth, adding bounding benchmarks (including consistent scale at ground level, latitude/longitude, etc.). Individual and corporate entities purchase the data and use additional software to add demographic and other information to produce the maps they value. For example, maps of the Dadaab refugee camps depict the administrated space of the camps, demography, and other data. Everyday ecologies and materialities - wells, homes, and seasonal surface water - are less transmissible through this process.

Things on the ground are imaged by the jagged cloud of a satellite's glitchy motion and extracted to form the dashed lines of the administrative boundaries. The satellite producing public imagery from 1999, USGS-NASA's Landsat-7, has a sensor failure producing an uneven picture with both gaps and overlaps. This demonstrates some of the compositional logic behind the technology, betraying its nature as neither photographic nor veristic, but instead, like all maps and representations of mass data, an authored picture.

Figure 6. Elsa MH Mäki, *Satellite Study*.

Figure 7. Cave Bureau, *Camp Context Study*.

Biography

Anooradha Iyer Siddiqi is an architectural historian at Barnard College, Columbia University, and author of *Architecture of Migration: The Dadaab Refugee Camps and Humanitarian Settlement* (Duke University Press, 2024), on the spatial politics, visual rhetoric, ecologies, and long colonial traditions of the UNHCR-administered camps at Dadaab, Kenya. Siddiqi is the coeditor of *Feminist Architectural Histories of Migration* and *Spatial Violence.* Her book manuscript "Ecologies of the Past: The Inhabitations and Designs of Anil and Minnette de Silva" analyzes the politics of heritage environments through the work of Sri Lankan architect Minnette de Silva and art historian Anil de Silva-Vigier.

Notes

[1] The scholarship represented in this book is dedicated to the communities and elders in Dadaab, whose lives and work hold meaning for us all. It is indebted to the generous frameworks of the Lenape communities, whose unceded land has enabled my institutional position. Ideas in this article build on those in Anooradha Iyer Siddiqi, *Architecture of Migration: The Dadaab Refugee Camps and Humanitarian Settlement* (Durham: Duke University Press, 2024); Anooradha Iyer Siddiqi, "Drawing the Dadaab Refugee Camps: A Critical Archive," talk in the Columbia University Graduate School for Architecture, Planning, and Preservation Historic Preservation Lecture Series (2023); Anooradha Iyer Siddiqi, "A Restitution of Academic Freedom / Dadaab Commons," paper in the Cornell University Institute for Comparative Modernisms symposium, Reparations for Colonization Carbonization, organized by Esra Akcan (2023); Anooradha Iyer Siddiqi, "Heritage as Restitution," *Curator: The Museum Journal* 65, no. 3 (July 2022): 673–77; Anooradha Iyer Siddiqi, "Ephemerality," *Comparative Studies of South Asia, Africa, and the Middle East* 40, no. 1 (2020): 24–34.

[2] W. E. B. Du Bois, *The Souls of Black Folk* (Oxford: Oxford University Press, 2008).

[3] Warsan Shire, "Home," in *Bless the Daughter Raised by a Voice in Her Head* (New York: Random House, 2022), 24.

[4] Edward Said, "Identity, Authority, Freedom: The Potentate and the Traveler," *boundary* 2 vol. 21 no. 3 (Autumn 1994): 1–18.

[5] Said, "Identity, Authority, Freedom," 7,

[6] Said, "Identity, Authority, Freedom," 10.

[7] Said, "Identity, Authority, Freedom," 12.

[8] Said, "Identity, Authority, Freedom," 13.

[9] Said, "Identity, Authority, Freedom," 17.

[10] See discussion in Siddiqi, *Architecture of Migration,* esp. chap. 2, "Land, Emergency, and Sedentarization in East Africa," 97–138.

[11] Most people who engage with Dadaab from outside, even artists, enter the camps through agencies and nongovernmental organizations involved in the management of populations or control over the free migration of others.

[12] Please note recent studies by scholars (sometimes themselves refugees) using architectural methods in displacement contexts in order to recast drawing or mapping as a collaborative technique for knowledge building and healing. Ayham Dalal, *From Shelters to Dwellings: The Zaatari Refugee Camp* (Bielefeld: Transcript Verlag, 2022); Julien Lafontaine Carboni, "(From) the Repertoire: An Architectural Theory of Operations: Oral and Embodied Knowledge in Architectural and Spatial Practices" (PhD diss., École Polytechnique Fédérale de Lausanne, 2022).

[13] Neil Carrier, *Little Mogadishu: Eastleigh, Nairobi's Global Somali Hub* (London: Hurst, 2017), 27.

[14] Deqa Abshir, "Foundation," http://deqaart.com/?portfolio=foundation (accessed February 8, 2022).

Space and Heritage Roundtable Transcript

November 22, 2022, The Richard Eden Suite, Clare Hall, University of Cambridge

[Editor's Note: The roundtable was structured in three parts: two separate panel discussions, a general discussion, and Q&A session. Each panel, as transcribed here, includes short presentations by each of the panelists, brief comments from respondents, and an open discussion among panelists.]

TAO DUFOUR: Welcome to this roundtable discussion on the theme of "Space and Heritage," and thank you to all for joining us—here in person and those with us online. I would like to open the roundtable with a few acknowledgments, followed by summary comments on the context for the event and the theme.

This event has been organized through the kind assistance and support of its hosts, Clare Hall and the Department of Architecture at Cambridge University. I would like to thank the President of Clare Hall, Professor Alan Short, and the College Registrar, Tam Marshall-Watts, for their support, as well as Professor James Campbell, the Head of the Department of Architecture. My time here as a Visiting Fellow at Clare Hall has been made possible through research leave afforded by the College of Architecture, Art and Planning at Cornell University, for which I thank Dean Meejin Yoon. My research assistant, Gracie Meek, worked on the graphics and publicity for this event; thank you, Gracie.

This roundtable is organized as a contribution to the special issue of the journal *Future Anterior*, which I am guest editing on the kind invitation of Professor Jorge Otero-Pailos, with the assistance of an editorial team led by Christina Sun, to whom I extend a special note of thanks for her careful and thoughtful work on the issue. The title of the special issue is "Space and Heritage: On the Generativity of Environing Worlds." The theme for the issue takes its cue from a basic observation and description of perceptual experience by the philosopher Edmund Husserl, which is that in the flowing temporal life of the embodied subject, she acquires, accrues, and sediments certain practices, sensibilities, styles of thought, and, in sum, ways of being that *inhere* as embodied habitus. The issue aims to draw attention to the spatial quality of these embodied acquisitions as a kind of "heritage." Taking as its point of departure this phenomenological sense of heritage as the embodied becoming of the subject, the theme of the issue dilates, recognizing that the subject exists always already in

Future Anterior
Volume XIX, Number 2
Winter 2022

relations with others, whether these others are present "in the flesh"; in some way experienced or understood as having been present during or before one's lifetime; or as those yet to be encountered. In this expanded way, the concept of heritage is approached as intersubjective and implicating relations across generations. The aspect of the *spatial* conditions of this intersubjective and intergenerational relationality is what is indicated by the theme's subtitle: "On the Generativity of Environing Worlds." The phrase speaks to the problem of the lived experience of one's surroundings as an inheritance, encountered directly in their material presence, or in mediated ways and historically through narrative, and visual and aural images; or what is perhaps actually the case, in inextricably intertwined ways that affectively implicate the perceptual, memorial, imaginative, the wide spectrum of the representational, emotions, moods, and so forth. In light of the breadth of the theme, the roundtable has been organized to bring different disciplinary perspectives into conversation. It is a pleasure and honor to have the interest and participation of my colleagues, to whom I am deeply thankful for their generosity, time, and thought.

Panel 1

ANDREAS PANTAZATOS: In this short presentation, my aim is to shed light on the relationship between heritage and the idea of environing world.[1] I present three points, which I would like to see more as three provocations to kick off our discussion. The first point seeks to understand the meeting point between heritage and environing world. The second point invites us to reflect upon the ethical question that heritage raises in conversation with environing world. The third point reminds us of the epistemic aspect of the relationship between heritage and environing world.

Contemporary approaches to heritage defend the idea that heritage is a process and therefore it is not static and cannot be locked in its material fabric.[2] Heritage as process involves an understanding about heritage according to which heritage is always in flux, and it is a constant process of negotiation. We negotiate what and how we select/choose what we inherit from the past. Then, we negotiate what and how we interpret what we selected/chose to inherit from the past, and we negotiate what we transit from this process to the future.[3] Therefore, heritage is constantly in *becoming* or is constantly in transition as I have argued elsewhere.[4] This idea invites two further interrelated thoughts. One is that the negotiation does not take place in a vacuum, but it takes place in our lived world including our own experiences and the experiences of others. The other thought involves the web of relationships that we develop with our world and with others. The web of these relationships with the world and others are the background, the environing world,

Figure 1. UK Parliament, the Palace of Westminster. Photo: Andreas Pantazatos.

where heritage negotiation takes place. A good example here is the World Heritage site of the British Parliament, the Palace of Westminster in London. The UK Parliament is a significant space because it is considered the founder of modern Western democracy. This is one aspect of the background of the UK Parliament that helps us know how to negotiate the different web of relationships that the Parliament heritage site reveals. For instance, political decisions that were voted in the UK Parliament had a significant impact on the lives of people who lived in colonized states beyond London. The lives of these people and their future are entangled with the UK Parliament and are part of the environing world of the Parliament heritage site.

Heritage as constant *becoming* takes place in the environing world and shapes the continuity of our environing world by revealing a web of relationships. This web includes the relationships we form with things that we find in our world and our responses to them, and the relationships we develop with others with or without the things of our world. If we accept that heritage reveals this web of relationships, an ethical question invites itself.[5] How should we live our lives as part of the web of relationships that heritage reveals via its constant mode of negotiation? To respond to this question, we can appeal to Nozick's scheme about ethical pull and ethical push.[6] We are pulled by what we owe to other negotiators of heritage and their understanding of their own relationship with the world. At the same time, we are pushed by our own motivations as negotiators of heritage and our own understanding of the world and its environs. Recall again the example of the British Parliament. Our response to how we should treat the Parliament heritage site entails an answer to the question how should we live our lives acknowledging the variety of stakeholders who have a stake in the site beyond London, and the role of their voices in our understanding of what does the Parliament stand for?

An answer to the previous question turns our attention to the epistemic aspect of heritage.[7] Heritage as constant *becoming* is shaped by the environing world within which it takes place. At the same time, it shapes the environing world as the process of heritage negotiation develops new layers of understanding of heritage, and new layers of our understanding about the interaction between heritage and the environing world. Hence, heritage contributes to the creation of knowledge about our relationships with the environing world and our relationships with others that shapes our future. If this is the case, there are three questions that invite themselves. Who are the participants that contribute to heritage negotiation for the creation of this new knowledge? Is every participant equally trusted to get involved in providing testimony that informs and enriches the heritage negotiation? Is there space for every participant to play a role in how new understandings of heritage are transited into the future?[8] Let's recall again the heritage site of the UK Parliament. Participants' contributions to the negotiation of the Parliament's heritage are central to the environing world of that heritage. It is this environing world that informs the interpretation of the heritage site of the UK Parliament and shapes the future of the heritage site.

ANTHONY STEINBOCK: Phenomenology is a special kind of reflection that does not want to take things for granted, but strives to examine the meaning of things as they are given in experience, as well as to describe their structures. What we call the natural attitude is that attitude that takes the world for granted in a *commonplace* way such that we become forgetful of the very emergence of meaning for us. This forgetfulness, which becomes like "second nature" to us, constitutes its "naiveté," and makes it philosophically susceptible to critique.

Radically shifting attitudes from straightforwardly accepting *what* something is to *how* this something is given, phenomenology clarifies this very "what" or being that was taken for granted. Enquiries into both aspects, the "how" and the "what," make up the process of phenomenological investigation: questions concerning meaning constitution (modes of givenness) and essential structures (being). For example, perceiving a world, we do not taste our tasting, see our seeing, or immediately think our thinking. We do not immediately (if at all) notice that the whole of the object is given through sides, that sides are given through aspects (smooth, soft, straight), that aspects are given through adumbrations (before, after, wooly red), that adumbrations are given through phases (present, retention, protention).[9] We don't see how sense orients us toward being or gives being an orientation such that this being makes a difference, or how meaning is that "aspect" under which being speaks to us, is comprehensible, and is grasped as such. We might take for granted a body/soul dualism without realizing the distinctive role that the lived-body plays, or again, assume a spirit/nature dualism without accounting for how the earth as ground gives meaning to the lived-body and how we orient ourselves spatially and temporally.

Important to recognize is that the phenomenological shift in perspective is carried out so as no longer to presuppose what being is, and instead to understand the *meaning* of being in which we already *participate* and to participate in being creatively. Such a postural shift allows the attitude of taking things for granted to come into view *as* the "natural" or "mundane" (or naïve) attitude. It is from such a phenomenological perspective that we can in fact identify our perceptual and intellectual relations with being *as a participation in being as* meaningful (or *as* not meaningful), *as* sense-filled (or *as* nonsensical).

In short, phenomenology acknowledges the naïve basis of reflection, but distances itself from this basis in order to gain it in a new way, critically. Phenomenological reflection steps back from this basis in order to bring it into relief in its fullness, to witness the initial strangeness of meaning in what has become for us so obvious, and thus to describe the process of meaning-formation in its opening unfamiliarity—a dynamic process that has long since been taken for granted within routine practicality. Further, the phenomenologist does not merely reflect "on" experience, but *within* experiencing itself as it is being lived-through. By reflecting on and within the sense-giving process itself, we grasp it in its living process so that we can glimpse how and what this process "means," "intends," or "accepts."[10]

If we take a quick glance ahead now to *generative* phenomenology, we can say that it is a philosophical method that is open to the sociocultural, historical, geological, and normative generation of meaning in our lives together. It treats the normative significance of territories and terrains, the earth as ground of bodily beings, the world as horizon of objects that emerge for us; it shows how traditional notions of normality and abnormality take on a richer, dynamic and subtle form of concordance of sense and even optimality, which means it is not reducible to statistical averages, to what is natural as opposed to what is artificial, or to what is ordinary. A generative phenomenology shows how norms arise within experience itself. And it describes the intersubjective relations of home worlds and alien worlds as they develop dynamically and intertwine over the generations, and how the meaning of home or our worlds are mutually dependent upon and co-originate with alien or other worlds.

That's one understanding, one significance of generativity, that I introduced earlier. But I also understand generativity in another sense, namely as the very movement from which emerges the relation of home and the alien world. And in this sense, generativity is not any thing, but instead, the dynamic movement, the infinite becoming or origination. So, there are two senses of generativity and two senses of generative phenomenology.

On the one hand, there's a generative phenomenology, in the lowercase, that covers all generative phenomena that I just mentioned. And then generative phenomenology, in a different sense, capital "G" Generative phenomenology that covers all the thematic dimensions that are interrelated and that are co-generated statically, genetically, and generatively. So in this sense, even the generative—the phenomenologist—even the attempt to cover generativity stands within the very movement of generativity itself as it attempts to grasp the generative movement in its unfolding.

So, the two senses are the one generative method that covers certain generative or historical phenomena, and generativity, the Generative phenomenology that covers the generativity itself. So, this gives rise to a particular question: In what sense generativity is historical; and the sense that it takes place in history, but it's not reducible to history or to particular historical moments?

So, as a clarification, generativity is both an essential structure, and yet its revelation is peculiar to a certain cultural and historical tradition. Most broadly, I would say the Abrahamic/Greek tradition. Generativity, as a kind of historical essence, as it were, is revealed in this broad tradition, and is the very process by which there are normatively significant structures that have a unique and irreducible orientation.

And in and through their difference, generativity makes an historical difference. But generativity becomes articulated normatively, socially, and geo-historically, in the very structure of the home and alien. It is that movement through which home and alien dynamically coexist and are co-relative. So, when we speak of the generative nexus of home/alien—the relation of the home and the alien—we are describing the movement of generativity and in this sense, the entire generative framework. But this means that generativity cannot be described from a putative, objective third-person perspective, but always from within the home. And, in this case, within generativity. I don't mean by this that there is a home world within a generative framework, but that generativity in this respect is itself home. So that the structure of generativity, as I've expressed it here, does not merely account for differences that would be alien to a particular home, but for the possibility of something radically alien, even to generativity itself.

So, to summarize, there are two senses of generativity, one that pertains to the relation of home and alien, and then the other deeper sense of generativity as home itself that accounts for something that does not even articulate its own self-understanding as home or alien, or as generativity.

OLA UDUKU: This is very much a meditation, which I thought I would offer to the symposium as a provocation as well. I'm looking at the more concrete, so to speak; and this is to do with the idea about narrative and heritage in trans-generational and trans-historical events, very much focused on the Oil Rivers in South East Nigeria. These are centrally located around the Niger Delta region, and have a long and historic relationship to local culture. This has been prior to, during and after the slave trade. These historical traces are evidenced by delta rivers and creeks retaining their Portuguese names such as Sombreiro, Escravos and Forcados. The coastal region of South Eastern Nigeria, into which the Niger River forms the delta that flows through creeks and lagoons to the Atlantic was central to much of the transatlantic slave shipping route; from the interior of South Eastern Nigeria to the coast and out to the New World.

Eerily also, at Nigeria's British colonization; from the 1820s and '30s onward these riverine water courses were also the routes by which the palm oil extracted from palm trees in the eastern Nigerian hinterland, was shipped to ports like Liverpool for processing into domestic products such as soap and detergents. They also happen to be in the same location where initial drilling for crude oil and its exploration took place in Nigeria. The issue around this is that these flows of extraction and international encounters, have formed the background to the formation of this rich coastal culture which, I would say, can only be considered as transitional and transgenerational in its relationship with various forms of exploitation and culture. Clearly, the longest engagement this region has had now is indeed its link to Shell and other oil exploration companies, which has gone on for more than half a century. This has both involved locals and the international agents involved in oil exploration who have now become enmeshed into this coastal culture, which has enriched some but also impoverished and created environmental disasters for others. This cosmopolitan coastal culture remains very much in existence, which is the feature I wish to highlight in this piece.

This traditional coastal culture in eastern Nigeria thus was very much influenced by encounters with other cultures. In fact, the material cultures of those from that area are very influenced by Victorian dressing for example the Bowler Hat is still a significant part of official male traditional dress in the Niger Delta region. But it also transcends the purely cultural and permeates the socioeconomic and historical livelihoods in terms of family structure, and education, so for example family units are often known as "houses" and the leaders are "chiefs" who still wield significant political power and presence in their continued control of many parts of the Niger Delta region. So, the devastation and plunder of the region is intertwined with family histories and cultures which are socioeconomic and political with these historic events over centuries. These rivers, literally of blood, prosperity and life have both enriched and impoverished the societies in which they exist. Furthermore the discourse around freedom, inheritance, and acquisition of wealth are all intertwined in ongoing narratives about what the rivers mean and how these relate to the important and prominent individuals of this area.

Probably most known to us culturally would be the fact that literary heros such as Ken Saro-Wiwa, are from this region as well. Saro-Wiwa was tragically hanged by the then military government for complaining about the rape and environmental destruction of the Niger Delta region and his and other coastal riverine communities by the oil companies. The delta region remains one of the most polluted parts of Nigeria today. But there are also narratives around the civil war, which happened in the 1960s, where we've got the work of people like Elechi Amadi, Chimamanda Ngozi Adichie. So, this space is contested in the sense that it in many ways, still is probably the most expensive piece of land or areas of land in Nigeria because it still continues to bear oil called Bonny Light, one of the best kinds of light crude oil, apparently, in the world.

But also it's tainted, and it has always been tainted with these encounters, be it with slavery or with forced labor, sometimes involved in extracting oil palm and more recently with the links to Shell, and so on. So, these narratives keep being recreated and reinvented by those who encounter this land, or this link to the land. So, whether they are of the land or encounter the land, this is part of the narrative that continues and culturally, therefore, it becomes a very transitional and contested space.

So, who owns the land? There are interesting interviews that have gone on to say that, indeed, when Shell/BP arrived in Lagos; in the Oil area in Oloibiri in South Eastern Nigeria, certain chiefs were given large amounts of money and they did quite well. Their sons—they were mainly sons—got into many management jobs and so on in the Shell industrial complex. Whereas other parts of the same community had their land literally taken from under their feet. But still, culturally, that link to another, I would say a metaphorical other, influences the way in which the delta region of Nigeria is still understood. Even the fact that etymologically the names of these rivers still remain Portuguese shows this continuous transition of cultural ideas and narratives. This also shows that this is in no way solely located in notions of the past or for that matter in the present, there's often the past as well that's being invoked.

As a final counter-provocation, further east of the delta region, and close to the southeastern city of Calabar is a location called Tinapa, which was planned to become an Export Processing Zone (EPZ) which would enable it attract foreign investment to become a film making location hosting local film studios and becoming a location for other film enterprises, indeed for, further imaginaries such as the Nollywood film industry. This location is somewhat further northeast, in all fairness, from the Oil Rivers delta region,—but the idea that you can imagine this space again as having yet further links to what I can only call extraordinary versions of fantasy and fiction. But then I believe that coastal regions such as the Oil Rivers are enmeshed in cultures that remain present and still very contested, and in which generations have had to keep weaving their stories through, unfortunately, probably more the tragic than the uplifting narratives of the past and future ambitions.

LESLIE HEWITT: The following presentation and set of installation images are selected from a recent project that I did with the Dia Foundation in New York. Specifically, Dia Bridgehampton with even more specificity thinking beyond title and deed, it is also the site of the Shinnecock Indian nation who have lived on the east end of Long Island in close contact with the Atlantic Ocean for approximately thirteen thousand years. And in the purview of freeman's towns, of which most notable Freetown and East Hampton, Long Island and Eastville, Sag Harbor, Long Island, and other residues moving beyond settler colonialism beginning in 1640.

The images are set as a counterpoint to the quotes and questions, titles, research vignettes, and studio notations that follow. The title of this short presentation is *Untitled Birthmark: Sculpture as an Analgesic Acting to Relieve Pain*. Inspired by the chapter "Manual [meaning of or pertaining to the hand or hands] for General Housework" from Saidiya Hartman's *Wayward Lives, Beautiful Experiments: Intimate Histories of Social Upheaval*.

There are seven sections: Untitled Birthmark, How to Handle Ruptures and the Unimaginable, How to Riff, How to Mend, How to Reposition, How to Embody, How to Ritualize.

Untitled Birthmark. Try describing the alienation and bizarre sensation one feels while looking, reading, a map of this work. The banality of its charting and impressive marks

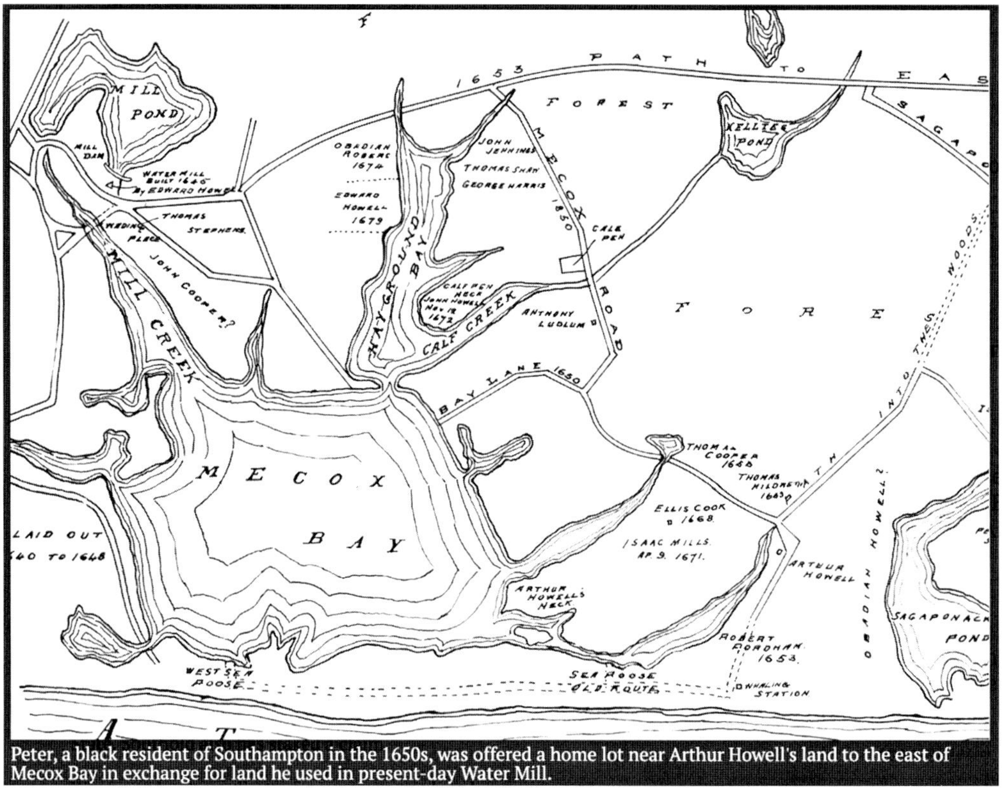

Figure 2. The Plain Sight Project. "A Free Black Man at Mecox in 1659." *The East Hampton Star*, February 27, 2020. https://www.easthamptonstar.com/villages/2020227/free-black-man-mecox-1659.

delineating, measuring, a striving for an exactness relating to the depths of the Atlantic Ocean. Aiming to soften its currents, subdue its waves storms and eerie calm through lines and angles, a system of making sense, flattening space and time. What happens to the uncharted? The unpictured? The irresolute, yet resolute, sites of catastrophe, sites of new beginnings, births, illnesses, desires, struggles, collaborations, love, longing, fighting, healing, and sensing despair all entangled, yet laying their flat, still unpictured, underdeveloped beyond image capture. How to square or to encircle the drawing map with the sensation of knowing, a kind of welling up and sensing there is more, there is more here? How to handle ruptures and the unimaginable?

Art historian Griselda Pollock explores the concept of "encounter event as a model to move beyond the restrictive dichotomies of word and image. Verbal and visual language, object and text, and into the politics of difference via an understanding of interpretation as a collaborative activity solicited by an artwork, as an event, that precipitates an encounter with difference."[11] After discussion about the nature of my current research and studio explorations, curator Oluremi Onabanjo made the suggestion to read *The Black Shoals: Offshore Formations of Black and Native Studies*, by Tiffany Lethabo King, a poignant section of her book titled "Beyond the Iconicity of Black Labor," deepens and expands this question of how to

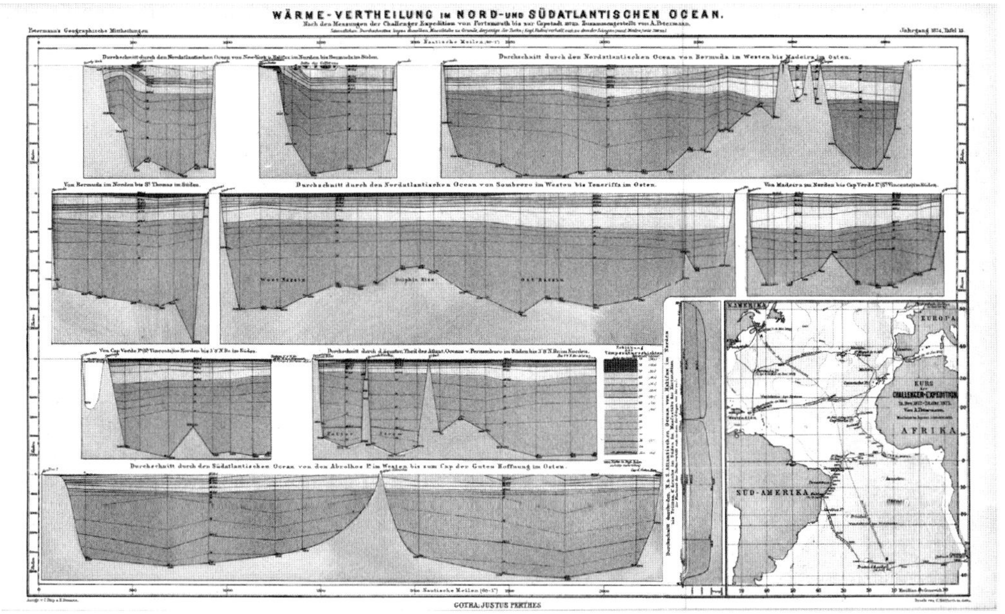

Figure 3. A. Petermann. "Wärme-Vertheilung im Nord-und Südatlantischen Ocean. Nach den Messungen der Challenger Expedition von Portsmouth bis zur Capstadt 1872/3." Published by Justus Perthes in Gotha in 1874 (in *Mihhheilungen us Justus Perthes Geographischer anstalt uber Wichtigue Beue Erforschungen*, vol. 20).

handle ruptures and the unimaginable in the following precise ways: "While labor is important, when it is used as an exclusive, governing analytic in the scholarship of US slavery and US settler colonialism, it hides more than it reveals, specifically labor as a governing frame obscures other processes, relations, locations and symbolic economies that black bodies, and representations of black embodiment, produce and sustain. Labor, though one particular and useful frame of analysis for analyzing colonial and subsequent capitalist contexts, imposes its own totalizing regime of reason and visuality."[12]

To obscure, to sustain and to subvert. Totalizing regime. Totalizing regimes of reason and visuality describes forms of navigation, a choreography of sorts, made by individuals or large masses of people, and forming spatial terms toward our freedom. A freedom of movement and building of a multiphonic, multi-rhythmic cacophony. *How to Riff. Untitled Base.* Hmm, hum, or hymn this is hmm, hum, or hymn spelling each word. H-M-M, H-U-M, H-Y-M-N.

"Sinnerman," released in 1962 by artist Nina Simone, acts as a reminder of the poetics and poignant echoes in transformation. The transformative power of words, utterances, and sound modeled and handled to evoke all the unsaid, but felt deeply in the between; the negative spaces; the boundlessness of silences across generations; living in the realm of postmemory. "You know it, you know how it goes. Where you gonna run to? Please hide me. I run to the rock. Please hide me. I run to the rock. Please hide me. All in that day. But the rock cried out." *How to Riff. Untitled Shinnecock Bay Atlantic Sound.* "I run to the sea. I run to the sea, so I run to the river." *How to Riff. Untitled Bay Valley Riff. How to Mend. How to Reposition.*

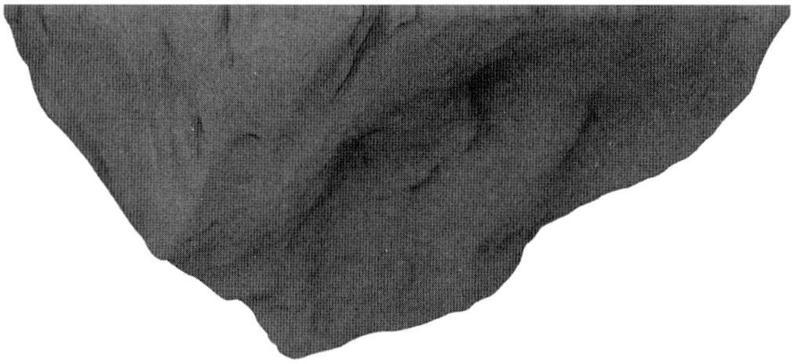

Figure 4. Computer generated research image, Leslie Hewitt | Studio © Leslie Hewitt.

Figure 5. Computer generated research image, Leslie Hewitt | Studio © Leslie Hewitt.

By approaching image and object repositioned as interrelated and as inseparable modalities, it is expanding. It is expanding and mutable. It is then expanding and mutable form in space to expand a form of address, and address toward spatiality that includes geologic time. Pointing to a deep time measure. Can these happen through the exploration of ideas of light, sound, and inertia as they are pulled into the spatial matrix of image, object, echo? A close parallel to an idea, feeling, or event. Amalgams are echoes are of a different sort, merging fragments of the depths of the topography of the Atlantic Ocean floor with the contours of calm water bays, inlets where land curves inward to receive the memory of currents that traveled long distances. You know, ocean waterways. *How to Embody? How to Ritualize?* Resonance is worth defining here, it is the quality in a sound of being deep, full, and reverberating. It is the reinforcement, the prolongation of sound by reflecting from a surface, or by this synchronous vibration of surrounding objects. *How to Ritualize*? For solo piano, alto saxophone, or tambourine, this score may be realized in any imaginative way or in conjunction with or in response to the recording of Thelonious Monk's song, *Evidence, Justice*.

Figure 6. Leslie Hewitt and Jamal Cyrus, *For Solo Piano, Alto Saxophone, or Tambourine (This Score May Be Realized in Any Imaginative Way, or in conjunction with or in response to the recording of the song* Evidence (Justice) *00:07:55 on the album* Monk in Tokyo, *Columbia Records (1963) with Thelonious Monk on piano, Charlie Rouse on tenor saxophone, Butch Warren on bass, and Frankie Dunlap on drums or* Evidence *00:04:41 on the album* Thelonious Monk Quartet with John Coltrane at Carnegie Hall, *Blue Note Records (1957) with Thelonious Monk on piano, John Coltrane on tenor saxophone, Ahamed* [*sic*] *Abdul-Malik on bass, and Shadow Wilson on drums or* Evidence *00:05:00 on the album* Evidence, *New Jazz (1962) with Steve Lacy on soprano saxophone, Don Cherry on trumpet, Carl Brown on Bass, and Billie Higgins (Abdul Kareem) on drums,* Evidence, 2022. © Leslie Hewitt and Perrotin.

Figure 7. Leslie Hewitt, *Untitled (Landmark)*, research image, 2021. © Leslie Hewitt.

TANIA SENGUPTA: In December 2021, UNESCO inscribed the annual festival Durgapuja of Kolkata (Calcutta), eastern India, in its Representative List of Intangible Cultural Heritage of Humanity, a category instituted through UNESCO's 2003 Convention.

I have been part of a collaborative project entitled "Mapping Ephemerality" with Swati Chattopadhyay of the University of California Santa Barbara (lead-investigator) and Arijit Sen of the University of Wisconsin–Milwawkee, which looks at how this festival, its transient material processes and manifestations, as well as its emotive and performative dimensions interact with the Kolkata's more perennial urban fabric and life, producing an intense sense of locality, community and city. UNESCO's Durgapuja inscription prompted, for me, reflections on certain instutionalized taxonomies and epistemologies related to heritage.

Kolkata's Durgapuja is a ten-day festival (with five core days of celebration) to mark the worship of Durga—the main female goddess for Bengalis—who vanquishes Mahishasur, an evil demon, to save humanity. The story and iconography consist of Durga, her four children (Lakshmi, Saraswati, Kartik, and Ganesh), Mahishasur the demon, and all their (mythical bird/animal) vehicles or consorts. The idols are created over months by often hereditary clay-idol makers based in Kolkata's Kumartuli area. More than three thousand temporary pavilions—called "pandals," and made of bamboo or steel frames, fabric, straw, paper, plastic, metal sheeting and various waste-material—are erected throughout the city to house the idols, enable rituals, absorb millions of visitors and collectively present an urban spectacle, spanning the diminutive to the grand. The entire process is mobilized bottom-up by para(neighborhood)-based communities through local youth clubs and formal and informal resident groups. People dress up in festive clothing and visit other pandals in the city with friends and relatives ("pandal-hopping"), often taking all-night-tours—mobilizing crowds, accumulation of bodies, and collective claim on city. Decorative lighting and stalls selling snacks, handicrafts and everyday consumer items line up streets and fairgrounds. The whole city is re-worked as a gigantic new material, spatial, experiential and performative assemblage. Durgapuja also involves multiple forms of labor—idol makers, pandal makers, decorative lighting providers, dhakis (traditional drummers), priests, hawkers, cleaners, cooks (for communal meals)—many of them coming temporarily from provincial regions. Funded originally by residents, Durgapuja also increasingly absorbs corporate and global capital, sponsors, advertisements, and imagery. Highly agile and adaptive, there is equally continuous discourse on loss of vital traditions or physical elements, new aesthetic themes

Figure 8. Pandal, residential street and crowd, Mudiali Puja (2022). Photo: Subhrojyoti Mukherjee.

of pandals or commercialization, and engagement with a host of social issues and increasingly, environmental concerns and initiatives. The clay idols are immersed in the river Ganges on the tenth day (bisharjan). The festival and immersion of thousands of idols are also major urban governance exercises; the pandals are dismantled, materials often kept for annual re-use, and already, anticipation begins for the next year. Material traces of Durgapuja remain within the city's fabric after the festival ends; fragments reappear and people galvanize back into action as the event is re-performed the year after.

The curious aspect of the UNESCO inscription is that Durgapuja as a phenomenon embodies an intense level of urban spatial and physical (re)making, and materiality and tangibility. It is in fact a highly complex material and spatial production and performance. This involves deeply interrelated sociocultural, economic and material relations and political dynamics: from fundraising, political and other patronage, 'para'-politics and social relations; and civic governance and policing.

Figure 9. Mudiali pandal facade being constructed and the labors involved (2022). Note also the cart and cart-pullers in the foreground, delivering mustard oil, used for both cooking and ritual purposes. Photo: Subhrojyoti Mukherjee.

Hence, Durgapuja's slotting into the category of the "intangible" seems somewhat perplexing. Being anything that is not tangible, the "intangible" seemingly bears infinite possibilities, yet it is circumscribed by what it is not—the tangible. How, then, does one account for the deep entanglements of Durgapuja's intense, tangible materiality with its associated practices, and the social, experiential, imaginative and affective worlds that are produced by, but also produce, its material, spatial and corporeal formations? Must we necessarily inscribe heritage through mutually exclusive taxonomies? If the inherent referent of the "intangible"—the world of the tangible, can be touched, felt or seen, Durgapuja certainly would lay a strong claim to that world as well. Conversely, is the material heritage of monuments, buildings or natural/cultural sites free of embodied, imaginative, affective, storied, narrative dimensions?

The notion of intangible cultural heritage (ICH) arose, as Amanda Kearney reminds us, out of a concern with the preoccupation of the West and UNESCO World Heritage listings (originating in the WH Convention 1972) with monuments, buildings and physical (natural and cultural) sites, where numerous cultural practices did not find a place.[13] This would have understandably been welcome for cultures and geographies marginalized through colonial hegemony and postwar/postcolonial international geopolitical and cultural regimes institutionalized, for example, by the United Nations or UNESCO.

However, I think there is something deeper at stake here: the marking of ICH is arguably also a way of accounting for and delimiting the "other" within a distinctly "othered" space—rooted in and in continuation of, a colonial and white Western epistemology premised on a Cartesian divide between the material and immaterial, materiality and practice, matter and mind, environments and experience, stable temporality and ephemerality, self and other—formalized and consolidated through a postwar capitalist geopolitical and thereafter, neoliberal, order. Perhaps ICH delineates a space for the "other" that will not erode or threaten in any fundamental way the marking of stable, tangible—mostly white Western—heritage. On looking at a sample of ICH inscriptions, we find that about 80–85 percent of the nearly five hundred items inscribed since 2003 belong to non-Western—often ex-colonial—geographies and contexts, culturally "exotic" to the Western gaze. A small bunch maps roughly onto the ex-Soviet or Central/Eastern European nations and cultures, and only a tiny proportion falls within Western Europe and North America—e.g., French Pyranese bear festivities (2022), Hungarian string dance (2022), Danish Inuit singing-dancing (2021), Slovakian and Czechian puppetry (2016), or Belgian shrimp fishing on horseback (2013). The latter ones often relate to cultural practices or traditions that are nominally peripheral to the mainstay of Western European or North American life—the West's internal "other." The list of (tangible) World Heritage sites is on the other hand still disproportionately populated by European and North American examples (in August 2022, there were 58 sites in Italy and only 98 in all of the African continent; 498 in Europe and North America, 195 in Asia and the Pacific). Juxtaposed this way, the ICH list also emerges as a catalogue of seemingly exotic practices and worlds, not unlike the late-nineteenth or early-twentieth-century anthropological, collection, and museum practices that gathered, exoticized, and othered diverse worlds in relation to the West.

Figure 10. Workers rolling leaves of the betelnut tree to create panel, Bakulbagan Puja (2018). Photo: Swati Chattopadhyay.

Alongside its complex materiality, Durgapuja has particular cyclical and durational temporalities—it is ephemeral, evoking Edmund Husserl's conceptualization of embodied heritage as thickened temporal experience and their reiterations. Is it its elusive temporality—also a characteristic of many of the other ICH inscriptions—that fuels its, or their, conflation with the "intangible"? This brings into question heritage designations' competence in handling the nuances of temporality. Chiara Bortolotto (2007) notes that the main innovation of ICH was not really about its intangibility—it clearly wasn't—but in fact about understanding these in terms of time, "as evolving processes."[14] ICH is also equated with "living heritage" in its own representations.[15] But it also equates fluid temporalities and "living practices" with exotic and othered cultures, not letting these permeate or mess with the "stable" sites-and-monuments based World Heritage categories.

Crucially, I want to note here that the myriad cultural practices across the world that do sit under UNESCO's ICH category (and many others that don't make it to the list), in fact, mostly straddle and challenge the type of binary life-worlds and taxonomies foundational to international heritage frameworks. But it is the fundamental epistemological frame through which these are seen and inscribed as an exotic, other-worldly "other," and which then prefigure our directions of knowing, that is problematic. It is telling that UNESCO uses the word

Figure 11. Female sanitation workers cleaning up, Mudiali Puja (2022). Photo: Swati Chattopadhyay.

"inscription"—suggestive of the power and instrumental role of such engravings—writing over, writing into. The process of inscription is arduous, hard earned, but also deeply etched and projects conceptually divided worlds.

Anyone interested in a project of equity for marginalized cultures, practices and knowledges also need to be vigilant of the type of othering and continuations of colonial frames that UNESCO inscriptions and modern heritage management reaffirm and inscribe in newer ways. It would instead be liberating to imagine heritage through more agile formations, where tangible and intangible; materiality and practice, experience, imagination, affect; the materially stable and the ephemeral, are not incommensurable or even "complementary" conceptual domains, but rather part of the same wider and fluid formations.

Respondent

MAXIMILIAN STERNBERG: I would like to point to two brief questions that, to me, run across the presentations. One is a tension between an emphasis on the *relational* in heritage—each of you pointed out heritage is always in state of movement, heritage is malleable, subject to changes over time—versus a more *normative* conception of heritage. Most speakers spoke explicitly or at least implicitly about norms in conceiving of heritage. I am not suggesting that the two conceptions are necessarily conflicting, but it's perhaps worth pondering over their relationship. For those speakers that presented more concrete instances of heritage and space, how do they see that tension playing out, between the relative dimension of heritage and a conception that presupposes a firmer ethical outlook. In other words, where does the ethical dimension sit within the relationship between the relational and normative? Does it sit within this relationality or is the normative underpinned by other considerations? Or both? For instance, Andreas's points one, two, and four appear to raise explicit moral questions and I was curious about how these emerge from the relationality, thereby creating their own norm? Anthony made that very striking comment about norms arising from within experience itself. I would have liked to hear more about this assertion. How does that pertain to generativity with a small "g" or a capital "G"?

The other cross-cutting theme that intrigued me is a dialectic within representation itself, or concealing and revealing. I was very struck by Ola's comments about the river enriching, but also impoverishing, the shift in heritage and experience of the river. Or, Leslie speaking about labor concealing the ripples in the sea of currents that started very far away and make their way to the shore, that there was a process there that the totalizing concept of labor does not capture. So on the one hand, the concept of labor seems to be pushing back against the totalizing vision of Humboldt's cross-section through the Atlantic, but on the other hand seems again to conceal as much as it seeks to reveal. Similarly, this notion that the intangible is in fact profoundly material and that ultimately again the notion of intangible heritage becomes a way of somehow segregating the colonial from totalized heritage.

Discussion

ANDREAS PANTAZATOS: I found it fascinating, the framework that Anthony gave us about generativity for the very reason that these kind of concepts when we try to embrace them—moving away from their starting point and the philosophical realm in which they were created—you always take a leap of faith in the dark thinking "will they work?" or "will they not work?" So I think it was very helpful to put this forward about particularly the idea of historicity and the nature of experience between the home world and the alien world.

Now I'm going back to the questions that you put forward to me, Max: two points. Now, I see points 3 and 4 related. And I will explain why. When you try to find out how knowledge is saved and who provides testimony or not, if you're excluded or included is an ethical matter. So from this point of view, you might say that the ethical might come first, in the sense that depending on which school of thought you're following, what one would have for somebody to be ethical, is the capacity to create relationships as the fundamental human thing because each one of us probably is considered as someone other's child in that kind of sense. So, if I want to go to have that approach, that has to do with the ethics of care; so relationality, is what builds the normative framework when we talk about the ethical. How you make the move from that to heritage? Is it because heritage is about relationships? The whole idea about past, present, and future then broadly construed, is an intergenerational relationship. And the whole idea about what kind of decisions you make, would you select to move to the future, has to do with how you manage and negotiate this kind of relationship. And that's why the distinctions that Tania brought forward earlier about the tangible and intangible, those kinds of distinctions blur the lines of how we negotiate this kind of relationships.

ANTHONY STEINBOCK: I had a question for Leslie, and Leslie's artwork. Are you suggesting, in the mapping that you showed us in the Atlantic near the harbors and the Bays of the Hampton, the Shinnecock area, that that's a mapping of the hidden or mapping of mystery, for example, of the depths? And that the flattening that you mentioned is the flattening of that rich vertical dimension? And is your work an attempt to rehabilitate that in a certain way or show it in a different light?

LESLIE HEWITT: Thank you for the question. I always find it hard to do a presentation about artwork, because it's meant to be experienced in your total self, not just through an optical presentation. In brief, my goal is to try to call up a multitude of histories that are often on the periphery. That are decentered for reasons that we know, and also try to show other kinds of relationships. So, for instance, my goal for that particular project was to show the kinds of kinship and strategic sharing of radical traditions that create an entanglement between the Shinnecock and the free people of color in that area. For me, merging the depth of the Atlantic Ocean in the sculpture with the bays that are named through Shinnecock logic create a new space. Because it's a space that doesn't literally exist, right? But it does exist through the kinds of relationships that were formed.

TANIA SENGUPTA: I would like to continue thinking about this whole idea of familiarity and ex-colonized populations—internalizing a lot of colonial knowledge, a degree of "self-colonization," and so forth—it's quite interesting that when, in 2003, the category of intangible cultural heritage was instituted, I remember in India we were very happy—my colleagues and friends working in heritage—that, finally, we have something that accounts for our experiences, our stories, our histories. So, it was seen as not just a victory, but a recovery of sorts. But equally, one gradually realizes the problem; and you see, this listing of Durgapuja really got me thinking: so, [for global heritage listing bodies] this is intangible. This festival, which is a highly intense phenomenon; so many aspects of it are so material, so embodied, so physical. We [project investigators] had some initial discussion, and then I started thinking further about the categories. Many of the UNESCO intangible heritage dossiers are submitted from global South contexts. So, to conform to the required rubrics, there's a whole international economy around how to submit UNESCO Heritage proposals and experts who would give you consultancy for that. It's a grand management of that international knowledge of heritage and international regulatory frameworks. But I'm also partly saying that Durgapuja still resists a lot of these categorizations and it is whatever it is; it's all that is put together, so you really can't separate tangible and intangible aspects. That's not to say that we need to stop categorizing everything and I don't mean a grand collapse of all categories into a black hole, but equally, these are vital genealogies of categories and therefore that is a key aspect. I found very interesting the idea of the home as the generative place or the journey that I think Anthony mentioned. The notion of ethics and relationality. So, processes that are already deeply relational are obviously great places to learn heritage ethics from, which you too raised, Max.

ANDREAS PANTAZATOS: Can I just add something about what Tania just mentioned about a gap between the tangible and intangible, which is it's this kind of interaction that does not really attract our attention when we talk about heritage in space. And I think it comes out very clearly from the discussion of the Oil rivers in Nigeria for the very reason that you have the river that counts as a river for the people who've been living there forever, then suddenly you have an oil company that actually are related to oil and this changes completely what kind of story we tell about the river and how they're related to it and what kind of legacy it creates, particularly when the names are Portuguese. So imagine if you do not know anything about Nigeria and somebody gives you three Portuguese names about rivers in Africa, you believe that this place can be Portugal. It is this kind of interaction because of the tangible dimension of the intangible that the lived experience, if it's not taken into consideration, is what is missing.

TAO DUFOUR: On that note, I wanted to ask if Ola wanted to respond, and then we will move on to the next panel.

OLA UDUKU: I've been listening to the discussion, and I do think the case studies of the Oil Rivers particularly bring all these bits together about it being space. But there is that translational and relational relationship between the actual rivers, but then also, what happens? It is very performative in the sense that you have Africans in bowler hats as their tradition, and we all know from King that tradition itself is invented. But clearly, this is a liminal zone. There's been a series of activities that have crossed the coast and the rivers themselves, which flow knowledge, so to speak. It is that confluence between the tangible and the intangible. And in this case, you have to then infuse the economic into that discussion. But clearly, the stories that are being told are dipping into that in terms of their relationship. It is something that I'm genuinely, anecdotally interested in myself because at some levels people think about the rivers exactly as that: they're names for these rivers, and in their mindset, they're related to one thing or the other. There's the cultural amnesia, obviously, as to what these rivers did over time. But clearly for us now we can see the effects in terms of the internationalization of the whole oil scandals in the Delta region of Nigeria. But the culture is still mediating between these things, and it's claimed as a culture; in this case, both its intangible things but also the very tangible in the dress, performative activities, and so on. So I think it is a really a very interesting example to look at and to explore and particularly because it does base back to the idea, in terms of the local language, about people having "houses"; so you have the house of the chief literally, some of which are more conceptual and there being an actual house there now. So, you've got these words that really discuss or engage with concepts, although they have very physical meanings as well. But yes, I thought it was really interesting to have the framing of the first speaker, thank you very much, which I think for those of us who don't necessarily think philosophically always, it really does begin to challenge it. But also, I think to frame forms of research in this area, which I think are actually lacking, there's just not enough of it. And Tania's point is very true as well. The whole idea about in theory intangible heritage was for the other, but the framing is very much from the West. What it's capturing is very different from presumably what its original ambition was.

Panel 2

JEAN KHALFA: Reading Tao DuFour's remarkable analysis of Husserl's description of perception of space as structured by sedimented experiences within temporal life, I thought that it gave a key to the works of a number of Caribbean writers and artists I have worked on, over the years, some of whom portrayed the alterations or the collapse of what Husserl described. In these works the structure of experienced space within the colonial context and then through a possible decolonization process, is not homogeneous and cannot be unified under a single gaze or description. This has been the focus of my research on Césaire, Fanon, Glissant, and Lam. Here are a few notes on how each described and used such a complex, sometimes apocalyptic experience of space.

The first great text Aimé Césaire published, in 1939, *Cahier d'un retour au pays natal (Notebook of a return to the native land)* opens on a sequence of about forty stanzas describing the alienation of the colonial consciousness via a description of the space of his island, Martinique, as essentially fragmented. This link between the structure of the space and that of consciousness, will be a crucial dimension of Césaire's work throughout his career. Here are a few examples:

"At the end of first light *burgeoning with frail coves* the hungry Antilles, the Antilles *pitted* with smallpox, the Antilles *dynamited* by alcohol, *stranded* in the mud of this bay, in the *dust* of this town sinisterly stranded."[16]

And: "an aged poverty *rotting* under the sun, silently; an aged silence *bursting* with tepid *pustules*, the dreadful inanity of our raison d'être."[17]

Here the heritage of slavery, a deep alienation of the self to itself and its own environment, is figured, imagined and represented, through detailed images of fragmentation on the one hand and cancerous growth and proliferation on the other. Readers of this poem always remember his astonishing mastery of the vocabulary of tropical medicine to describe material and mental lesions. It is a mental space without unity or direction, which corresponds to a physical space that is fundamentally pathological. However, beyond this first, gripping description, this is also a poem of liberation through the return to another land, qualified as "native"—*pays natal*, a land of origin but also one that gives birth. The nativity the poem announces and produces at the same time, is that of a new consciousness, which Césaire called *négritude*. Now this form of consciousness is also related to a perception of space, but a very different one. What this phenomenological poem evokes now is the materiality of the earth and its soil not as separatedness and fragmentation but as mystical flesh. In the revised versions published after the war, notably that of 1956, which has become the standard edition, Césaire shed some aspects but not all, of the spiritualist dimension of his work. But of negritude he wrote the following in all versions:

it takes root in the red flesh of the soil
it takes root in the ardent flesh of the sky[18]

There are long variations on this theme in the poem, which are always variations on spatial-temporal structures. I have endeavored to show that this work is thus structured around a dual opposition, which can be read geometrically or geographically: geometrically, there is a constant opposition between division in a discrete space and experiences of unification expressed through the models of the spiral and of the cycloid.[19] This corresponds geographically in Césaire's imagery to the opposition of the mangrove in the South of the island,—the tropical vegetation at the interface of sea and land represents corruption and disease—and the volcano in the North, which, in spite of the catastrophic 1902 eruption, is presented as a manifestation of the birth and revolution of matter, both the production of being in itself and, for Césaire, an image of poetry as *dire volcanique*. The three dimensions of imaginary, writing, and political disalienation are always linked in Césaire. Toward the end of his life, Césaire collected his final poetry, under the title *Moi Laminaire* (*I laminaria*, 1982). At first sight this odd portrait of the self as seaweed points to a reconciliation with the liquid element and the maritime landscape, but laminaria are a kind of algae that attaches to rocks and remain in place in spite of the turbulence, the laminarian flows imposed on them over time. Indeed the images of the poem are often of rocky structures, and this poetry that is essentially of the experience of the mineral, echoes more the poetry of presence of the fifties and sixties than the Surrealism of Césaire's youth. This collection perhaps strengthens the early oppositions dynamically organizing Césaire's writing through an imaginary structured by spatial determinations.

As regards Frantz Fanon, one of the main foci of my work has been his psychiatric thought, not just because it was as revolutionary as his politics but because Fanon thinks revolution as a process of disalienation in the same terms as he conceptualizes the psychotherapeutical process within the asylum.[20] It seems clear to me that both fed each other and that it would be difficult to understand Fanon's political texts without understanding his psychiatric works. He also often considered his own work in psychiatry (which he continuously practiced) under the terms of his revolutionary thought, which led him to pioneer his own experimental ethnopsychiatry.

Though he admired Césaire as a poet he thought that negritude at best responded to a pathology of identification and was at worse a mystification.[21] It is notable however, that as in Césaire's poem, all the oppositions in his thought are linked to opposite structures of space. The space of the colonial city is described as a space of division, between the "European" and the "indigenous" parts, the latter a space of constant control and enclosure where the colonized can only experience free bodily movement in dreams and in states of trance—sublimations of the movements they cannot engage in. The idea of "corporeal schema" was imported in philosophy by Maurice Merleau-Ponty from prewar psychiatry in France, and interpreted in relation to Husserl's phenomenology: an embodied experience of the environment as the generative space of movements and projects for the individual. For Fanon the corporeal schema collapses, and the body of the colonized becomes a thing within his space, a "compartmentalised, Manichean, and petrified world," "a world of statues,"[22] and under the pitiless gaze of the colonizer. In the same way the traditional psychiatric institution amplified the initial neurological or psychological disturbances that brought the patient there, through containment and the prevention of all free movement. It developed the illnesses it was supposed to cure, produced the agitation or violence that came with it, as well as the repression and enclosures needed to control them. In this circle the patient had been made a thing by the institution, which needed to be radically transformed if any disalienation was to occur, and this transformation implied a complete reorganization of its material structure. This is why the antipsychiatry of the '50s started with a reflection on the structure of the space of the asylum. Creating autonomous social structures run by patients, social therapy implied a thorough reorganization of the space of the asylum so that bodies could circulate and operate freely within it. Fanon actively contributed to this new model of mental health care (under the influence of the pioneer François Tosquelles, as did Jean Oury). Similarly, he portrayed the independence struggle as a process of individual disalienation as well as of institutional transformation. This is what made it a revolutionary process: the struggle was also a process of therapy of the social. His penultimate book, *Year V of the Algerian Revolution* (1959) defended that view through the analysis of sociological case studies. Conversely, his final book, *The Wretched of the Earth* (1961), considers the risks for a national struggle to fail as a truly revolutionary, disalienating process. The danger for a postcolonial state was the rapid solidification of the initial process into inert social institutions and bureaucratic machineries of power justified by some identitarian ideology. It is striking from this point of view that at the end of the famous first chapter of the *Wretched of the Earth* Fanon should differentiate the true revolutionary struggle in spatial terms by pointing out that liberation is a liberation from any single-centered power structure and from hierarchical machineries of power: "Even if the armed struggle has been symbolic, and even if they have been demobilized by rapid decolonization, the people have time to realize that the liberation was the achievement of each and every one and no special merit should go to the leader. Violence hoists the people up to the level of the leader. Hence their aggressive tendency to distrust the system of protocol that young governments are quick to establish."[23]

Édouard Glissant also moved away from the negritude of Césaire, which he defined as a thought of identity on to the model of the root, in favor of the model of permanent processes of becoming, which he defined metaphorically via the complex ecosystem of the mangrove, in Martinique, and conceptually through the theory of the rhizome in Deleuze and Guattari's work. The point is to imagine a form of development in space that has no center, no specific point of origin or lineage, but rather consists in lateral relations that alter each element in a whole to a good degree but without totally erasing their differences. Glissant named this structure *La Relation*. In this model the world is, at each of its points the *Tout-Monde*, defined as "Our universe inasmuch as it changes and continues through exchange, and at the same time the 'vision' that we have of it." In this universe, each point contains a multiplicity of overlapping identities and differences, and from this perspective Martinique and more widely the Caribbean can be seen as a laboratory of the evolution that faces the rest of the world, where individuals share with many others in different parts of the world at least as much as they do with those in their vicinity, a situation that entails a complex process of becoming. Again here historical processes are conceptualized through a reflection on the generativity of space, in this case that of the island, but, against Césaire and his quest of metaphysical and mythical origins (the volcanic eruption and negritude). To transform the present, the mangrove has become the model, valued in its proliferating heterogeneity.

These three writers admired Wifredo Lam. Fanon chose a painting by Lam for the décor of one of his plays, *L'Œil se noie* (*The Drowning Eye*)[24] and both Césaire and Glissant wrote on him and, in important artists' books, with him. Lam was an artist of many origins (Cuban of Chinese, African, and European ancestry), who refused to be reduced to any as well as to their multiplicity itself. Now, in his best known work, *The Jungle* (1943),[25] what is interesting is not just the complicated perspectival organisation of the surface, but also the questioning of painting as a spectacle offered to an external eye. From then on, the surfaces, were to be organized as the interaction of planes that could not exist in the same physical and historical reality. This is particularly striking in the later part of his work,

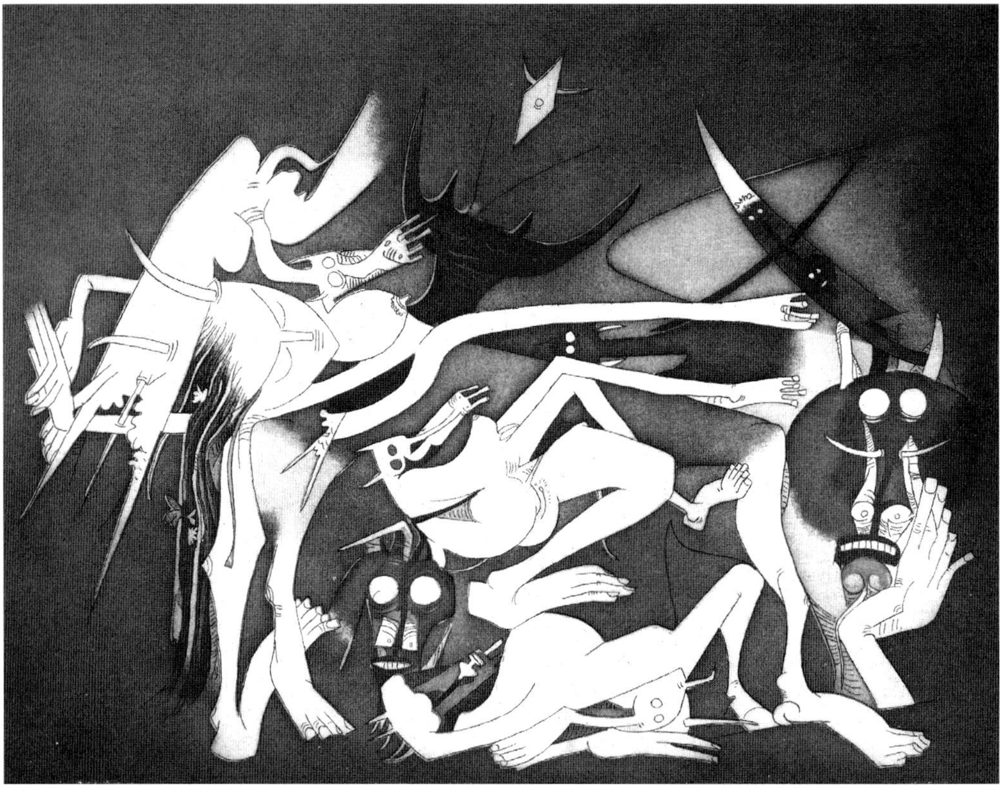

Figure 12. Several "Nouvelle Bonté" in Aimé Césaire and Wilfredo Lam, *Annonciation.* Milan: Giorgio Upiglio, Grafica Uno, 1967. Seven etchings by Lam, a sheet with ten poems by Césaire and an epigraph by Lam. CR. 225.

which is largely made up of etchings for collaborative dialogues with poets, remarkable artists books, of which there is a complete collection in the Wren Library in Cambridge.

Several printing passages are necessary to produce the etchings Lam produced with the help of the great master printer Giorgio Upiglio, in Milan: first for the drawing and then for texture and sometimes different colors when the artist uses aquatint, possibly in planes of different densities. Lam uses this complex process to superpose a multiplicity of planes rather than compose any depth that would be unified by an external perspectival gaze: the characters in a dream, or a trance, in a Santería ceremony, where they are "mounted" by the gods that they communicate with, coexist with the content of the trance, which can be a series of fears and hopes symbolized by the condensations within singular floating beings, of animal, divine, human aspects together with inanimate artifacts, without any ground, so that the print can be looked at from any angle. The nativity theme and the fragility of life were personally important to Lam and graphically what his *annunciations* stage are the interaction of a multiplicity of obscure forces, dangerous or protective.

But engaging with such a theme through his knowledge of the complex experiences of a religion based on a mythology was not for Lam a simple ethnographic exercise (if such an exercise is ever simple). It had for him a historical and

Figure 13. Alain Jouffroy and Wifredo Lam, *Lames de Lam* (print). Seven etchings by Lam and a poem by Alain Jouffroy. Unpublished. The portfolio was never assembled CR 372.

political significance. He saw it also as refusing the colonial situation where the spaces in the world are organized in relationship to an exterior and dominant gaze. He aimed to represent the coexistence of different spaces, and, importantly, parallel temporalities, which Glissant saw as a defining feature of the art of the Americas. The work of art is to be perceived as absolute, complete in what it presents, and it does not refer to anything beyond the surface: "We leave this admirable depth of Western painting, melancholy and solitary, we enter another expanse, which unleashes the infinite work of Relation. Lam leads us there."[26] Lam's political reading of his own aesthetics was in fact proposed very early on by Pierre Mabille, in 1944, in the Césaires' journal *Tropiques*. In his study of *La Jungle*, Mabille stated that the organization of a representation in relationship to a central point (anywhere on the painting's surface) reflected a general conception of the organization of the world by a unique God, and of society by a supreme chief, structures totally foreign to the Afro-Cuban cults he studied, where a multiplicity of deities or spirits intervened randomly in ceremonies where individuals experienced their own possession independently of the others. He opposed this space of proliferation, cohabitation and transmutation to the "sinister nazi jungle" with its Führer, its mechanized divisions and the resulting "rigorous parallelism of endless cemeteries."

Figure 14. Jean-Dominique Rey and Wifredo Lam, *L'Herbe sous les pavés*. Six etchings by Lam. CR 401.1982. © Wifredo Lam Estate, ADAGP, Paris and DACS, London 2023.

The last artists' book Lam published, in 1982, with Dominique Rey (*L'Herbe sous les pavés*, *Grass under the cobblestones*) was of a much smaller format than most of the previous ones, because he was by then partly paralyzed and could no longer work on large plates. It is a *mise en abyme* of painting itself and the return to the classical theme of the painter with a model, but in an astonishing reversal where the mythical characters of his previous paintings paint self-portraits as neoclassical beings. Here perspectival representation seems to return, but it is immediately negated by the incommensurability and yet the communication of the incongruous worlds he stages.

Each of these works pays great attention to the historical "heritage" that shapes the consciousness of space. We saw that they do it in very different, sometimes opposed ways, but never just in an illustrative manner. They reveal and explore a much "thickened" spatial perception in order to imagine and contribute to alternative historical processes.

NATALIE MELAS: This will be a small philological thought experiment, or, with Leslie Hewitt's presentation in mind, a riff. The broad question I would like to pose is: Can there be a generativity of disinheritance, a generativity that is outside filiation, or emerges from the destruction of filiation?

"The Open Boat," the opening chapter of Edouard Glissant's *Poetics of Relation*, gives an account of the abyssal middle passage of the Atlantic slave ship where inheritance is not transmitted through generational filiation, but in rupture—a continuity in discontinuity [*continu-discontinu*]. Amidst the terror experienced there, what is lived is the disappearance of everyday life.

> The asceticism of crossing this way the land-sea that, unknown to you, is the planet Earth, feeling a language vanish, the word of the gods vanish, and the sealed image of even the most everyday object, of even the most familiar animal, vanish. The evanescent taste of what you ate. The hounded scent of ochre earth and savannas.[27]

Glissant's account of the slave ship adopts the language of generativity, that is, of birth and generation.

> This boat is a womb, a womb abyss. It generates the clamor of your protests; it also produces all the coming unanimity. Although you are alone in this suffering, you share in the unknown with others whom you have yet to know. This boat is your womb, a matrix, and yet it expels you. This boat: pregnant with as many dead as living under sentence of death.[28]

Birth and death are not sequential but conflated in the womb/abyss paradoxically pregnant with the dead and those alive only through deferment (*vivants en sursis*). Most notably perhaps, the word "generative" occurs here in reference precisely to the womb. The French is even more direct: The womb/abyss is "*génératrice de ta clameur. Productrice aussi de toute unanimité à venir.* More or less literally: generative of your clamor. Productive also of all unanimity to come."

What is generated in this ruptural inversion of generation, is clamor or cry. Resistance perhaps, or protest as the translator supplements, but in the form of sheer sound. Something is also *produced*; something emerges from the broken natural temporal flow of generations, something that is not given but made. Glissant names it here "a coming unanimity" that derives from the sharing of the unknown. In the chapter's final paragraph, that madeness perhaps verges into poetry: "This is what holds us in poetry . . . we cry the cry of poetry. [*C'est cela qui nous tient en poésie . . . Nou crions le cri de poésie*].[29]

Notably, this unanimity is "shared" rather than "transmitted" or handed down. Sharing takes the place of generativity's transmission, and implies an open-ended parity. This parity detours around the hierarchy of generations on the boat even as it confounds both the temporal linearity of inheritance and its potential analogy with the exclusivity of private property. The passage's direct address to a "you" enacts this sharing, even as the predominance of the present tense blurs the line between the enslaved on the ship and the reader in the present as potential addressees.

Glissant makes a grand claim for the sharing of the "unknown-absolute" [*inconnu-absolu*] that is "the projection of the abyss." In time, he writes, that sharing "grows" in the "frequenting" of the abyss, becomes knowledge of the Whole [*le Tout*], and "within the Whole liberates the knowledge of Relation."[30]

Relation is here the inheritance of the abyssal rupture of the middle passage. Poetically dense, this writing seems at first reading highly abstract, a philosophical fable distant from the embodied particularity of lived experience and distant indeed from the lived present. Glissant's language throughout the passage often closely approaches the lexicon of phenomenology—the insistence on "experience," for instance, and on the *vécu* or "lived experience." It may be that the generativity of rupture requires an abstract accounting or imagining of the womb/abyss and its original victims since they are not given as ancestors capable of direct transmission to their descendants. Many of them, Glissant underlines, did not survive the middle passage at all. The experience at issue here is not "lived" in clear distinction to death and the dead, nor is it locatable in a single or singular "living" present.

The abyss also seems to require an active, almost productive forgetting. The people who have frequented the abyss "live Relation, which they clear as one would a plot of land, in the measure that forgetting of the abyss comes to them, so also their memory is strengthened [*à mesure que l'oubli du gouffre leur vient et qu'aussi bien leur mémoire se renforce*]."[31] The phrasing is ambiguous and slightly opaque, but the terms suggest a paradoxical inversion and discontinuity: it is by forgetting the abyss that memory is strengthened. Is forgetting the abyss itself an *experience* of the abyss that strengthens memory and thereby makes possible continuity in discontinuity?

> For if this experience made of you, original victim floating in the abyss of the sea, an exception; it has become common in order to make of us, the descendants, a people amongst others. Peoples do not live from exception. Relation is not made of foreignness but of shared knowledge. We can say now that this experience of the abyss is the thing best exchanged [. . . *a chose le mieux échangée*].[32]

At issue in "The Open Boat" is specifically the *experience* of the abyss. Over the centuries it is this experience that is best or easiest to "exchange." The word is striking. We can read it as a loose synonym for sharing, along the lines of the "shared knowledge" that makes up Relation in the previous sentence.

Or we can read it more forcefully, more transactionally as an exchange of something for something else. It stands in stark contrast to the linearity and the irrevocability of "heritage" or "transmission." At its most radical this exchange implies that the abyss of the open boat in Relation is the inheritance of all us, "us without exception" [*pour nous sans exception*].[33]

ŁUKASZ STANEK: I am going to say a few words about our project recently shown at the Biennale of Architecture in Rotterdam. We worked on it with the geographer Michael Dziwornu based in Accra, Ghana, and with the photographer Eric Don-Arthur based in Winneba, also in Ghana.

Our project is focused on Asutsuare, which you can see in this drone footage. It is a rural settlement at the Volta River in Ghana. After Ghana's independence in 1957, the government of Kwame Nkrumah decided to invest in sugar production. A sugar plant was built at Asutsuare and a sugarcane plantation was laid out supported by an irrigation system. An estate was constructed, consisting of housing and social amenities. The project reflected Nkrumah's vision of a state-led economy and Ghana's exchanges with socialist countries. Engineers and technicians from Ghana, Poland, Czechoslovakia and Cuba contributed to the project.

The factory opened in 1965, just a few months before Nkrumah was toppled. It continued to work until the early 1980s, when it was closed down. In the late 2000s the factory was bought by Chinese investors. Today, it manufactures paper and plastic products. The old sugarcane plantations were repurposed for the farming of rice and bananas. The former administrative buildings and the distillery lab are used by a secondary school.

A few months ago Michael and I interviewed the inhabitants of Asutsuare and Eric took photographs of the people and the places. We asked retired employees of the factory about their memories and, in particular, about how they imagined their future during their work in the factory. Among them was Mr. Edward Addo, pioneer and retired surveyor. We also asked younger people about their visions of the future. Our project consisted of bringing together these intergenerational conversations, which were deeply *related to* and *linked through* specific spaces in the estate, the factory, the fields, and the river.

These imaginations of the future, today and sixty years ago, were in many ways different. Asutsuare was shaped by state-socialist investment in the territory and in the people. These investments, notably the irrigation system, profoundly shaped the landscape. People told us about their memories of collective work but also of collective enjoyment, often across class and racial divides. These memories were closely related

Figure 15. Asutsuare, Ghana. Hostel building. Still from *Asutsuare Rebound* by Michael Gameli Dziwornu and Łukasz Stanek, with photography by Eric Don-Arthur. Aerial video by Barrak El Mahmoud.

to spaces. Mr. Seth Akligo, retired engineer, specifically mentioned the swimming pool. Others talked about the fields, the factory, the canteen, and the community center.

Several people recalled the training that they received. For example, Madam Paulina Addison told us about her training as a tractor operator. After sixty years she was able to name the producers of the various machines that she used. Managerial and technical staff remembered their training in Ghana and in Eastern Europe. The ambiguous counterpart of these memories is the old laboratory of the sugar factory, which was transformed into a secondary school.

This temporality of state-led planning and the futures that it entailed *contrasts* with the 1980s, marked the structural adjustment program. Our project is very much about the ways in which the people appropriated the inherited buildings and infrastructures—but also about how they appropriated the memories about the period of socialist modernization. This is what we talked about with Madam Christina Adjei, headmistress of the Osudoku Senior High School.

Younger people shared with us more individualized and more entrepreneurial life projects. Among them was Mr. Prince Selasi, environmental and safety officer at the factory. But he and others also mentioned a sense of community. This sense did not refer to socialist-era collective identities. Rather, it conveyed a pride about the ability of the inhabitants to make use of the inherited spaces in Asutsuare.

Let me finish with a quote from one of our interviews. This is Mr. Anthony Ramzey, a retired lab technician. He told us: "If not for the Chinese it [the factory] would have been left in the bush. So I am just happy that presently it has employed some people. But I was hoping it would have been used for a better

Figure 16. Asutsuare, Ghana, estate and factory. Still from *Asutsuare Rebound* by Michael Gameli Dziwornu and Łukasz Stanek, with photography by Eric Don-Arthur. Aerial video by Barrak El Mahmoud.

Figure 17. Asutsuare, Ghana, factory, rice fields, and Volta River. Still from *Asutsuare Rebound* by Michael Gameli Dziwornu and Łukasz Stanek, with photography by Eric Don-Arthur. Aerial video by Barrak El Mahmoud.

purpose. The government has to revive it. . . . It is a monument by itself." I think that there is a lot to unpack here, but let me just emphasize his hunch *that monument is something that deserves a better future*. That way of thinking is closely related to the central concern of our project, which is the intergenerational experiences of the future *in and through* specific spaces.

IULIA STĂTICĂ: I will speak to the theme of this roundtable from the perspective of an architectural historian, working within the context of socialist and post-socialist studies, and will draw on aspects of a documentary film that I produced together with my colleague, Adrian Câtu.[34] The film is titled *My Socialist Home* and approaches the socialist apartment from the interior, focused on women's lived experiences of their homes in ways that have produced a distinct relationship between the sense of interior space and women's bodies. Filmed almost entirely within the domestic space, the documentary project makes reference to two main legal frameworks that were initiated during the dictatorship of Nicolae Ceaușescu: one, a law that criminalized abortion; and the other aimed at the mass production of standardized housing blocks, precisely to accommodate the increased population derived from the former measure.

I will focus on two of the subjects in the film, Magdalena and Andra, a mother and her daughter. Magdalena first moved into the apartment in 1976 from the countryside in Eastern Romania, while Andra, who was born in 1987, has known the apartment as her only home. Their attachment to their home, although manifest in different ways, speaks to the duration of the effects of these political processes of the socialist past, and perhaps in the most evocative way, points to the spatial affectivity of the socialist apartment: to its familiarity as the space of lived experience, and at the same time to its *phantasy structure*, that is, the ideological project that was the background to its design and material construction. By "familiarity" I mean both the immediacy that is implied in one's bodily experience, as well as a process of becoming accustomed to these interiors in such a way that the socialist apartment becomes the paradigm of home for many generations, and in this way a "heritage." Insofar as the apartment is the space of shared experiences, including Magdalena's past experience of living in it under socialism, this past is also shared across generations, whereby norms that emerged continue through processes of normalization that are immanent and embodied. This notion of normalization highlights also the way in which the "phantasy structure" enabled by ideology is experienced as *reality,* becoming synonymous with lived experience.

The sense of security associated with the home carried with it a generational significance suggesting the potential for passing down one's own home to one's children. Andra, acknowledged in the documentary, that inheriting her mother's apartment could be her sole avenue to homeownership: "Sometimes I dare to think about . . . a house, but I think the tendency is to be practical and imagine that I will probably come back to this apartment." The essential aspect of home ownership during socialism, and at the same time its acquisition through labor—in the dual sense of productive and, in the case of women, reproductive labor—appears thus to imply the formation of a new tradition that is concerned with a long term projection and establishment of lasting roots (Figure 19).[35] The home transformed into a tangible proof of the lasting importance of the

Figure 18. Magdalena and her daughter, Andra, in the kitchen of her socialist flat. Still from *My Socialist Home*. Iulia Stătică and Adrian Câtu, 2021.

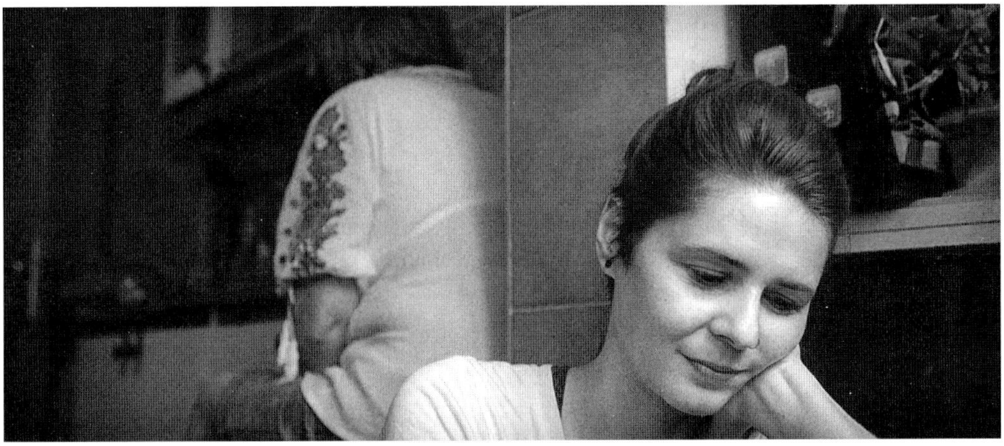

Figure 19. Andra visiting her mother, Magdalena, in her childhood flat. Still from *My Socialist Home*. Iulia Stătică and Adrian Câtu, 2021.

family and functioned as a symbolic representation of kinship.[36] The legal framework indicates the principle of generational inheritance that was embedded in the home, and that is being preserved in a post-socialist condition. In particular, I want to point out the idea of the home as an inheritance that was made available by the state. The home, as experienced during socialism can mostly be reconstructed only as a post-socialist condition, as before 1989 all its representations were idealized projections, of the modern family, maternity/natality, and state-delivered care. The question of natality is essential, especially in this context, insofar as the home is not only a space for care, but also because it functioned as an accomplice to subversive actions. While Magdalena confesses in the film that "I had no abortions, except one," Andra, states at the end that she wished her mother had told us more about her abortion, as she herself wanted to know. The way Magdalena spoke about this matter also highlights the normalization of this clandestine practice in the interior of the home, as these practices did not happen in isolation. Instead, the woman was entwined in a complex network of interconnected gendered relations that emerged in the opaque space of the home. Hannah Arendt speaks about this precisely in relation to the question of natality: "The only efficient way to guarantee the darkness of what needs to be hidden against the light of publicity is private property, a privately owned place to hide in."[37] The way Andra's generation internalized the practices that her mother's generation had normalized, as exceptional, can be glimpsed especially in her shared conversations with her secondary school friends: "We would tell each other, like, how many abortions we knew they'd had. . . . We were terrified, but also amused by the madness of things . . . and by the fact that it was about our mothers!" The minimal, but evocative account of both characters suggest in many ways a generic gesture, and points to a certain commonality, nevertheless, capturing at the same time the subjective implications.

In ending this brief contribution, I would like to point again to the idea of a reconstruction of the interior from within post-socialism, insofar as it had constituted an opaque receptacle of memories, practices and habits that shaped specifically women's subjectivities. Clandestine art that was not made public before the 1990s, suggest also the uniqueness of this space. In the work of Romanian artist, Ion Grigorescu, the interior of the socialist apartment marks a thematic interest creating a strong connection with the corporeal aspect of the subject. His own body is opposed to the collective body—the body politic—omnipresent in the official art of socialism, presenting it in the simplest domestic actions: sleeping, washing, eating.[38] In one of his short videos titled "Our Home," Grigorescu anticipates not only the hierarchy within domestic spaces but also replaces the prevalent portrayal of a woman consistently in the kitchen—a common theme in post-socialist cinema—with that of a man. Grigorescu's work challenges and complicates the traditional matriarchal representation of women, eroding its conventional contours. In contrast, the sleeping woman evokes a link to the dream realm, casting the apartment as a possible space imbued with dreamlike qualities.[39] Simultaneously, the man engaging in routine domestic actions implies the shared nature of the domestic experience. Although our understanding of the woman and the dynamic between the two characters is limited, she functions as a guide in the realm of the domestic space, suggesting the multilayered nature of the material and experiential character of the socialist home.

SOPHIE LOIDOLT: I would like to add two thoughts to the discussion on "Space and Heritage: On the Generativity of Environing Worlds" that connect to my work on Hannah Arendt: first, that activities and visibilities shape *spaces of meaning*, and they do so over generations; and second, that *natality* is a concept that *politicizes generativity.* I believe that this is something we need when talking about space and heritage.

Let me first address the idea of "spaces of meaning": Hannah Arendt has often been criticized, e.g., from a feminist perspective, for her tripartition of activities into labor, work, and action. If one takes her analysis to be putting certain activities into certain boxes or worse, putting people who are attributed certain activities into certain boxes, this criticism would certainly hold. I would like to propose a different reading, however. What I see in her work is a phenomenological analysis of how certain types of activities, with a certain intentionality, a certain temporality, a certain form of sociality etc., generate spaces of meaning: spaces in which we are fundamentally oriented. Think about how making music together orients space and time with respect to an inner logic of combination, rhythm, harmony and disharmony, volume, sound level and intensity etc.—this is what I would call a *space of meaning.* Another basic example is that we are living organisms who are existentially geared into the metabolism of our bodies: this of course structures our environment, not just biologically but as a space of meaning, of labor and rest, of change and repetition, of needs and their satisfaction. This is what Arendt calls labor, for example, answering to the human condition of life. And this is only one human condition, besides birth and death, worldliness and plurality. Arendt wants to show that, as human beings, we are pervaded by *all* human conditions, and that this brings an incredible dynamic with it, of how we can refer to the world and one another. What adds to this dynamic is that *visibility* also creates specific spaces of meaning: public and private spaces. I think that the whole architecture of the human condition lies in describing how these different spaces of meaning (activity-based and visibility-based spaces of meaning) interfere, boost, or harm each other as well as the activities and forms of sociality taking place in them.

The second focus I would like to take in this context is that of natality. If we think about generativity and space, we have to consider the possibility that harmful, suppressive, patriarchal, sexist, racist, etc., practices are deeply embedded in the bodily, spatial nature of heritage. (I am thinking, for example, of a whole genre called "Critical Heimatroman" in Austria, which thematizes this. Often the plot is connected to the Alpine nature, whose portrayal and embedded generative historicity is definitely a lot darker and gloomier than in *The Sound of Music.*) This makes me think that we might not only want to retrieve the generativity of places but also break their chains. Natality seems to be able to do both. This is why I think it is a valuable idea in our context.

Generativity, I would claim, manifests itself everywhere in Arendt's core notions: in plurality, as well as in life and worldliness. But natality is especially fascinating in this context, not only because it is clearly a generative notion, but also because it promises the power to rupture tradition, to renew it, to keep it open.

With natality, I would claim, Arendt entails an existential-phenomenological reformulation of human spontaneity: by linking it to birth, instead of building up detached transcendental structures. With this, a whole—still transcendentally relevant—setting opens up that includes topics like *corporeity*, *vulnerability*, and *generativity*, as well as a revised interpretation of existential *temporality and spatiality*. Arendt, in the German version of *The Human Condition*, *Vita activa,* speaks of the "fact of natality founding all human togetherness."[40] By this she means that *human* togetherness is essentially shaped by *generativity*, i.e., by the fact that generations before have endowed the world with meaning to which we can refer, and that new generations yet to come open up a horizon of unpredictability and renewed possibilities. Arendt emphasizes that the uniqueness of each newcomer is "not so much a matter of fact of certain qualities or of the unique combination of already known qualities."[41] Rather, it rests on "natality, by whose virtue every human being once has appeared in the world as something uniquely new."[42] How is this possible? Arendt describes the condition of the possibility for the new to appear in the world as the interplay of a *stable place of appearance* (a spatial category) and the *movement of generativity*:

> The birth and death of human beings are not simple natural occurrences, but are related to a world into which single individuals, unique, unexchangeable, and unrepeatable entities, appear and from which they depart. Birth and death presuppose a world that is not in constant movement, but whose durability and relative permanence makes appearance and disappearance possible, which existed before any one individual appeared into it and will survive his eventual departure. Without a world into which [men/humans] are born and from which they die, there would be nothing but changeless eternal recurrence, the deathless everlastingness of the human as of all other animal species.[43]

Hence, it is the *world* that allows for *natality*: This place, enriched by generation after generation with their endowments of meanings and their artifacts is formed in a historical and spatial sense as the *human* world. Its objective time is constituted by those presently *in it, remembering its past as well as projecting its future*. Innerworldly time is thus a constituted linear timeline of historic, "objective" time that *belongs to* the stable place of the world. On the other hand, the world is a "stage": To be "on" it, is to be in the "light" shining in the place of appearance.[44] To "disappear" from it means leaving this place at a certain point in innerworldly time (and space), but into a darkness that also transcends this timeline (and space). Equally, "appearing" in the world means appearing at a certain point in innerworldly time and space, but also entering it "from nowhere," as it were. In this sense, the world as a "stage," with its innerworldly time, is *crossed* by generations from darkness into darkness. By having a past, the human world is thus open for the new—this concerns time in its innerworldly sense. By being a stage that makes the difference between existence and non-existence, a "first unique appearance" is possible—this concerns how a procession of generations passes through the human world.

Natality, thus, is conceivable only in worldly plurality: It allows for the possibility of the *event*, the unpredictable, the incalculable[45]—simply because subjectivity is constituted as an openness, and not a closure, as is intersubjectivity in a generative sense. Natality is thus never a "capacity" we have at our disposal like the movements of our bodies, even if some passages in *The Human Condition*might sound as simple as that[46]; it has the same an-archic quality as all that occurs in the space of plurality. Thus, it is a "capacity" and "faculty" only in the sense that I can "respond"[47] to my beginning by inserting myself into the world, by taking a risk, by *appealing* to others.[48]

Respondents

FELIPE HERNÁNDEZ: First of all thank you, Tao, for organizing this session, I think that it has been a fascinating, really stimulating conversation from the beginning. This panel has been very intresting. Let me try to make sense of the presentations the way that I saw them. I'll start with Sophie and the notion of "spaces of meaning." Even though it was the last presentation, it articulates to a large extent the central topics of preceding conversations: how is it that spaces of meaning are generated? It happens through different forms of sociality and interaction across generations, something that we saw in all the presentations, which started with a summary of the three leading Martiniquan and Caribbean thinkers: Césaire, Fanon, and Glissant. I think the main issue here is the notion of broken space [if] you like, shattered space, shattered by the histories of forced dislocation, histories of slavery, the brutality of what happened in the islands of the Caribbean at the time of colonization. The story is in the work of each one of these three authors who examine how it was registered; how it was represented. And, then, of course, how is it that spaces of meaning emerge? Which would be another question in this fascinating survey of literary representations and interpretations of that very complex history of the Caribbean. Natalie revisits Glissant, emphasizing the aspect of contrast conflict in this continuum. Something that is "pregnant with death," and the idea of the "generativity of rupture," two mesmerizing concepts that lead us to question profoundly how is it that we are constructing a heritage here which is somewhat different from the rather facile interpretation of the notion of heritage as something celebratory, or optimistic.

I would argue, the latter question contains the main challenge of this panel, in which there were two types of presentation. The first, looking at issues to do with socialism, which is fascinating. Łukasz is looking at the implementation of this tremendous enterprise of sugar production. Sugar production is very closely connected to histories of colonialism all over the world, in the Caribbean as well in the Americas and Africa, where he works. A system of production, which at the scale that he talks about, starts with the expansion of Europe to the West. How is it that after independence, Nkrumah's vision of an economy, Nkrumah's vision of progress is actually one that in one way or another perpetuates the principles of colonialism, the principles of control?

In the case of Iulia, socialism reemerges in relation to the intrusions in/on/into women's bodies and their domestic spaces. And then you said something that was very interesting: the idea that the apartment appears as a heritage, and yet it is an apartment created and made available by the state that contains memories of oppression, control. And yet it is the heritage that is going to be passed on. So in a way, you're introducing us to another kind of heritage: property as heritage that is going to be passed on. So this opens up the discussion to engaging with a much broader view, various connotations of the idea of heritage.

Given the wealth of topics and themes –slavery, death, monopoly, the body and property—I wonder whether I could push back a little on the notion of heritage? Because I remember Anthony's notion of "generativity as home"; if we were to look at generativity as a home in the context of these presentations, these challenging topics, I think "the home" would be a very uncomfortable one. And I am also wondering if the idea that Andreas suggested of this becoming and attachment, where the difficult notion that heritage is always new, may be contradictory in so far as it is always connected to something traumatic and destructive.

So the way in which I'd like to push back is perhaps thinking about the notion of heritage, which is always tarnished by violence: the violence of colonialism, the brutality of slavery, the hierarchies of socialism, and even the terms in which development agendas reproduce colonial principles. I wonder if in those terms heritage is actively generative, or if it can truly acts as generativity.

IRIT KATZ: The ongoing creation of space, its constant change and ephemeral dimension, are revealed as a fundamental aspect of the intergenerational heritage discussed in all the interventions of this special issue. They pull out heritage from its immediate connotation with fixity and permanency to show its necessary relational, intersubjective, and ever-changing attributes.

I would like to contribute to this discussion by offering the idea of inhabitation as generative heritage enacted to constantly reaffirm different forms of life, while linking the idea of inhabitation to the multifaceted perspectives presented by the different contributors. The idea of inhabitation here could be seen as generated by the heritage of people's everyday actions related to their specific forms of life, while heritage is being formed and reformed by the creation of environments of attachment and belonging based on people's traditions and habits, with which they literally in-habit the world.

The Agambenian notion of "form of life" (*forma-di-vita*),[49] based on Wittgenstein's concept of *Lebensformen*, binds together regularities, configurations, and patterns based on the fabric of human life, activity, and existence on earth. Different forms of life, with various traditions, cultural approaches, beliefs, habits, and social values materialize in different architectural forms through which people inhabit their specific human world. Through these particular spatial forms of inhabitation, different forms of life might go beyond the control and violence of any biopolitical and necropolitical machines, creating private and public human worlds based on unique ways of being. These worlds are based both on the heritage inherited by new generations from previous ones inhabiting the same environments, and their always new conditions and relationalities of living in the world.

Discussing the meaning of heritage in our challenging time, when resistance to violence and injustices of inequality and exclusion are urgently needed, the contributions to this special issue circle around the question of inhabitation as indeed an opposition to these forces and also a search for ethical ways to inhabit the world through spaces of inclusivity, joy, and poetic creations. Examining the dynamic relationships of co-existence between home worlds and alien worlds, Anthony

Steinbock understands generativity as an ongoing movement that creates homely environments through constant becoming that simultaneously excavates familiar origins and alien environments it links to.

Ola Uduku, Leslie Hewitt, Tania Sengupta, Jean Khalfa, and Natalie Melas discuss the violence of colonialism and coloniality, showing how traditional situated forms of life were displaced and eradicated by extractive colonial regimes. In Uduku examination of how the palm oil trade and slave trade around Nigeria's delta and rivers have created the narratives that impoverished local communities, inhabitation could be seen in the ways generations continue to contest this history by weaving their tragic stories while relinking to the land. Inhabitation could also be seen in the form of the poetic expressions of traumatic worlds enacted through words, music, and embodiment and ritualization, which are revealed by Hewitt as a way of those robbed by the violence of US slavery and settler colonialism to mend and reposition themselves.

The idea of inhabitation as a form of poetic creation through space and words reappears in Khalfa's discussion of Césaire's work describing the colonial fragmentation and alienation of his island of Martinique, reflecting how the divisive space of the colonial city, where the colonized Indigenous are separated from the colonizing Europeans, could be inhabited by free body movement enacted only in dreams and in states of trance. By reflecting on Glissant's *Poetics of Relation*, Melas also shows how poetics might be the only way through which the terrorizing space of the Atlantic slave ship, shifting between the womb and the abyss, could be reinhabited in a nomadic or fugitive way seen by Moten as "moving through the landscape without claiming it."

The temporary existence on the landscape is also identified by Sengupta as an ephemeral mode of inhabitation, identified in the intangible heritage of the Hindu festival of Durgapuja in Kolkata. It shows how inhabiting the world through ephemeral architecture supports a form of life in which temporary creation enables local communities and economies to continuously create themselves through the ongoing spatial making and remaking of their worlds. This reminds us how, when thinking about heritage, the ephemeral is no less important than the permanent, allowing for the ongoing engagement of generations in enabling temporary environments to cyclically reappear.

If the architectural vernacular heritage of colonialism is modernism, then Łukasz Stanek shows how the colonial heritage continued in Ghana with the post-independence Nkrumah government, creating a sugarcane plantation and factory near the Volta River. These modern forms become inhabitable through enjoyments and future imaginations, both in the past and in the present. Iulia Stătică shows how familiarity, created by an embodied experience of the socialist apartments, becomes paradigmatic of the home for many generations that create heritage through their inhabitation. The adoption and adaptation of these spaces of modernity, it seems, both in Ghana and Romania, generates heritage through the daily activities of embodied inhabitation which add a necessary layer to what otherwise could be seen as uninhabitable, with heritage being the actual ability to inhabit them in specific forms.

The political thought of Hannah Arendt discussed by Sophie Loidolt brings together these different forms of inhabitation existing between the poetical and the political. Arendt's idea of natality connects between the heritage of past generations and between the generativity of new people and insights, enabling us to understand that the fundamental connection between forms of life and heritage is constant generativity, which forms and reforms its spaces through their inhabitation rather than by framing spatial heritage in a way which is fixed and permanent, and therefore dead and uninhabitable. Even if, for Arendt, our human world is created by more permanent traditions and structures that exceed our short human lifespan, we inhabit these worlds as living beings, bound to our particular life yet with the crucial potential of change and transformation. This means that our world-making actions of inhabitation, being based on repetitions of ourselves in-habit, are never fully repetitive but also have the potential of radical adjustments and change, including our spatial forms, according to our shifting and dynamic forms of life. This reveals the strong link between heritage and inhabitation, based on the generative power and patterns of daily life but also on the power to overcome the tragic ruptures, injustices, and vulgarity of our times through the regenerative pulses of poetics that might allow us to engage with the world in an affirmative way.

Discussion

SOPHIE LOIDOLT: There was one thing that I wanted to get into the conversation again: what Iulia said, which now that you mention it as well, that property is really an excellent category of heritage, apparently, and we had it in this private sense, but of course we can also see it in that biggest sense. I was just recently at a talk where somebody suggested, regarding political philosophy and the idea of utopia, that we have a basic income and 100 percent inheritance tax, which means that nobody would inherit anything anymore. That, of course, would dramatically change some workings and meanings of spaces of generativity. But if you don't have anything, you can't inherit, so I mean that really structures the way in which we also think about heritage and if that was, as a political decision, taken away because in the socialist state, it stays of course, and it stays apparently in a very pronounced sense. So I just found that interesting how much the property question actually relates to how space and heritage are structured, especially for those who don't own property.

IULIA STĂTICĂ: In the socialist context—I'm speaking from the Romanian context, which represents to a large extent a unique case of socialism, precisely in the period of late socialism from 1965 until the end of the '80s—I think that the state had a very purposeful idea of what heritage is and how that could be used in an instrumental way to produce an attachment in people to the infrastructure that was ultimately a space of care. It mirrored this idea of the state as a carer for the population. And then from here, this inherited infrastructure, which was the image of the modern home, had also to be paired with the modern body, that would have been again passed on as heritage through practice. And it was all tied together. So I think there is an institutional, state rhetoric of heritage, in that sense that aims to reconstruct an idea of tradition that the socialist regime had demolished, built upon the ruins.

Precisely in this context, as Felipe was also pointing to, I think there's a distinction to be made between two forms of heritage. One is the institutional variant of heritage manifested through infrastructure. The other is a more subjective form of heritage, often found in obscure places, as highlighted by Arendt. This subjective heritage is passed down through generations, primarily through oral tradition, practice, and lived experiences.

ŁUKASZ STANEK: I would like to address Felipe's and Iulia's comments. I was struck by the multiple relationships between our two presentations, Iulia. Both of them focused on post-socialist contexts in a broad sense. They touched upon tensions that perhaps could be unpacked by distinguishing, in a fairly arbitrary way, between inheritance and heritage. The starting point for our project with Michael and Eric was the status of Asutsuare as an inheritance from a past generation. Some of it was lost—people on the estate recall how dysfunctional machinery was buried on the factory grounds—while some buildings, the irrigation system, the fields, and specific skills are being repurposed. They are being made productive in life projects that are much more individualistic than the vision of Nkrumah. This brings to the fore the question: who exactly has the claim to this inheritance? Asutsuare resulted from a national effort, and the land on which the sugar factory was built and on which the plantations were laid out was expropriated from the local community, which is still awaiting compensation. And so the category of inheritance is contested. One way to rethink this situation is to consider Asutsuare not as inheritance but as heritage, the latter implying a claim to a shared, collective future. This is how I understood the statement by Mr. Ramzey about the factory as a "monument," which I quoted before.

Concerning Felipe's comment on the sugar industry and colonialism: The sugar industry was set up in Asutsuare as a part of centrally planned agriculture in Ghana. The Polish companies that advised on the project had no experience in sugarcane production, since in Poland sugar is not produced from sugarcane, but from sugar beets. And so they referred their Ghanaian counterparts to Cubans as experts in sugarcane in the socialist world. It was through the networks of global socialism that the long memory of the plantation system and slavery came back to Asutsuare.

TAO DUFOUR: Fascinating. My colleagues and I were in Trinidad recently for a research project, where this question of the "inheritance" of sugar is very much present.

NATALIE MELAS: This has been so fascinating; there are many things to try to pull together. But the question, Sophie, of spaces of meaning. I have a question about "meaning," and whether that's necessarily where one wants to be or wants to go, versus description or even stepping aside from meaning, which may be something that's at stake in what Łukasz calls "complex relation between inheritance and heritage," if heritage is the moment of meaning. A moment of consolidation, meaning that may even require a stage or something like that. I'm thinking on this morning's presentations about intangible heritage and things like that. So, that's one question I come away with.

And the other one is this question of the future. I think that's really interesting. Łukasz, your presentation—I'm thinking of Reinhart Koselleck's idea of futures past, the future that certain regimes imagine but that don't materialize, but they exist in a very interesting relationship in a certain sense to heritage. It's almost a future as a lost heritage. So, I like very much this idea of thinking about the future, or that moment that the temporality is "not yet" or not yet materialized or never materialized in some sense.

SOPHIE LOIDOLT: Thank you Natalie. With "meaning" I actually have in mind something very broad. In the sense of what you talked about as lived experience—*expérience vécu*, I think. In that sense, I would claim that we're never outside of spaces of meaning. So we're not stones just rolling down a slope. There is something that is like for us to be wherever we are. And meaning, in that sense, does not mean that it has to be harmonious, but it can be. So only if you're in a space of meaning, this can be experienced as broken and fragmented. The strong picture that resonated a lot with me was the boat pregnant with death. And that sort of resistance and fragmentation and turning around is only possible as a distortion of meaning. That itself I would describe as a space of meaning. In a very broad sense, it's not something we have to get to—it's not a teleological notion—but rather a way of trying to describe how we are in spaces.

JEAN KHALFA: Perhaps I can continue on these themes—Natalie's, of natality and spaces of meaning. There's a passage in a chapter of *Black Skin, White Masks* called the "The Lived Experience of the Black Man" ("lived experience" [*experience vécue* is Husserl's concept of *Erlebnis*]) where Fanon says something like "I came to give birth to the world" in a very Merleau-Pontian way. Then, when suffering racial insults, he realized, "I have become a thing within that world." Giving meaning, creating a meaning for the world, or giving birth to a meaning for the world, has nothing to do with the preexistence of meanings that can then be transmitted. It's more the opening of a space where meaningfulness can be introduced. That made me think of two things. One is that you could distinguish two types of negritude. Negritude, in a way, is the archetype of an heritage. We want to find and celebrate our "roots" or origin in Africa, which is difficult. But the Césairian form of negritude is simply the celebration of—like Tao said—a land of birth or of giving birth or of the possibility of a subjectivation. While the negritude of Senghor is in effect this talk of inheritance—solidified history—which Fanon then criticized first as alienation and then as an ideological instrument of power in postcolonial societies. So the other is that there's a difference between potential and power, if you want, between subjectivity and history that is solidified in heritage. But of course, I'm looking at all that from the point of view of Fanon who was himself very influenced by Sartre. What Sartre says when he looks at the poetry of negritude—he wrote a famous introduction to an anthology of negritude poetry by Senghor—he says that poetry is the only genre for a revolutionary thought, because it's the medium through which or in which subjectivity can be established, subjectivity in language. Sovereignty within language. That allows us to distinguish between a body of work, which constitutes a heritage, and the practice of the creation of a space of meaning that cannot be reduced to that inheritance, or to any inheritance. That's where the question of the future and of natality comes in. Which—you're right Tao—is half of the work of Wifredo Lam, as either annunciations or maternities.

Participants

The roundtable has been organized, introduced and moderated by Tao DuFour (Assistant Professor in History and Theory of Architecture, University of Cambridge). In the first panel, colleagues presenting are Andreas Pantazatos (Assistant Professor in Heritage Studies at the Department of Archaeology, University of Cambridge), Anthony Steinbock (Professor in the Department of Philosophy at Stony Brook University), Ola Uduku (Roscoe Chair and Head of the School of Architecture at the University of Liverpool), Leslie Hewitt (Associate Professor of Art at Rice University), Tania Sengupta (Associate Professor and Director of Architectural History and Theory at The Bartlett School of Architecture, University College London), and Maximilian Sternberg (Associate Professor at the Department of Architecture, Cambridge University).

In the second panel, colleagues presenting are Jean Khalfa (Fellow of Trinity College and College Senior Lecturer in French and the Faculty of Modern and Medieval Languages and Linguistics at the University of Cambridge), Natalie Melas (Associate Professor in the Department of Comparative Literature at Cornell University), Łukasz Stanek (Professor of Architecture at Taubman College of Architecture and Urban Planning at the University of Michigan), Iulia Stătică (Lecturer in Urban Design at the School of Architecture at the University of Sheffield), and Sophie Loidolt (Professor of Philosophy and Chair of Practical Philosophy in the Institute of Philosophy at the Technische Universität Darmstadt), Felipe Hernández (Associate Professor at the Department of Architecture and Director of the Centre for Latin American Studies, Cambridge University), and Irit Katz (Associate Professor at the Department of Architecture, Cambridge University).

Notes

[1] T. DuFour, *Husserl and Spatiality: A Phenomenological Ethnography of Space* (London: Routledge, 2022).

[2] L. Smith, *Uses of Heritage* (London: Routledge, 2006).

[3] J. E. Tunbridge and G. J. Ashworth, *Dissonant Heritage: The Management of the Past as a Resource in Conflict* (Chichester: John Wiley and Sons, 1996).

[4] A. Pantazatos, "Heritage, Epistemic Injustice and Identity Formation," in *Cultural Heritage, Ethics and Contemporary Migrations*, ed. C. Holtorf, A. Pantazatos, and G. F. Scarre (London: Routledge, 2018).

[5] A. Pantazatos, "The Normative Framework of Stewardship," in *The Ethics of Cultural Heritage*, ed. T. Ireland and J. Schofield (New York: Springer, 2015), 127–44.

[6] R. Nozick, *Philosophical Explanations* (Cambridge, MA: Harvard University Press, 1981).

[7] Pantazatos, "Heritage, Epistemic Injustice and Identity Formation."

[8] Pantazatos, "Heritage, Epistemic Injustice and Identity Formation."

[9] See, for example, Robert Sokolowski, *Husserlian Meditations: How Words Present Things* (Evanston, IL: Northwestern University Press, 1974).

[10] In this sense, phenomenology is not "normal," because it does not follow the flow of experience as it is *simply* taken for granted. But in another sense, phenomenology is "normal," or better "hyper-normal" to use Husserl's term, in the sense that it describes the very ways in which the mundane activities unfold.

[11] Griselda Pollock, "What if Art Desires to be Interpreted? Remodeling Interpretation After the Encounter-Event," Tate Papers, no. 15, Spring 2011, https://www.tate.org.uk/research/tate-papers/15.

[12] Tiffany Lethabo King, *The Black Shoals: Offshore Formations of Black and Native Studies* (Durham: Duke University Press, 2019), 118.

[13] A. Kearney, "Intangible Cultural Heritage: Global Awareness and Local Interest," in *Intangible Heritage*, ed. Laurajane Smith and Natsuko Akagawa (London: Routledge, 2008), 209–26.

[14] Chiara Bortolotto, "From Objects to Process: UNESCO's 'Intangible Cultural Heritage,'" *Journal of Museum Ethnography*, no. 19 (2007): 21.

[15] "UNESCO—Intangible Heritage Home," Intangible Cultural Heritage, https://ich.unesco.org/en/home.

[16] Aimé Césaire, *The Complete Poetry*, ed. and trans. A. James Arnold and Clayton Eshleman (Middletown, CT: Wesleyan University Press, 2017), 13. My emphasis.

[17] Césaire, *The Complete Poetry*, 13.

[18] Césaire, *The Complete Poetry*, 43.

[19] Jean Khalfa, *Poetics of the Antilles* (Oxford: Peter Lang, 2017), 43.

[20] Jean Khalfa, "Éthique et Violence chez Frantz Fanon," *Les Temps Modernes* 2, no. 698 (2018): 51; "Introduction: Fanon, Revolutionary Psychiatrist," *Frantz Fanon: The Psychiatric Writings from Alienation and Freedom*, ed. Jean Khalfa and Robert J. C. Young (London: Bloomsbury, 2021).

[21] Frantz Fanon, *Frantz Fanon: The Political Writings from Alienation and Freedom*, ed. Jean Khalfa and Robert J. C. Young (London: Bloomsbury, 2021), 152.

[22] Frantz Fanon, *The Wretched of the Earth*, trans. Richard Philcox (New York: Grove Press, 2004), 15.
[23] Fanon, *The Wretched of the Earth*, 51.
[24] Frantz Fanon, *Frantz Fanon: The Plays from Alienation and Freedom*, ed. Jean Khalfa and Robert J. C. Young (London: Bloomsbury, 2021), 71.
[25] A work acquired by MoMA in 1945, https://www.moma.org/collection/works/34666.
[26] Édouard Glissant, *Iguanes, Busards, Totems fous; L'art primordial de Wifredo Lam*, in *Lam Métis* (Paris: Éditions Dapper, 2001).
[27] Édouard Glissant, *Poetics of Relation*, trans. Betsy Wing (Ann Arbor: University of Michigan Press, 1997), 7.
[28] Glissant, *Poetics of Relation*, 6.
[29] Édouard Glissant, *Poétique de la Relation* (Paris: Gallimard, 1990), 21.
[30] Glissant, *Poétique de la Relation*, 20.
[31] Glissant, *Poétique de la Relation*, 20.
[32] Glissant, *Poétique de la Relation*, 20.
[33] Glissant, *Poétique de la Relation*, 21.
[34] These ideas are expanded upon in my book *Urban Phanstasmagotias: Domesticity, Production and the Politics of Modernity in Communit Bucharest* (London: Routledge, 2024) and in my article, "From Biopolitics to the Lived Body: Maternity, Reproduction, and the Domestic Space of Socialist Bucharest, 1965–1989," *Architectural Histories* 10, no. 1 (2022).
[35] Daniel Miller, *Modernity: An Ethnographic Approach: Dualism and Mass Consumption in Trinidad* (Oxford: Berg, 1994), 135.
[36] Krisztina Fehérvary, *Politics in Color and Concrete: Socialist Materialities and the Middle Class in Hungary* (Bloomington: Indiana University Press, 2013); Frances Pine, "Naming the House and Naming the Land: Kinship and Social Groups in Highland Poland," *Journal of the Royal Anthropological Institute* 2, no. 3 (1996): 443–59.
[37] Hannah Arendt, *The Human Condition* (Chicago: University of Chicago Press, 1958), 71.
[38] Alina Asavei, "Estetica rezistenţei şi persistenţei/The Aesthetics of Resistance and Persistence," in *Ion Grigorescu: The Man with a Single Camera*, ed. Alina Şerban, 188–213 (Berlin: Sternberg Press, 2013), 191; and Ovidiu Ţichideleanu, "Ion Grigorescu: A Political Reinvention of the Socialist Man," *Afterall: A Journal of Art, Context and Inquiry* 41 (Spring/Summer 2016): 10–21.
[39] Juliana Maxim, "Corpusul lucrărilor şi lucrarea corpului/The Body of Work and the Work of the Body," in *Ion Grigorescu: Bucharest*, ed. Alina Şerban, 18–31 (Bucharest: P+4 Publications, 2020).
[40] Hannah Arendt, *Vita activa oder vom tätigen Leben* (München: Piper, 1981), 21.
[41] Arendt, *Vita activa oder vom tätigen Leben*, 217.
[42] Arendt, *Vita activa oder vom tätigen Leben*, 217. See also Arendt, *The Human Condition*, 178.
[43] Arendt, *The Human Condition*, 96.
[44] Arendt, *The Human Condition*, 62.
[45] Arendt, *The Human Condition*, 177.
[46] Arendt, *The Human Condition*, 9, 178, 247.
[47] Arendt, *The Human Condition*, 177.
[48] For the whole passage on natality, slightly modified, see Sophie Loidolt, *Phenomenology of Plurality: Hannah Arendt on Political Intersubjectivity* (New York: Routledge, 2017), 204–5.
[49] G. Agamben, *Means without End: Notes on Politics* (Minneapolis: University of Minnesota Press, 2000).

Book Review
Ana Gisele Ozaki

In the Skin of the City: Spatial Transformation in Luanda

António Tomás
Durham: Duke University Press, 2022

António Tomás's *In the Skin of the City* provides an urban history of Luanda, Angola, through the idea of the "skin" as a physical, social, and organic boundary. Tomás, a cultural anthropologist by training, weaves a historical narrative, chronologically organized, in which the "skin" that has historically separated colonizer and colonized, white settlers and Black natives, rich and poor, has also been transformed and negotiated over time, from the first colonial encounter to its contemporary form.

Tomás states that rather than dwelling on the divide between interior and exterior, his interest lies in "how certain notions of physical and social boundaries that denote limits and edges in the city came into being" (1). "Skin," in this context, comes from Tomás's reading of local artist Antonio Olé's work and exhibition, whose name inspired the book's title. For the author, Olé's *musseque* (shacks) photographs, specifically, speak to an urban and national history of the social and spatial forces that have left marks on the city's "skin" (3). From this perspective, Tomás establishes the colonial period's "*fronteira do asfalto*" (the asphalt frontier) as the original marker for Luanda's "very particular repertoires for enforcing difference" in its urban environment (4–5). Rather than a top-down approach, however, Tomás claims a narrative from the margin, aware of its "malleability" and "undecidability" (8) and how Luanda's residents have been "enclosed, cut off, encircled, or removed from the various urban units," which include "the fort, the street, the apartment, the *bairro* (neighborhood), and, in the national reconstruction lexicon (after the period 2000–2010), *urbanização* (urbanization), *centralidade* (centrality), and the *reserva* (land reserve)" (6).

For Tomás, the "skin" also serves as an analogy to reconcile "major tenets of mainstream urban theory" (9) in the Global North and South regarding segregation and dichotomies. The author, in fact, targets explicitly their generalizing categorizations while acknowledging their clear Eurocentric bias (specifically concerning Paris). Claiming to contest both sides, Tomás builds a narrative that, while it does not refute the teleology of classical urban theory—dividing the chapters chronologically from a centralized to a decentralized city—it relies on social theory's understandings of singularity and contingency (16).

Countering the overwhelming purchase of "skin" in the architectural field, Tomás's appropriation is inspired then by the embodied experiences of the city, in Olé's and the writer Ondjaki's work, for example, as well as Tomás's ethnographic and personal perspective as a Luanda native.

Following his interest in destabilizing urban theory staples, Tomás focuses primarily on what he calls the "metaphysical" associations to issues of citizenship and the "over-utilized" concept of "right to the city." To do that, the author emphasizes the role of the squatter and their relation to the law as what makes the practice—and not its physical condition—particularly precarious. In this way, the author aims to problematize assumptions linking citizenship to land, particularly in how postcolonial Angola pursued social housing as a way of political manipulation and alienation, with the rise of national authoritarianism, considering that beneficiaries did not automatically own the land they inhabited. This way, Tomás justifies his choice by stating that squatters have been the ones standing "on the margin, or the skin, for they always arbitrate and negotiate boundaries, not physical boundaries but legal ones as well," that is, they have managed to "simultaneously exist inside the government and outside the law" (15). In fact, the city's limits and skin have been "drawn and redrawn" because of their historical challenges (15). Therefore, a critical analysis of Luanda's skin is only possible through historical and ethnographical approaches and "lateral thinking" (15). Ultimately, according to Tomás, the book synthesizes Luanda's "defining urban principles" from a perspective of "separation" rather than "agglomeration" (21), unlike the urban theories staples.

The book is divided into three parts. The first one, "Formation" (chapters 1 and 2), is based on archival work on the colonial occupation of the city. Chapter 1 focuses on the construction of Luanda as a colonial city when the city's foundational "social taxonomy" (22) came about through the centrality of the slave trade, which produced squatting as an intrinsic urban condition. Through the case of downtown Luanda's Elinga Teather and his rework of Fernando Batalha's *Casa Luandense* theory (78), Tomás establishes a conceptual primer to understand the city's situated and enduring dynamics of colonial difference and coexistence. Based partially on Portugal's colonial mythology regarding assimilation and hybridity and further supported by the slave trade, the *sobrado* (two-story) characterizes the colonial typology for "the cohabitation of enslavers and the enslaved" (31). In this chapter, Tomás also sets up a framework to understand social mobilization, squatting, and the urban colonial legacies he focuses on in future chapters. Chapter 2 describes the formation of Luanda as a modernist and white settler city, marked by the work of Portuguese modernists, particularly enchanted by Le Corbusier's urban promises. Concerning the establishment of Portugal's authoritarian *Estado Novo,* urban migration, and occupation of the colonial territory, starting in the early twentieth century, Luanda saw an increase in infrastructural projects and the "expansion of the modern grid" (23). It is foundational to this period, the *Estatuto do Indígena* (Indigenous statute) (1926), which formalized the legal and racist differentiation between white settlers, new Africans (civilized), and Natives (uncivilized), as well as their associated spaces, the formal city, and the *musseques,* respectively.

The second part, "Stasis" (chapters 3 and 4), relies heavily on Tomás's ethnographic work on the city's postcolonial transformations. Chapter 3 focuses on the disintegration of the Portuguese empire and the effects of a national "power vacuum" (95) from decolonization and the civil war. In this chapter, on the one hand, Tomás's ethnography accounts mainly for the squatting of formerly white settler residences, when, "through sovereignty," "Angolans were righting the rights to the city" (93), and on the other, how the apartment unit's "skin" reconfigured the transition to a postcolonial state. Chapter 4 describes the infrastructural and administrative collapse of the city following decolonization and the emigration of thousands of Portuguese settlers as the perfect storm for the culmination of an informal economy embodied in the Roque Santeiro marketplace, "a mixture between a marketplace and a refugee camp" (132). As a new center within the previous periphery, it allowed peripheral connections outside the colonial center and characterized the leading force for urban decentralization between the 1980s and 1990s.

The third part, "Fragmentation" (chapters 5 and 6), conveys a "collage of disparate bits of information" (20) to shape Tomás's concept of the "bifurcation of the urban" (14, 180) and how postcolonial political and land regimes have established the dissociation between citizenship and property ownership. Chapter 5 deals with the fragmentation and reorganization of the city through the rise of authoritarianism, privatization, the instrumentalization of urban expertise, and legal mechanisms regarding land rights and ownership through the construction of Cidade Alta, the presidential complex, and gated communities expanding the urban borders southward. Chapter 6 scrutinizes the rise of presidential power and neoliberal market economy in the city's transformation, mainly through legal accommodation to foreign investment, especially by China, in clearing informal settlements and implementing new *centralidades.* Tomás reads the Kilamba residential complex, built through Chinese capital and planning, as the "formalization of the state of emergency" for urban and national developments since it was "built outside the framework of any city's master plan or outside the control and oversight of any locally based institution" (198).

Finally, the book's coda circles back to Tomás's musings and critiques of classical urban theory, making a case for singularity, association, combined methodologies, and the squatter's role in understanding the "contingencies of the African urban condition" (26). Unlike the flanêur, who traces "continuity and permanence in the city" in Paris and the Global North, the squatter "is about its continuity and fragmentation" (211). Through Luanda's contingencies, Tomás justifies the fragmentation of his reading and methodology in tracing Luanda's history, singularities, and patterns.

An incredible contribution lies in how the book translates and engages throughout its chapters with dominant Portuguese scholarship regarding the colonial period, largely inaccessible in English, while providing a nuanced and critical analysis of their biases and blind spots. Known among scholars of the Lusophone world, discussions on Portuguese colonialism are still incredibly limited to the Portuguese language and mainly metropolitan scholars and institutions. In this sense, Tomás's voice and thorough analysis, based on his lived and local experience, is a breath of fresh air in a sea of nostalgic Portuguese dominance. As a counterpoint to metropolitan voices, Tomás's study shows a mastery of local mechanisms, archives, and spatial analysis intimately connected to his local personal experience in the city. Tomás masterfully expands local issues, previously studied within a limited and metropolitan framework, on global and national scales, which brings richness and nuance to his analysis, especially concerning the colonial period.

Another highlight is Tomás's analysis of urban toponomy and postcolonial re-inscriptions in chapter 4, in the context of central attempts to establish proper postcolonial urban borders while faced with the center's inability to serve as the gravitational force it once was. Tomás's examination of residents' mental maps as disjointed from the physical and ideal postcolonial city projected by the state elicits a critical depth that seems only possible through a deep and situated engagement with the city and its users. Tomás's methodological and theoretical approach reveals the sociopolitical complexity beyond the physical and infrastructural purchase of urban borders and limits.

At the same time, while not as central to Tomás's project, the defiance of his analysis of the metropolitan scholarship could have been further emphasized, especially to unfamiliar scholars. Tomás could have more critically assessed embedded colonial hierarchies in the knowledge production concerning formerly Portuguese Africa. Colonial archives, institutional knowledge, and resources are still heavily located in the metropole. In this sense, Tomás's theoretical framework based on the "skin" could have expanded to a global perspective of the colonial logic of knowledge production and rights to memory, especially considering contemporary discussions regarding the repatriation of stolen heritage and reparations.

Similarly, Tomás's provocative "skin" analogy, which aims to expand architecture's obvious currency related to building technology and materials, seems to have missed the opportunity to problematize it further as the product of the social logic of colonialism. While Tomás analyzes the social construction of such "skins," often from planning, legal, and political perspectives, the "skin" seems to serve as an open discursive mechanism loosely acknowledging its most broad and evident connection to the social construction of racial difference. Tomás approaches it briefly in chapter 1, connecting it to Portugal's mythological colonial narrative based on Gilberto Freyre's lusotropicalism and Portugal's evasion of a local and creolized elite. According to the Brazilian sociologist, Portugal was particularly prone to hybridity and racial mixing, unlike its British and other Northern European counterparts. However, the reader is left curious about how such legacies carried on (or not) in the postcolonial period when Tomás seems to suggest a shift from race to class, in the spatial antagonisms between the rich and poor, the formal city and the *musseque* in later chapters.

Still, Tomás's book is groundbreaking and essential in bridging discussions across European colonial powers, geographies, and language boundaries, especially in the context of African cities. Overall, this is an inspiring contribution to urban and postcolonial studies on urban Africa. It invites further research and exchanges from similar geographies, previously limited by Portuguese-speaking studies. This book ought to be thoroughly assigned to architecture, architectural history, and urban studies courses for undergraduate and graduate students, as it expands historical methods and theories from anthropology and social sciences to those fields, advancing Tomás's call for revisioning the terms of urban comparison, association, and attention to singularity and local contingencies.

Biography
Ana Ozaki is the Inaugural Mellon Race, Place, and Equity Postdoctoral Fellow at the University of Virginia's School of Architecture and will be joining the University of Pennsylvania's Art History Department as Assistant Professor in the fall of 2024. Ozaki's research investigates the complex ways racial ideologies have interfered with architectural understandings of climate and the environment within the Black Atlantic. Centered on Brazil's construction of an architectural ideal for the rest of the tropics, her current book project examines the country's connections to West and Southern Africa, specifically Nigeria, Angola, and Mozambique, albeit often mediated by Europe. She has previously held positions at Princeton University, Barnard College, Columbia University, UCLA, Cal Poly San Luis Obispo, and Cornell University.

Michael Gameli Dziwornu and Łukasz Stanek
Photography by Eric Don-Arthur
Interviews by Michael Gameli Dziwornu and Łukasz Stanek

Artist Intervention

Asutsuare Rebound

After Ghana won its independence in 1957, the village of Asutsuare became the focus of state-led, socialist-inspired agricultural and industrial development. A sugar factory was built, along with a residential area, a sugarcane plantation, and the required irrigation system. Twenty years after its closure in the 1980s, the plant was bought by Chinese investors. Today, it manufactures paper and plastic products, while the sugarcane plantation was repurposed for the farming of rice, bananas, and fish.

Asutsuare Rebound, first presented at the Rotterdam Biennale of Architecture (2022), studies the reuse, reappropriation, and revalorization of modernist planning in Asutsuare. We have interviewed retired employees of the sugar factory and younger inhabitants who explained to us how the material infrastructure and memories of the plant are a resource for imagining and producing a collective future. By juxtaposing their voices with images by photographer Eric Don-Arthur, this project revisits concepts of long-term planning beyond dominant narratives of postcolonial melancholy and postsocialist nostalgia.

Asutsuare Rebound begins to reassess the ambiguous impact of long-term planning on the landscapes of Asutsurare. While the irrigation system has became a crucial resource for the villagers, it has also been undermined by conflicts around land taken over by the state sixty years ago. While the repurposed buildings are not always adequate to new programs, they have often become nodes of new activities for which there was no funding available. While many inhabitants in Asutsuare appreciate the state-led development from the Kwame Nkrumah period, they appropriate it for individual entrepreneurship. We understand these ambiguities not as evidence of failure, but as an invitation to rethink the future in a way that moves beyond both modernist techno-utopias and neoliberal short-termism.

Future Anterior
Volume XIX, Number 2
Winter 2022

Figure 1. Asutsuare Estate, Ghana. A view of rice fields and an irrigation system from the Kpong Irrigation Scheme at the foothill of the Osudoku mountain. Photo © 2022 Eric Don-Arthur.

I think it was considered very seriously before [the factory] was sited here because of the river and the water. . . . In the laboratory we had our own water works and we supplied water to every part of this community.

—Mr. Anthony Ramzey, retired lab technician, 2022

Figure 2. Asutsuare Estate, Ghana. Mr. John Awuku Dziwornu, a farmer and business consultant, shows the process of manufacturing egg crates at the paper processing plant of Shinefeel Ghana Ltd. In the late 2000s, Chinese investors purchased the old GHASEL factory buildings and began producing paper and plastic products. Photo © 2022 Eric Don-Arthur.

The collapse of the company [GHASEL] was a blessing in disguise. The infrastructure was there and [people] became owners of their own enterprises: whether that's farm enterprises, or they set up a place to provide vulcanisation services, mechanisation services, the repair of motorbikes, bicycles, shops of spare parts, and the rest. The place has become very vibrant. Each and everybody has something to do. But all this could be attributed to the initial investment in the construction of the sugar factory and the irrigation infrastructure that was put up.

—Mr. John Awuku Dziwornu, 2022

Figure 3. Asutsuare Estate, Ghana. Paper recycling depot at Shinefeel Ghana Ltd. Photo © 2022 Eric Don-Arthur.

At first, GHASEL was employing people from the community, they were also contributing to the economy of Ghana. And Shinefeel has come and is doing the same thing.

—Mr. Prince Selasie Tong Kurug, environmental and safety officer at Shinefeel, 2022

Figure 4. Asutsuare Township, Ghana. Ms. Paulina Addison, pioneer and heavy vehicle operator at the sugarcane plantation, shows grandson her family photographs. Photo © 2022 Eric Don-Arthur.

I remember that when we started the job, it was fine. . . . Because the sugar cane was there. . . . The outgrowers would come and report at the end of the day. At that time people from the North would collect them and harvest the sugarcane. They would load the trailers, they had six trailers or eight trailers. At that time, we used the machines. They called it Ulysses. That machine we used. And another one was MF.

—Ms. Paulina Addison, 2022

Figure 5. Asutsuare Estate, Ghana. A view of the former GHASEL laboratory currently serving as the boys' dormitory of the Osudoku Senior High Technical School (OSUTECH). Photo © 2022 Eric Don-Arthur.

This school was initially housed because of the [GHASEL] structures available. [They include] the boys' dormitory, the main structure that houses the boys, and then, part of the accommodation has also been leased to teachers to live in. And then I can also say that other people, even the primary school here, they all have places that they squat, so to speak.

—Ms. Christina Adjei, headmistress of the Osudoku Senior High School, 2022

Figure 6. Asutsuare Estate, Ghana. Ruins of the GHASEL hospital reclaimed by nature. The hospital served the staff of GHASEL and the wider community. The structure briefly served as classrooms for pupils of the Asutsuare Estate D/A Basic School. Photo © 2022 Eric Don-Arthur.

We have the banana farm, fishpond factories, and a Chinese company that recycles waste materials into reusable products. But we need many things here. What we need most are a hospital and a doctor. Also, the roads are in a poor state.

—Ms. Paulina Addison, 2022

Figure 7. Asutsuare Estate, Ghana. Repurposed sugarcane fields of the erstwhile GHASEL for the cultivation of rice and bananas. Photo © 2022 Eric Don-Arthur

In the late ’60s, there was this irrigation project which was undertaken by FAO [Food and Agriculture Organization] about some six miles from Asutsuare. They called the place Padlock Area A. They experimented with rice production and irrigation. People became used to the rudiments of rice cultivation.

—Mr. John Awuku Dziwornu, 2022

Figure 8. Asutsuare Estate, Ghana. Mr. Seth Akligo, pioneer and engineer at the water works shows a swimming pool used by both foreign and Ghanaian staff of GHASEL. Photo © 2022 Eric Don-Arthur

The place was very lively, we had a swimming pool over there, and you could see white men and there were blacks together, enjoying themselves. There was also a canteen and a workers' canteen. It was Kwame Nkrumah's time. We enjoyed a lot.

—Mr. Seth Akligo, 2022

Biographies

Michael Gameli Dziwornu is a research scientist with the CSIR-Institute for Scientific and Technological Information (CSIR-INSTI), a public research organization in Ghana. Michael joined CSIR-INSTI in June 2021 after completing his PhD in Urban Studies from the University of Milan-Bicocca in Italy. He is particularly interested in crime geography, geographic information systems (GIS), urban studies, migration studies, and the postcolonial geographies of Africa.

Łukasz Stanek is Professor of Architectural History at A. Alfred Taubman College of Architecture and Urban Planning, University of Michigan, Ann Arbor, USA. Stanek authored *Henri Lefebvre on Space: Architecture, Urban Research, and the Production of Theory* (Minnesota, 2011) and *Architecture in Global Socialism: Eastern Europe, West Africa, and the Middle East in the Cold War* (Princeton, 2020). Stanek taught at the ETH Zurich, the University of Manchester, and held guest professorships at Harvard University and the University of Ghana. He co-curated the exhibition *The Gift: Stories of Generosity and Violence in Architecture* at the Architekturmuseum der TUM (2024).

Eric Don-Arthur is a photographer based in Winneba, Ghana, whose artistic practice, as he describes it, "visually investigates the physical and psychological intersections of love, light, and logic." His work has been widely published and exhibited both in Ghana and internationally, most recently at the International Architecture Biennale Rotterdam (Netherlands), the Victoria and Albert Museum in London (UK), and the Architekturmuseum der TUM in Munich, Germany. Eric Don-Arthur's current research interest is in photography as liberation pedagogy.

Submission Guidelines

Future Anterior is a peer reviewed (refereed) journal that approaches the field of historic preservation from a position of critical inquiry. A comparatively recent field of professional study, preservation often escapes direct academic challenges of its motives, goals, forms of practice and results. Future Anterior seeks contributions that ask these difficult questions from philosophical, theoretical, and critical perspectives.

Articles should be no more than 4,000 words (excluding footnotes), with up to seven illustrations. It is the responsibility of the author to secure permissions for image use and pay any reproduction fees. A brief abstract (200 words) and author biography (around 100 words), and a list of numbered image captions with credits must accompany the text. Acceptance or rejection of submissions is at the discretion of the Editorial Staff. Please do not send original materials, as submissions will not be returned.

Formatting Text: All text files should be saved as Microsoft Word or RTF format. Text and citations must be formatted in accordance with the *Chicago Manual of Style,* 15th Edition. All articles must be submitted in English, and spelling should follow American convention.

Formatting Illustrations: Images should be sent as TIFF files with a resolution of at least 300 dpi at 8" by 9" print size. Figures should be numbered clearly in the text, after the paragraph in which they are referenced. Image captions and credits must be included with submissions.

Checklist of documents required for submission:

__ Abstract (200 words)
__ Manuscript (4000 words)
__ Illustrations (7)
__ Captions for Illustrations
__ Illustration Copyright information
__ Author biography (100 words)

All submissions must be submitted electronically, via email to Future.Anterior.Journal@gmail.com

Questions about submissions can be sent to the above email address or mailed to:

Jorge Otero-Pailos
Editor, *Future Anterior*
GSAPP
400 Avery Hall
1172 Amsterdam Ave
Columbia University
New York, NY 10027

https://www.arch.columbia.edu/future-anterior

Become a *Future Anterior* Sponsor

Future Anterior is funded by grants and distributed in the spirit of making knowledge available to everyone. Donations are critical to helping us accomplish this mission. If you would like to become a sponsor, please fill out this page and mail it, with a check payable to Columbia University, to:

Future Anterior
Graduate School of Architecture, Planning, and Preservation
400 Avery Hall
1172 Amsterdam Avenue
Columbia University
New York, NY 10027

Or contribute by credit card online at:
https://arch.givenow.columbia.edu/#

All sponsors will be recognized in each issue of *Future Anterior* and receive a one-year subscription to the journal.

Please check the appropriate sponsorship level:

Individual Sponsor: ❑ begins at $100/year
Institutional Sponsor: ❑ begins at $500/year
Patron: ❑ begins at $1000/year

Name*: ______________________________

Address: ______________________________

____

City: ______________________________

State: ______________ Zip: ______________

Country: ______________________________

Institution/Office: ______________________________

E-mail: ______________________________

*please provide your name exactly as you would like it to appear in print